The Commercial Manager

The complete handbook for commercial directors and managers

Tim Boyce and Cathy Lake

THORO*g*OOD

Published by Thorogood

10-12 Rivington Street

London EC2A 3DU

Telephone: 020 7749 4748

Fax: 020 7729 6110

Email: info@thorogoodpublishing.co.uk

Web: www.thorogoodpublishing.co.uk

A CIP catalogue record for this book is
available from the British Library.

PB: ISBN 1 85418 358 3
    ISBN 978-185418358-3

Cover and book designed in the UK
by Driftdesign

Printed in the UK by Ashford Colour Press

Special discounts for bulk
quantities of Thorogood books
are available to corporations,
institutions, associations and
other organizations. For more
information contact Thorogood
by telephone on 020 7749 4748, by
fax on 020 7729 6110, or e-mail us:
info@thorogoodpublishing.co.uk

Contents

Part one

THE COMMERCIAL MANAGER

Commercial awareness

Introduction

The key words of the commercial view of business are profit, cash, order book, intellectual property, risk and contracts.

A purist might say that the first three only are the real core. These three may be considered in terms of their relative immediacy. The most immediate need in successfully running most businesses is cash. Cash is needed every month, every week and every day to pay the workers and to meet creditors' demands. The next most immediate need is for the company to produce good profits. Profit is measured in the annual accounts but for many companies, the half-year and quarterly results are anticipated and watched equally closely by the company, by investors and by the City. Internally to the company, profit forecasts are monitored monthly or at more frequent intervals depending upon the company's financial health. Poor profits means reduced investment by the company and loss of confidence by shareholders, who expect their dividends and bonuses. To be active at all, a company must have orders to process. It is arguably artificial to make this the third most immediate priority. Some companies, such as supermarkets, may receive (and need) hundreds of orders a day, with a complete order processing and delivery time measured in hours or days only, with an inventory holding of no more than forty eight hours' worth. On the other hand there are companies, such as shipbuilders, who may need only one or two orders a year in order to maintain the order book. But it is not just a question of maintaining the order book. Most companies aspire to growth. Provided commercial performance is maintained, a bigger company means bigger profits.

A company that considers only the first three of the commercial components may be highly successful and may be described, perhaps, as highly focused. However it will have no future unless it constantly refreshes itself with new ideas. New ideas will generate tomorrow's orders, profit and cash.

The management of risk has a major influence on profit, cash, orders and the commercial exploitation of ideas. Most managers will be familiar with programme risk management aimed at identifying and eliminating or mitigating technical risks that potentially impact upon time (and therefore money). But there are also commercial risks and the management thereof – in a way that is not divorced from programme risk management – is crucial to success.

Similarly, the opportunity to maximize profit and cash, to eliminate threats to the successful performance of orders, and to protect ideas for the future hinges on the terms of 'the contract'. Companies operate by receiving contracts from customers and placing contracts with suppliers. Contracts from customers are sometimes called sales orders and contracts with suppliers are usually called purchase orders. Of all the transactions into which the company enters, the contract is the one with which the commercial manager must be most familiar. The contract must be good, sound and familiar to all those concerned with it. There is an old maxim to the effect that if the job is going well the contract is left to gather dust in a forgotten drawer. If the job goes badly the contract does nothing to help. In enshrining two extremes, the maxim neglects the majority of contracts, which lie somewhere between the two, and indeed in practice many problems are caused by people *thinking* they know what is in the contract without bothering to check. Also, if problems do arise then a solution, which is arrived at other than by recourse to the courts, will be based around what the contract says, even if the contract does not expressly address the specific problem.

Profit

Accountants use many measures to monitor the financial health of a business. Expressions such as 'gross profit', 'net profit', 'operating profit', 'margin', 'contribution', 'recovery', 'revenue', 'earnings', 'earnings before interest and tax' and several more all have a distinct meaning. Profits are also expressed as percentages of cost, of sales, of turnover and as a return on capital investment. The percentage range across these various measures can be quite large. 5% return on sales may equate to 200% return on capital. Bandying such numbers can inadvertently cause embarrassment. The customer who hears that his job generated 75% profit for the company may be concerned that he was overcharged. But if this figure is simply the margin between the selling price (which includes overheads, material handling charges, financing costs, warranty, third party royalties, packaging, freight and insurance) and the basic works cost (direct labour and materials) then the net profit on the job may only be 10% and the customer should be quite content. No financial figures should ever be used outside of the company other than properly approved prices.

For the purposes of this book the single word 'profit' will be used both to mean how well the business has done over a twelve-month accounting period and also how well an individual job has been done in financial terms. In both cases the objective is, in simple terms, the same. Everything the company does must be sold at a higher value than the sum of all of its costs. Accountants make adjustments to profit, for example, by making 'provisions', which is money kept in the kitty against some known contingent liability that may or may not arise. Special items in the accounts (for example, unexpected excessive costs of acquisitions) also affect profit. Profits retained for investment are still profits, although the shareholders forgo a higher next dividend in return for the promise of growth and higher dividends later. But for present purposes, the simple definition is more than sufficient. To maximize profit means minimizing cost, maximizing selling prices and finding a product/market where customers abound or are secure. The strategies towards this are as follows.

Increasing demand

Concentration on producing and supplying those goods and services where demand is increasing should lead to higher profits. This may sound obvious but sometimes product developments are pursued because of the inherent technical challenge – found attractive at the individual or corporate level – rather than because of a well-researched market demand.

Minimizing costs

Minimization of the cost of production by selecting the cheapest possible combination of premises, machinery, labour and services is an obvious goal. Thus, if substituting machines for labour is cheaper, this will be done despite the social consequences. Proactive supply chain management, value chain management, partnership sourcing and service outsourcing are all aimed at reducing cost in the overall value chain.

Optimizing output

Maintaining output at the level at which profits are maximized is a useful approach. For example, if a business produces widgets and the best machine runs most efficiently at 5,000 widgets per hour then producing only 4,000 widgets per hour is under-utilizing the equipment and recovering the cost of the machine more slowly – to attempt to produce 6,000 widgets an hour may incur higher maintenance costs and longer downtime periods.

Market/price influencing

Where a single organization is dominant in its own area of activity it can affect the price of the goods it produces by varying the amount it supplies to the market. It is therefore able to adjust either price or output to suit its own profit-maximization objectives.

Niche markets

Supplying in a niche market can provide secure profits. Whether there are many or few customers, the fact that there are few suppliers or a single supplier will support high prices provided the niche is for essential, high value adding products. The niche may disappear as technology or business practice changes, but there are no foolproof ways of making good profits over an extended period of time.

High price markets

Supplying in a market where prices are kept artificially high can appear attractive. There are a few markets – for example perfumery – where regulatory bodies appear happy to allow artificially high prices to prevail.

Low risk markets

Supplying in a market where risks are low is a worthwhile consideration. Some markets (arguably business consultancy) are at the high profit, low risk end of the spectrum, but sometimes low risk business may mean low rates of profit. However, the attraction is in the certainty of profit and the avoidance of events that could threaten not only profit, but also the very existence of the company.

Mergers and acquisitions

Merging with or acquiring other businesses is a frequent route to intended higher profits. The aim may be to eliminate part of the competition, to acquire new customers and products or 'simply' to realize higher efficiencies through the synergies (for example, increased purchasing power) of a combined operation.

Some of these strategies are not without their obstacles and pitfalls. For example, abuse of market position can fall foul of competition law as will be seen in Chapter 4 and many an acquisition has both proved more costly than anticipated as well as more difficult to convert into predicted benefits.

Cash

Healthy cash flow is the essence of good business management. In its start up phase, a company will have some of its loan capital set aside for paying the workers and meeting other creditors' demands. But a business breathes through its cash. At the earliest moment, regular cash income from its customers must exceed its cash expenditure or the company stands a considerable risk of going broke. Lord Wienstock of GEC fame boasted (over the company's 'cash mountain') that his shareholders and the City could count annual profits as real money sitting in the bank. This is an admirable ethic. Those businesses that produce their profits reliably and consistently as cash (and not 'paper' profit in the accounts) are considered to be well run. Even if the level of profit is not spectacular, such companies are a safe bet. For investors and in the take-over stakes, companies producing profit in hard cash are frequently a more attractive option than the more speculative enterprises. The bubble burst over many dot.com companies who seemed to have a good product portfolio, a large customer list and bags of good ideas, but many had cash flow problems as well as never making a profit. A strong order book and business founded upon well-made contracts and other sound business practices may well allow a company to secure loans, but if these are to cover running costs, rather than capital and other investments (for example, training) for the future then the company is likely to suffer. Burning away profit (and increasing liabilities) by financing loans to cover running costs is one of the worst commercial 'crimes'.

There are many factors affecting cash-flow, including:

Employee terms

Almost every aspect of employment has a cost and therefore a cash flow implication. It is not just a question of whether staff are paid on a weekly or monthly basis. For example, payment of bonuses linked to individual performance may be earned ahead of or behind schedule. Payment of bonuses for company performance may become due before the company's accounts have been audited, leaving a difficult question over payment based upon submitted accounts with the risk of under payment or overpayment if the audit approves a different set of numbers.

Customer payment performance

Not all customers pay on time even though invoices are valid and payment is due. In some companies it is worth the additional staff cost in having a credit control department whose job it is simply to chase customers for payment and where necessary to take further steps to ensure that payment is made.

Customer payment arrangements

In simple transactions the payment terms may be a quite straightforward – 'payment in full 30 days from receipt of valid invoice'. In larger contracts there may be a choice of advance payments, stage payments, progress payments, payments on account and combinations thereof. The selection and negotiation of these more complex arrangements is absolutely essential to the successful management of cash.

Supplier credit periods

Payment practices with suppliers are an important factor in managing cash flow. Despite legislation aimed at ensuring companies pay their debts to suppliers within thirty days of invoice, many companies still seek to have extended credit periods from their suppliers. This may be achieved either by negotiating extended credit periods (possibly with an increase in price) in the terms of purchase orders or by the simple expedient of ensuring that all bills are 'sat upon' for a period of time. This latter practice is to be deplored in modern business. Another approach, which tends to be employed on larger contracts, is for the buyer to seek a 'pay-when-paid' term in his purchase orders. The idea is to ensure that the company is not bound to make payments to its suppliers unless and until payments have been received from its customer. In some circumstances such arrangements are actually outlawed, although in some commercial arrangements this approach is quite valid and can be helpful to all concerned.

Contractual performance

Provided that the contract payment terms have been negotiated to optimum advantage before the contract is signed (not to be taken for granted – future events such as payment can sometimes be overlooked in the eagerness to secure the order in the first place!) then the most crucial aspect to managing cash flow is to ensure that the contract is performed on time and to specification. Key milestones, deliveries and any other events that trigger payment must be achieved according to the contract. It is sometimes thought that delivering ahead of schedule must be advantageous to the company, provided the customer is willing to accept delivery. This may or may not be true. It is not unknown for canny buyers to negotiate provisions into purchase orders that give them the option to accept early delivery if such is proffered, but to have no obligation to make payment ahead of schedule.

Other payment obligations

Whilst the aim is to concentrate on those commercial aspects where the manager will have most influence, there are other financial obligations where cash flow management is also important. In addition to paying suppliers, companies also have to make payments of VAT, corporation tax, business rates, licence fees and levies, energy and telecom charges. All these will be managed to ensure the optimization of cash flow.

Order book

As well as generating cash and profit from performing existing orders, many companies will have a deliberate policy of growth and expansion. This necessarily may be accomplished at the short-term cost of reduced profit, as profits must be ploughed back into the business as a source for financing expansion. The possibilities for developing the business include the following:

Expanding markets

Expansion within existing markets and spreading into adjacent markets brings about growth. This may be achieved by developing new products and by increasing output combined with greater advertising, publicity and marketing activities.

Successfully performing existing contracts

There is considerable value in terms of reputation in being seen to complete contracts on time and to specification. Goodwill is established and contented customers will come back for more. Every opportunity should be taken to let the customer (and the world) know what a good deal he has had from you, as he may not know himself!

Acquiring technology

Licensing designs, manufacturing rights, dealership, agency and franchise rights from other companies are sound ways of potentially increasing the order book over a shorter period of time (and probably at lower cost) than would be the case if the new technology or markets were developed from scratch. Granting such rights to other companies is also a convenient way of increasing revenues, although it may do little for growth.

Mergers and acquisitions

Naturally combining two or more enterprises has the effect of consolidating the separate order books into one. Although very major contracts may contain terms preventing merger without agreement of the customer (who may have legitimate rights in not wanting to find himself in a contract with a party whom he would not otherwise choose) mergers do bring about a sound way of not only increasing order book but also increasing the customer base.

All well-run businesses will have defined plans for growth and expansion. Individuals will be responsible for drawing up specific plans and programmes for existing and new products and technologies. This will be geared towards existing and potential new customers and markets. The single most important thing is for every employee to keep in mind these fundamental growth strategies. Ideas should be put forward and every opportunity taken in talking to and meeting customers, suppliers, associates and colleagues. All contacts are people and all people like to sound knowledgeable and informed about their organization. All intelligence gained needs to be shared to discover and exploit its value. Even if ostensibly worthless it may nevertheless corroborate, confirm or deny some other information.

Intellectual property

The company's ideas have a significant commercial value and the company owns the ideas and has the right to exploit them. Generically the ideas are known as 'intellectual property'. The rights to protect their form and application and exploit them are known as 'intellectual property rights'.

Some new ideas may be limited to purely internal matters such as business process improvement, but many ideas will be connected with the company's product portfolio. Whatever it sells (products, knowledge, advice, design) it's future will depend upon it's ability to innovate, even if only in its marketing strategy. Commercial success from innovation has an engineering aspect, a marketing perspective and this other odd perspective known as 'intellectual property'. The importance of the protection of intellectual property cannot be overstated. Without the intellectual property rights which the law provides, a company may not succeed in protecting and commercially exploiting its ideas or it may not succeed for very long. Intellectual property is an esoteric subject that continues to grow in complexity through changes in national and international law and regulation, as well as through changes in the fields of information and communications technology.

Value

The essence of all intellectual property law and regulation is to encourage innovation (because it is considered to be in the general good) by allowing those who apply their intellect to protect the results of their efforts from others and to exploit their efforts for gain. In some cases (copyright) the test of intellectual application is quite low. In other instances (patents) the test is higher. But the deal is just the same. The application of intellect is rewarded by exclusive rights to exploit the result. The owner (or 'proprietor') of the intellectual property does not have to exploit the result for material or financial gain. He can make the results available to others entirely freely, for example 'Linus' software.

The value of intellectual property can be realized in many ways. Intellectual property can be bought or sold as any other property. Intellectual property is referred to as 'intangible' property to distinguish it from other, tangible forms of property. An inventor who has no desire or the means to take his intellectual property into industrial application and who wishes a windfall income may simply sell all the rights to the highest bidder. Intellectual property can be licensed, which means that the proprietor retains ownership, but grants rights in the intellectual property to another for money or other commercial gain. The intellectual property can be applied industrially to sell products or services, to establish marketplace identity or to enhance reputation. Intellectual property rights can be used merely to prevent others from its exploitation. Intellectual property can be acquired through merger or acquisition. The intellectual property of others (for example, the publicly available technical information of a patent) may provide a springboard for new research or development.

Infringement of an intellectual property right is, in the eyes of the law, an infringement whether or not the infringing act was intentional, except where there is an express permission (for example a licence) or an implied permission (for example, where a contractual obligation can only be performed by one side by making use of the other side's intellectual property) from the intellectual property owner.

Patents

A patent protects an underlying invention. In the case of Mr Dyson's vacuum cleaner there will be a patent that covers the concept of the filter less cyclone as a means of removing dust. A patent is a 20-year monopoly grant by the Crown in return for public disclosure of the technical details of the invention. This disclosure is not intended to allow someone else to replicate the same idea, but to provide a springboard for the development of yet new ideas. For the patent applicant the aim is to draw up the description of the invention as widely as possible in order to limit his competitors' springboard opportunities. The aim of the competitor is to work his way around the patent so that he can make the maximum use of the patented idea without infringing the patent. The drawing up of a patent application is thus a task that is best left to specialists within a large company or, for the smaller company, to a patent agent. The application and grant process can be time consuming because, for example, the patent authority must undertake an extensive search to make sure that the application does not replicate an existing patent. For a patent application to succeed the invention must:

- Be new

- Have an 'inventive step' – meaning that there is a new idea that is not obvious to someone skilled in the relevant subject matter

- Be capable of industrial application

- Not encourage offensive, immoral or anti-social action

- Not consist of a scientific theory, computer program (although some applications may be patentable) or aesthetic work

- Not have been disclosed publicly.

The final test is of great interest to an engineer. In the excitement of discovery there is a natural tendency to want to tell the world about a new invention as soon as possible. However, from a business point of view no public disclosure should take place until the patent has been filed and no discussion should take place with any other commercial organization unless effective obligations of confidentiality are in place. Breach of a patent entitles the patentee to an injunction against the infringer, delivery up of any infringing articles (the infringer must hand them over to the patent holder) and financial damages.

Copyright

Copyright gives a 70-year period of protection in respect of original literary, dramatic, artistic or musical works, including sound recordings and films. Copyright exists from the moment the work is created, regardless of the media (paper or electronic) in which the work is held and does not involve any process of registration. Infringement is infringement regardless of the method. Thus copying by hand, photocopying, photography, electronic scanning and printing information from the Internet are all potential infringements. Copyright also embraces material of much more interest to the commercial engineer than literary, dramatic, artistic or musical works. For example, copyright covers engineering drawings, specifications, plans, risk networks, test schedules and the results of tests. The manufacturing drawings (even if held in CAD/CAM) of Mr Dyson's vacuum cleaner are copyright work. In practice, the sharing of technical information between companies can imply a right to use copyright material, but it is much better if the necessary licence is in place before this happens. Computer software is considered to be copyright work and infringement includes activities such as electronically storing or displaying the software or adapting the software, including translation from one computer language to another. The copyright protection for software subsists only for 50 years!

In addition to copyright protection, there are 'performers' rights' that are intended to protect the intellectual property in the performance of a work (for example, on the stage). This is likely to be of little professional interest to the commercial manager.

Database rights

A database is a 'collection of independent works, data or other materials which are arranged in a systematic or methodical way and are individually accessed by electronic or other means'. The database right gives fifteen years of protection and aims to protect against unauthorized copying, adaptations or dealings in the database. The right prevents unauthorized extraction or re-utilization. 'Extraction' means that the contents (in whole or in part) of the database are permanently or temporarily transferred to another medium by any means or form. 'Reutilization' means the unauthorized disclosure to the public. In addition, information in a database may be given a limited degree of copyright protection provided that the selection and contents are original, meaning that they are the author's own intellectual creation. If a database falls outside of the above definition or was created before 1 January 1998 then the database is protected by copyright.

Design rights

Design rights protect the appearance of an object. A registered design gives 25 years of protection and covers the aesthetic appearance of an object. An unregistered design gives a maximum of fifteen years of protection and covers the purely functional aspects of a design. Thus the shape and colour combination that gives eye-appeal to Mr Dyson's vacuum cleaner may be the subject of a registered design. The shape and configuration of the motor assembly may be an unregistered design. There is an important exclusion to unregistered design protection. This is known as the 'must fit must match' exclusion. It is accepted that a buyer acquires an implied right that enables him to use, repair and maintain his purchase without necessarily going back to the owner of the design. This means that he is free to buy spare parts from whomsoever he pleases (taking the risk of invalidating any warranty). Thus Mr Dyson cannot use his unregistered design to achieve exclusivity in the supply of spare parts since any manufacturer is entitled to make a spare part to his own design, copying only those parts of Mr Dyson's design that are necessary to accomplish a fit or match with the original. There is, however, nothing to stop a designer from so constructing his design as to make matching and fitting as difficult as possible. Intellectual property law simply prevents the designer from stopping someone else designing and making spare parts; it does not require him to make life easy for his competitor. This is an example where an understanding of intellectual property may guide an engineer's approach to his work. The 'must fit must match' exclusion relates only to the physical attributes (shape and dimensions) of the product. It does not extend to electrical, electronic or software interfaces.

Trademarks

Trademarks (including trade names) are words or symbols that are used in relation to goods or services that distinguish the owner from his competitors. There are rules that govern what types of words can be trademarks and it is as well to seek specialist advice on choosing a mark. Marks can be registered or can come into protection simply through the use of the mark over a period of time. The aim of the protection is to prevent someone from so using another's mark (either identically or similarly) as to cause confusion in the minds of the public. That is to say, a buyer may purchase goods or services from the seller using the infringing mark in the belief that the goods or services originate from the owner of the mark. This is said to be 'passing off' by the infringing seller. Companies choose, exploit and protect their trademarks very carefully. Upon the trademark may subsist the company's reputation that has been built up over many years. Reputation has a real, tradable value. Examples are everywhere: 'Dyson', 'Hoover', 'Virgin', and 'Orange'. In order to protect a trademark, the owner must ensure that it is always used in exactly the same shape (scale does not matter), style and colour. Detailed instructions and terms should always accompany any agreement between companies on the use of each other's trademarks (for example, in a consortium bid). Companies do not lightly allow others to use their valuable trade names.

Confidentiality

It might be thought that individually or in combination, patents, copyright, database rights, registered design rights, unregistered design rights and trademark rights would provide sufficient protection for a company's special information. This is not so. A company may have many trade secrets that do not fall under the protection of any of these regimes or the protection is weak – for example breach of copyright relies upon the injured party proving that copying took place. Examples of trade secrets are: price lists, supplier lists, customer lists, investment plans, merger and acquisition plans, bidding plans and expansion plans. Such information may be protected under the law of confidentiality. To achieve protection four tests apply:

Quality of confidentiality

This means that the information must be of the sort that would be expected to be confidential (for example, price lists). If the law is to provide protection and remedies for breach, it would be absurd to construe all company information as having this quality of confidentiality.

Circumstances importing an obligation of confidentiality

This means that there must be a relationship that carries the quality of confidentiality. Examples include a contractual relationship, an employer/employee relationship and fiduciary relationships.

Unauthorized use

This means use without the permission of the owner.

Not public domain

It is not possible to establish obligations of confidentiality over information that is in the public domain. In business dealings it is not usually possible to retrospectively apply obligations of confidentiality to information already exchanged.

The subject of confidentiality will be looked at in more detail in later chapters. However, there are three points of advice for the commercial manager at this stage. Firstly, do not provide or exchange company information outside of the company without there being established appropriate obligations of confidentiality. Secondly, mark all sensitive company information as confidential, or with the relevant company approved mark. Thirdly, begin all external meetings with a reminder that the discussions are commercially confidential.

Reverse engineering

Reverse engineering is the process of taking a competitor's product and learning from its design and construction for the purposes of producing a similar or better product. This is a perfectly legitimate activity, provided the reverse engineer does not infringe any of the rights of the originator described above!

The position of employees

If an employee invents something as part of his job there are two sets of circumstances in each of which the employer is entitled to claim ownership to the invention. Firstly, if the employee makes his invention 'in the course of his normal duties' it belongs to his employer. A research worker inventing a new concept linked to his work could not claim the idea as his own. On the other hand a machine operator who, out of the blue, sees how his machine could be improved probably could. Secondly, the employer can claim ownership if the employee, because of the nature of his work and responsibilities, can be said to have a special obligation to further his employer's interests. This is aimed particularly at senior staff. For example, a director of research and development might not be actively engaged in research but he would be expected to put his full skill and knowledge to his employer's service. In other circumstances the invention belongs to the employee and he is entitled to patent it and to receive any royalties arising from it. If the employer patents an invention made by one of his employees but which belongs in law to the employee, the employee is entitled to be named in the patent and enjoy its benefits.

Many companies put rules about employees' inventions into their employment contracts. Provided that the employee could reasonably have been expected to be aware of the rules when he entered into the contract, they bind him. However, the employer cannot use those rules to secure the right to an invention that has nothing to do with the employee's job. Any rule that seeks to deprive the employee of his rights in inventions belonging to him is void and unenforceable. Nor does the employer have the automatic right to an invention that, whilst partly related to the employee's job, does not arise directly from it and was worked upon by the employee in his own time, using his own materials and off his employer's premises. If an employee invents something that, by law, becomes the property of his employer he may nevertheless be entitled to a 'fair share' of any profits. To succeed in his claim, the employee must show that his employer has derived 'outstanding benefit' from patenting the invention. The size and nature of the employer's business would be taken into account when deciding if the benefit has been outstanding.

Contracts

Maximizing profit, minimizing risk and business development are all concerned with the carrying on of the business to the greater glory and profit of the shareholders. Nevertheless, this is achieved through the medium of winning contracts, on one end of which is the customer who is only concerned with acquiring the goods or services he needs at minimum cost and inconvenience. The important point is that under the contract the customer may be entitled to many things and all those involved in implementing a contract should be aware of those things and more importantly the extent and limitation of whatever the customer's rights are. The principle, however, is to know the customer's minimum and maximum entitlement. If in practice he is satisfied with his minimum entitlement then contract costs will have been minimized and profit maximized. On the other if he is dissatisfied with his maximum entitlement then it needs to be put to him, carefully and diplomatically, that if he wants more, he must pay more. Similarly the success of the business may depend upon the performance of the company's suppliers. Anywhere in the supply chain, the buyer/seller **transaction** is inevitably based, in simple terms, upon a conflict of interests – each of the buyer and seller appear to stand to gain at the expense of the other. Common sense dictates that the buyer/seller **relationship** must be managed so as to sideline that conflict, but the pursuit of profit for one's own organization is facilitated by an understanding of the limit of obligations and the extent of protection afforded by both sales and purchase orders.

Business analyses

It has been proposed that the key commercial words are profit, cash, order book (or growth), intellectual property, risk and contracts. Beyond the substance of these matters arises the question as to the means by which the company may analyze these issues on a continuous basis so that it appreciates the health and wealth of its business.

Profit analysis

Profit is analyzed in the profit and loss ('P&L') account. It indicates the profit or loss generated by the company's activities. The annual P&L looks back over time. In addition it is important to keep under review where profit is made. A surprising number of businesses, with a diverse range of activities, know that they make profit (because the P&L shows it) but lack a detailed understanding of which products and processes drive profitability. Henry Royce (co-founder of Rolls-Royce) said, 'every time material is handled something is added to its cost, but not necessarily to its value'. Not only does this show the importance of understanding what adds value so that non-value adding processes can be eliminated, but it also shows the thinking of another commercial engineer, for Royce was just a 'humble mechanic' when he spoke those words.

Cash flow analysis

Cash is the operating lifeblood of the company. All companies run an analysis of cash flow to predict receipts against disbursements. The analysis can be done daily or monthly (or on any periodicity), depending on the volatility and size of the company's operation. Positive cash flow generates interest and permits a good credit rating. Negative cash flow eats into profit and destroys not only creditworthiness but also shareholder, employee, customer and supplier confidence. The analysis of cash flow and, in particular, the forecasting of future cash flow is an important picture for the commercial manager to have, to help him/her give priority to achieving contract milestones and managing expenditure.

Order book analysis

The purpose of the order book analysis is to indicate both current performance (actual v anticipated orders and planned v achieved deliveries against orders received) and trends (to facilitate planning for capacity, resources, investment and other future expenditure). To sustain the operation on its present basis requires equivalent new orders to be won as existing orders are performed and completed. If the company's optimum performance is in delivering 1,000 widgets a month and the average customer orders

100 at a time for delivery the same month, then the company needs to secure 10 orders a month. Ideally, order-intake should run slightly ahead of deliveries. This provides some protection against problems and permits the steady growth of the company. If order-intake runs well ahead of delivery then there may be the danger that the company cannot cope with its commitments, or may run into cash-flow problems if raw material stocks have to be built up or further capital equipment bought ahead of receiving any payments from customers. On the other hand, if orders are trailing deliveries, then the level of output and performance for which the company is currently geared will be too high for the falling orders and output will have to be reduced, and if the level of order-intake is not increased this contraction can become an interminable process to the point where the company can no longer continue trading.

A consequence of this is that the quantity of stock may build up. Stock is a current asset within working capital but the value of that stock is related to its market value. If the market, or the share of it, is contracting then the value of the stock can rapidly fall. Even in a healthy business the general maxim is to keep stock to the absolute minimum consistent with meeting the most likely forecast demand. Observing the change in net order book value can see the measure of the problem. The gross order book is the summation of all gross contract prices. The net order book value is the gross order book value minus the value of deliveries already made under the orders held. A company delivering orders at a value of £30,000 per month against a gross order book of £300,000 has 10 months work. If the net order book value declines then trouble lies ahead, reinforcing the point made above.

Intellectual property analysis

It is important that companies maintain a thorough portfolio of their intellectual property. This can be easier said than done. Where a company has a tried and tested procedure for patenting its inventions, maintenance of the portfolio is largely a matter of routine and protection of the patent rights is largely a matter of vigilance. On the other hand, patents do **not** grant themselves. There must be awareness amongst the engineering community as to what may be a patentable invention and the things not to do until the right legal steps have been taken. This is a fairly simple example.

A more difficult feature of establishing the portfolio is grasping the myriad rights (and their governing terms and limitations) that may be covered in contractual (as opposed to statutory) arrangements. Incoming and outgoing licences all have both value and restrictions. Once work is underway under a contract new intellectual property may come into being. In some contracts one or both of the parties bring the intellectual property to the contract. Changes of ownership and control may complicate matters further. For such reasons an effective approach to maintaining the portfolio is essential and the engineer, whether working in the 'backroom' or in the frontline of the contract has much to contribute to this process.

Risk analysis

From an objective viewpoint it is important that whenever the company carries out formal risk analysis (for example, at the business level, at the contract tendering stage or at the contract performance stage) it ensures that all of the relevant categories of risk mentioned above are included. This will ensure that the processes of probability assessment, impact assessment, avoidance and mitigation planning can embrace all possible risks and not just those associated with technical or timescale risk. From a subjective viewpoint it is interesting to consider which of the above risks are within and which are outside the control of the company. On the face of it, common sense would say that political risks and acts of God are outside of the company's control, but most other risks are within the company's control. Some (wherever there is an external influence) such as customer risk, supplier risk and some aspects of personnel risk (e.g. trade unions) lie somewhere between the two. But this is not a very helpful place to start.

Another, more useful, way to segregate the elements in this list of risks is to differentiate between the ways in which they can be dealt with. The four categories are as follows:

- Risks within the company's management responsibility

- Risks that the company may seek to pass on to customers or suppliers under the terms of contract

- Risks against which the company may try to buy insurance

- Risks totally outside the company's ability to manage or to protect itself.

In practice, some risks may lay across more than one of these categories. In the area of technical risk the risks are largely within the gift of the company to manage, for example by acquiring the right level and mix of skills the risk of poor design or design being delayed or not completed can be reduced; by providing the right design aids and working environment the design process may be facilitated; by freezing the ultimate requirement specification before substantial design gets under way.

However, where the design objective is highly inventive or novel or where it is to meet special and unique requirements of a particular customer, it may be possible to pass some of the design risk on to the customer by phrasing the contract so that the work is not to meet the end-requirement but simply to work towards that goal to a predetermined level of expenditure. In this the customer takes the chance of the requirement not being met unless he chooses to spend more money. Similarly, in manufacturing, risk minimization is largely attainable by good planning, good shop-floor layout and industrial engineering. The customer may wish to share in the risk by providing funds towards the setting up or enhancement of the production facilities.

Financial risks are the responsibility of the company although some may be attenuated by passing a proportion of the risk to customers or suppliers. For example the customer may be persuaded to contribute to the alleviation of cash flow problems by providing upfront or interim financing on high value and/or long-duration contracts. Suppliers may be persuaded to provide abnormal payment credit periods. Where there is a foreign currency in the price, the customer may be content to make payments in whole or in part in the foreign currency, particularly if, as in the case of very large buyers or government departments, foreign currency can be bought more easily or more cheaply by the customer than by the company. Suppliers may be persuaded to absorb the risk of currency fluctuations in its prices. Foreign-exchange risks and/or general inflation risks may be shared with the customer on the basis of a formula allowing for the price to be varied in line with movements in exchange rates or inflation rates. On the other hand, estimating is largely a function of the skill of the engineers, surveyors and estimators and thus the financial risk must lie fairly and squarely with the company. Although matters such as tax liabilities and government financial support to industry are outside the scope of company management as such, nevertheless expert advice is available from bankers, finance consultants, and other experts in the field.

Commercial risks are essentially those flowing from, or associated with, the very nature of the particular enterprise or business. Thus choice of products, markets, customers and suppliers is a question of being prudent and exercising judgement and analysis. Monitoring market trends, the business columns and keeping watch for emerging competitors and products are all vital aspects. Taking steps to safeguard and exploit ideas and inventions are essential. Commercial risks are the very essence of being in business and require sound management. Contractual dealings also provide scope for minimizing not only commercial risks but also risks from many of the other categories.

Legal risks cover more than one category. It is possible, for example, to pass on to the customer the risk of a third party taking action in respect of an infringement of a patent or copyright. On the other hand, the company can actually take steps to ensure that it is not infringing such things by undertaking, for example, patent searches at the relevant authorities. Then again, it may be possible to insure against the risk of third party legal action. Some legal requirements are assumed by the very act of carrying on a business. For example, the employer has a duty of care (dereliction of which is negligence) to employees and customers.

Personnel risks are a matter for the company's own management. The employment of people is covered by a tremendous wealth of law and legislation. However, the risks to the success of the business are for the company to control and are bound by good organization, structure and management.

Political risks are outside the control of the company and are generally not insurable. The only real answer is for the company to be dynamic and flexible enough to respond quickly and effectively to political changes that influence the business.

Contracts analysis

On the face of it there may seem to be little of interest in analyzing contracts. However, most companies hold a 'contract review meeting' before a major contract is taken. This is a requirement under ISO9001 and is good business practice in any event. The purpose is twofold. Firstly there is an examination as to whether the contract now offered by the customer reflects the 'as bid' position, as may have been modified during authorized post-bid negotiations. The second purpose is to gain final ratification from the company that the contract may be accepted (and become a legally binding obligation) given the risks to the company that are expressed in, or implied by, the contract. There is an old maxim: 'the good news is we've won the bid, the bad news is we've got the contract'. There is much truth in this. Apart from the most obvious risk that the contract costs may exceed the contract price, the contract will convey to the company many risks that go much deeper than this. Hence the need, amidst the excitement of winning, to take a cold hard appraisal of the proposed contract prior to its acceptance. The engineer's role in the contract review meeting is essential (and in the earlier bid approval process). Unless he is commercially aware he may unintentionally skip over a matter that in his mind is trivial, but which would loom large if fully conscious of the commercial implications.

Furthermore, many risks are of finite duration. For example, a contract warranty (if drafted properly in the first place) will have a particular expiry date. It is important for the company to keep such matters under review such that individual risks may be closed off once the relevant date (or sometimes an event) has passed. This is especially so when a provision has been made in the company's books to continge against the financial consequences of the risk materializing.

Apart from criminal or negligent acts, the worst thing a company can do is to enter into contracts the provisions of which might spell disaster for the company. So important is this, that companies are required to draw to the attention of the shareholders those contracts that are 'material' to the good conduct of the business.

It is equally important to carry out a contract review meeting before placing any major subcontract or purchase order. This has many advantages that are similar to the customer contract review meeting. Firstly, there is the company sanction of the risks (to the company), which will arise because of the terms of the purchase order. Secondly, there is the opportunity to confirm earlier checks on the financial position and other matters affecting the viability of the intended supplier. Finally, there is the chance to do a thorough check on the consistency between the terms of the customer contract and the supplier contract. The word consistency is chosen carefully. In some cases there may be virtually no relationship between the two contracts. In other cases there may be extensive mandatory 'flow down' terms in the customer contract that result in the supplier contract having the appearance of a virtual photocopy of the customer contract. Indeed in some companies there is a practice of producing draft supplier contracts by starting with a photocopy of the customer contract. This is always dangerous. The danger lies not just in the 'commercial' terms but also in the detail of engineering aspects (for example in specifications). The danger is twofold. Firstly it may be appropriate to include terms in a supplier contract that are more onerous or demanding than in the customer contract. This is to ensure that there is some leeway (to the company's advantage) between the discharge of the company's obligations to the customer and the performance of supplier contracts. Secondly, by imposing requirements in the supplier contract that are really not necessary, the supplier's price may be higher (as he has to cover his contingent liability) than need be.

Other analyses

Apart from analyses relating to profit, cash, order book, intellectual property, risk and contracts, there are many other analyses that companies run. The following are some examples.

Balance sheet

The principal financial analysis, apart from the P&L account is the 'balance sheet'. Whereas the P&L looks back over the year to see what profit was made, the balance sheet presents a picture of the value, location and accessibility of the company's assets. It is essentially a snapshot at any given time and to this extent it is in many ways more useful than the P&L account.

Overheads

The accountants also spend much time poring over the monthly overhead analysis. This can be a more difficult analysis to understand and can generate even less interest as it can seem that individuals have little control over overheads. It is nevertheless important to get a grip of this subject. There are many different accounting systems in use (job costing and standard costing are examples) but many produce contract-charging rates that have both a direct and an indirect (overhead) element. If a manager is given a budget for his part of the overall job, his costs will be affected by the overhead rates. Many a manager has been disappointed to find that, when controlling his direct costs within budget, a sudden movement in overhead rates puts the total costs above budget. It is no use complaining that someone else is in charge of overheads. If the cost has gone up, it has gone up! Therefore the commercial manager must understand the company's overhead structure and become positively engaged in managing total costs.

Supplier base

In many businesses the supplier base is increasingly important. Supply chain management involves a range of techniques from the rationalization of supplier lists to the establishment of strategic partnerships with key suppliers. The information upon which such policies depend is up-to-date, complete and accurate data about the performance, products, prices, and stability of the company's supplier base. An analysis of this data, fed by hands-on experience of those – including engineers – dealing with suppliers is essential to success.

Checklist

- Profit, cash, order book (growth), intellectual property, risk and contracts are the key words of the commercial domain.

- Profit can be maximized by increasing demand, minimizing costs, optimizing output, influencing the marketplace, aiming at high price or low risk or niche markets and through mergers and acquisitions.

- Cash flow is influenced by employee terms, customer payment terms and performance, supplier credit and contractual performance.

- Growth is achieved through expanding markets, successful performance, acquiring technology and through mergers and acquisitions.

- Intellectual property is hugely valuable intangible property protected through patents, copyright, database rights, registered design rights, unregistered design rights, trademark rights and confidentiality.

- Risk can be allocated to or shared with customers and suppliers.

- Insurance can be used to cover some, but not all, categories of business risk.

- Contracts are the axis around which successful business performance revolves.

- Business analyses are an essential tool in monitoring the health and wealth of the company.

The contract

Introduction

It is possible to describe a wheel in terms of its end purpose but a complete understanding is lost without a description of the concept and operation of the axle. Similarly any detailed discussion of the commercial aspects of business without reference to contracts would be misguided. There would be many ways of describing business without such reference. It would be possible to talk about investment as an input and profit as an output, or resources as an input and product as an output. But without discussing contracts, a key part of the story is missing. It is easy enough to say that the manager should contribute to increasing profits by ensuring that contracts are delivered on time, to specification and at minimum cost because failure in these respects eats up money, which erodes profit. But the simple consequence – higher internal cost – of such failures is only a small part of the story. To fully appreciate the picture it is necessary to understand this thing called the contract. In this chapter coverage will be given to underlying legal principles, common contractual phrases and points of practical importance.

Law

Legal framework

Each country has its own system of law and within each system there are many divisions and subdivisions. English law is divided between public law and private law. Public law is concerned with the constitution and functions of governmental organizations, including local authorities, and their legal relationship with the citizen and with each other. Public law is also concerned with crime, which involves the state's relationship with, and power of control over, the individual. Private law is concerned with the legal relationships of ordinary persons in everyday transactions. It is also concerned with the legal position of companies. Private law includes contract and commercial law, the law of tort; law relating to family matters and the law of property.

Applicable law

A contract is subject to law. It is for the parties to the contract to choose the law that is applicable to their contract. If both were domiciled in the same territory, then the law of that territory would normally apply. If the parties are in different territories then they elect the law of one of the territories. Other possibilities are the law of the land in which the contract is physically performed, and the law of the land where one of the parties' parent companies is based. A final option is a 'neutral' jurisdiction. This may be a useful resolution where the parties cannot agree on which of their 'home' jurisdictions should apply. This is much more than an esoteric point for the lawyers. When a company proposes to enter into a contract that is subject to its local law, then the fullest appreciation of the risks in the transaction can be considered as part of the business decision to proceed. This appreciation can be seriously diluted if the transaction is to be subject to a foreign law with which the company is not familiar. To confuse matters further the parties may elect one jurisdiction to govern the legal formation of the contract, another to govern the performance of the contract and another to govern arbitration proceedings. The law in other countries varies dramatically in construction and application compared with English law. Only English law is considered here. Companies doing regular business with overseas customers or suppliers should familiarize themselves with the law which is applicable to their particular contracts. However, once one is familiar with contractual principles under English law, a commercial assessment of the risks and other implications of a foreign law is easier to make.

Appreciation of the law

The law as it affects the formation and performance of contracts, the duties, undertakings and obligations of the parties to each other and to third parties is a splendid mixture of common law, contract law, tort law and statutory law. Even in routine business transactions companies increasingly have lawyers on hand to advise, but legal complexity is no excuse for business people not to possess an appreciation of some basics of the law as it affects contracts. As consumers we all 'know our rights' when we go into a shop, so in business contracts we should know likewise – and it should be noted right away that consumer contracts and business contracts are not the same kettle of fish.

What is a contract?

But what is a contract? In the simplest terms a contract is a mutual exchange of promises. The seller promises to supply goods or services and the buyer promises to pay. If certain criteria are satisfied, this exchange of promises can be enforced in a court of law. As the court has said, 'Contracts when entered into freely and voluntarily shall be held sacred and shall be enforced by courts of justice'. This ancient statement not only captures the principle of legal enforcement but also illustrates, in its use of the phrase 'freely and voluntarily', a fundamental tenet of English law that contracts are made freely and not 'in terrorem'. This means that neither party may be forced into a contract or forced to perform a contract by threat. Amongst other things, this tells us that penalty terms in contracts are not enforceable, but as the text will show later, one man's penalty is another man's incentive! So contracts may not be made or carried out by force from the parties. However, a court may enforce a contract, meaning that it will require a defaulting party to perform, or failing such performance the court will allow the injured party certain remedies. But this is to jump ahead; to begin with we first need some principles.

Contract types

Although the principle of a contract is easy enough to state, contracts come in many varieties. So as an hors-d'oeuvres to this fascinating subject (sic) a short explanation of the different types of contracts as seen by lawyers is helpful.

Simple and speciality contracts

Contracts can be simple or speciality. Speciality contracts are also known as contracts under seal or deeds. Speciality contracts relate to certain classes of property leases and to contracts in which there is no consideration (see below). This type of contract accounts for a very small proportion of business and is not considered further. Regardless of complexity or volume the majority of business contracts with which this book is concerned are known as 'simple' contracts. Contracts of sale and contracts of purchase are examples of simple contracts.

Written and oral contracts

Simple contracts do not have to be made in writing. Individuals make the majority of contracts as oral arrangements only – whether it be buying a newspaper or purchasing a meal. Examples of contracts that are required to be made in writing are bills of exchange, the sale of land and consumer credit agreements. Although written contracts may be the preferred approach most companies will both place and accept oral contracts where the urgency of the situation demands. The aim will be to reduce these oral contracts to writing as quickly as possible. Nevertheless, to be valid even oral contracts must satisfy the basic legal requirements described in this chapter.

Signed and unsigned contracts

Simple contracts do not have to be signed, although many institutions prefer to require the formality and ceremony of personal signatures. Where a contract is signed then that in itself is strong evidence that the signing party intended a legal relationship.

Bilateral and unilateral contracts

The normal business contract that imposes obligations on both parties that must be discharged is an example of a bilateral contract. Somewhat oddly there can be a unilateral contract in which only one party is bound by his obligations. An example of this is the contract a householder makes with an estate agent to sell his house. If he finds a buyer the seller must pay the estate agent his fee. However, if the estate agent does not find a buyer the agent has no liability to the seller. Indeed the agent has no obligation to take any action at all! The business contracts in question are bilateral contracts.

Express, implied and quasi contracts

Another set of classifications distinguishes between express contracts, implied contracts and quasi contracts. In an express contract the parties commit the terms of their agreement to writing. In an implied contract it is their conduct that brings a contractual relationship into being. A quasi contract is one in which the law would impose an obligation to make a repayment where the beneficiary would otherwise be unjustly enriched.

Executory and executed contracts

Contracts may be termed 'executory' or 'executed'. An executed contract is one where the contract is fully performed. An executory contract is one that is wholly or partly yet to be performed. Somewhat confusingly a 'completed' contract means only that a contract exists in the sense that an offer of contract has been made and the act of accepting the offer creates or 'completes' the contract. So a completed contract will be either executory or executed. However, sometimes, completing the contract (in the foregoing sense) is referred to as 'executing' the contract!

Valid contracts

A valid contract is one that is of full effectiveness. It is not deficient in its construction in any way and is fully enforceable by the law.

Void contracts

A void contract is the antithesis of the valid contract and logically is a contradiction in terms. A void contract is no contract at all. The drawback is that in practice the parties to the contract may proceed to deal with one another as though the contract were valid probably in naïve ignorance of the void nature of their agreement. In such circumstances a court may try to deduce a contract so that the parties may end up where they intended. Indeed it is probably the case that a proportion of business 'contracts' are technically void albeit that no one notices because the parties achieve their intended aims with no difficulty and the effectiveness of the contract is never examined or tested. The essence of a void contract or a void contract term is that a court will not enforce it. The parties are free to continue with their arrangements but in the event of dispute about the arrangement or breach of the void term there is no legal enforcement available, although financial claims may be made if one side has suffered loss or been unfairly enriched at the hands of the other. A contract can be void for a number of reasons of which the following are the main examples:

Non-formation

If the contract is not correctly formed through the absence of one or more fundamental criteria (see below) the contract is void.

Public policy

A court will not enforce a 'contract' the purpose of which is against public policy.

Agreements to oust the jurisdiction of the court

It is fundamental that a party who considers himself aggrieved or injured in some way can appeal to the courts for judgment over a matter concerning his contract. Thus any contract that aims to prevent this will be void. However, it is permissible that the parties may include a contract provision that allows all disputes to be referred to arbitration for settlement with the parties binding themselves in advance to the outcome.

Restraint of trade

The court cannot enforce a contractual arrangement that is constructed in contravention of competition law.

Uncertainty

There can be cases when the agreement that the parties have made is vague or so incomplete that the contract is said to be void for uncertainty. In business contracts, however, the courts are loath to jump to a precipitative conclusion in this regard and will go to some length to find the parties' intentions.

Mistake

A contract may be void for a mistake of fact, which is known as an operative mistake. The nature of the operative mistake is not one of error of judgement where, for example, one side attaches an inaccurate value to some goods that he wishes to buy or sell. It is more of a fundamental failure to understand the nature of the contract or the identity or existence of the subject matter. Where there is a unilateral and fundamental mistake (made by one side only) the contract will be void if the other side knew or ought to have known of the mistake. If the other side is ignorant of the mistake the contract will be valid. If both sides make an identical fundamental mistake (a 'common' mistake) the contract is nevertheless valid. If they both make mistakes that are non-identical (a 'mutual' mistake) then the contract will not necessarily be void if the courts can find the 'sense of the promise'. This means what a reasonable person would have said was the intention of the parties. Thus to the law, mistakes come in a variety of types and a plain 'mistake' made by those drafting the contract (whether commercial or technical aspects) may have consequences quite unforeseen.

Voidable contracts

A voidable contract is one in which the contract appears to be properly formed, but may nevertheless be avoided by one party. An example of this is a contract that is entered into by one party being under duress from the other party. The party under duress has the option to escape the contract if he so wishes.

Unenforceable contracts

If a contract that is required by the law to be in writing is not in writing then it is unenforceable. In normal business contracts of the simple variety this is not going to be a concern.

Illegal contracts

The illegal contract is somewhat similar to the void contract in so far as if the purpose of the contract is criminal in nature or frowned upon by the public interest the contract cannot be effective. The law distinguishes illegal and void contracts because of their different consequences. However, it is presumed that business contracts are not illegal, nor against the public interest and on this presumption the illegal contract is not considered further.

Contract formation

All contracts must be correctly formed so that they will be of legal effect. There are five elements in the proper formation of a contract:

Offer and acceptance

On the face of it, offer and acceptance is simple and straightforward. A offers to supply ten widgets to B for £5 each. B accepts and a contract is created. However, if A advertises widgets at £5 each this is not an offer to sell but an invitation to treat. This would mean that B would have to offer to buy at £5 each and A's acceptance would create the contract. It is thus important to be certain when an offer is actually being made. Acceptance can also have its complications. For the acceptance to create a contract it must be given without qualifications or terms since to do so creates a counter offer which itself must be accepted before a contract can come into being. Quite commonly it is the practice for a company to say to a customer 'we accept the contract subject to the following...'. Strictly speaking this is a counter offer and no contract is made until the counter offer has been accepted without qualification. As a matter of custom and practice the two parties to the 'contract' may each proceed with the business of the contract – one to supply goods, the other to make payments – and a court may decide that a contract did indeed exist. The only question to be decided is whether or not *both* parties intended the qualifications given in the initial response to apply. Again this may depend upon the actions of the parties. For example, if the statement was to the effect that 'we accept the contract but will deliver blue widgets instead of green' and the customer, without having formally confirmed it, accepts deliveries of blue widgets then the qualification was mutually accepted.

A factor to be taken into account in determining the existence of a contract is the point at which correspondence on the matter rested. Where a matter has been debated without full resolution, whichever party had the final say in correspondence may well have the advantage. An example of this is seen in the 'battle of the forms'. In this, a series of forms – request for quotation; quotation; purchase order; order acceptance; delivery instructions; delivery advice note – alternate between buyer and seller and each form carries the buyer or seller's terms on its reverse. The terms are mutually exclusive on many points. What then are the terms of the contract? In such situations a general rule has emerged that the final piece of paper holds sway.

Offer and acceptance must be communicated. As far as the offer is concerned, once it has been communicated it must stand until the offerer revokes it prior to acceptance; the offeree rejects it; the offeree makes a counter offer; the expiry of a specified period (called the validity period); the expiry of a reasonable time having regard to the circumstances.

The act of rejection or counter offer by the offeree has the effect of cancelling the offer. If the offeree were to make a counter offer, for example, and then have a change of mind, finding the original offer acceptable after all, it would be too late for him to accept that first offer. As far as both offer and acceptance are concerned the effective moment is that of receipt. The exceptions are that for acceptance by post where the effective moment is that of posting (properly stamped and addressed), regardless of delay or even non-delivery. In some situations the actions of the offeree may be taken to effect acceptance although there is no formal communication. For example, a buyer taking and accepting deliveries and making use of the goods would have conveyed his acceptance through his actions despite having made no written or oral communication or acceptance.

Intention to create legal relations

As has already been said, a court can enforce a contract if the parties intended their promises to be binding. As a natural consequence of this, the court will provide remedies for the breaking of binding promises – known as breach of contract. In some circumstances it may be that promises made were intended to be kept but no one really expected or wanted a legal remedy for a broken promise – perhaps a cancelled invitation to dinner; in such cases a reasonable person (a standard if somewhat subjective test) would say that there could have been no intention to create legal relations and thus no contract is made. Business people must take care that their actions as individuals may not inadvertently be construed as intentions to create legal relations by the body corporate.

Consideration

Consideration is the legal word for the money that is paid for the supply of the goods or services under the contract. In fact, money is only one example of consideration, which has classically been defined as 'some right, interest, profit or benefit accruing to one party, or some forbearance, detriment, loss or responsibility given, suffered or undertaken by the other'. An example might be in a contract for software development where, in addition to payment of the contract price, the developer may be granted exclusive commercial exploitation rights in the software.

Consideration must be of value to the recipient; it must pass to the recipient; it must be legal; it must not be in the past – a post-event promise to pay for some service already completed does not satisfy the criterion.

Capacity

All adult citizens have the capacity to contract although there are exceptions. For example, there are circumstances in which contracts made by aliens, persons suffering from mental disorder, or drunkards are void. In business contracts, the question relates to the capacity of the company to be a party to a contract. Companies properly formed under the Companies Act have such capacity.

Legal and possible

The contract must not be illegal. For example, a contract to carry out a crime would not be a contract. The contract must also be capable of performance. For example, there could be no contract to supply a perpetual motion machine.

Types and formation of contracts – why worry?

So what practical advice can be extracted from this morass? For the commercial manager there are probably three points of interest:

Accidental commitments

Firstly, there is the danger of actions or words implying contractual obligations where no such intention was meant. Here then is a first warning to the commercial manager. His conduct may lead to unintended contractual obligations. If the manager appears to be acting on behalf of the company (having the company's 'ostensible authority') then a commitment may accidentally be made. The whole purpose to professional life is the pursuit of business and the creating of contracts. It might be said therefore that there should be no doubt that the intention is to create relations. However, it is frequently just the opposite. Marketing, sales, engineering and project management people will regularly discuss possible transactions with potential customers and suppliers with no intention to create legal relations. It is vital that in such matters the purposes of the discussions are clear to all so that legal relations are not inadvertently established. A letter confirming the discussions, but stating 'the discussions and the letter do not constitute an order or a commitment to place an order with you' is an example of a practical precaution. This belt and braces disclaimer points out that not only is no order created but also that no intention to place an order should be construed from the actions and discussions. Another safeguard in these matters is to use the expression 'subject to contract' which is a recognized expression that should exclude the risk of accidental legal relations.

Uncertainty

Secondly, there is the question of uncertainty. One of Britain's law lords once said, 'It is clear that the parties both intended to make a contract and thought they had done so. Businessmen often record the most important agreements in crude and summary fashion; modes of expression sufficient and clear to them in the course of their business may appear to those unfamiliar with the business far from complete or precise. It is accordingly the duty of the court to construe such documents fairly and broadly, without being too astute or subtle in finding defects… does not mean that a court is to make a contract for the parties, or to go outside the words they have used'. So there is a problem. If the contract (which includes any engineering, construction or manufacturing specifications) is unclear, a court may either decide what the parties thought they meant (which may be different from one or both parties' opinion) or may decide there is no contract at all. Equally dangerous is the habit in business contracts of leaving matters expressly as 'to be agreed'. Such 'agreements to agree' are generally unenforceable unless there is mechanistic process (not just 'good faith negotiations') that a court (or an arbitrator) could apply regardless of the wishes of the parties. So here is the reverse of the first point. A belief that a contract had been made, only for the parties to find it not so (or not so in the manner intended), again, caused through the way in which they conduct themselves.

Custom and practice

A court may take an interest as to whether the contract is a simple transaction or a transaction of a more complex type based upon the prior dealings between the parties. In a once-and-for-all contract the law sees a simple transaction standing by itself, governed by its express terms and within the general framework of contract law. Beyond this, and with great relevance to business contracts, is the idea of relations between parties who regularly do business, particularly if it is of a complicated or long-term nature. A law lord has said that 'in complex relations, obligations, often heavily binding ones, arise simply out of day to day operations, habits, thoughts, customs etc. which occur with precious little thought by anyone about the obligations they might entail or about their possible consequences'. So it can be argued that imputed into the contract are obligations, methods of working, conventions and mutual reasonable expectations that arise through a normal process of trade between contracting parties. However, a law lord has warned that 'an alleged custom can be incorporated into a contract only if there is nothing in the express or necessarily implied terms of the contract to prevent such inclusion and, further, that a custom will only be imported into a contract where it can be so imported consistently with the tenor of the document as a whole'. So there it is, perfectly clear – custom and practice might be implied into a contract or it might not! The lesson, nevertheless, is clear, if somewhat easier said than done – those drafting the contract (commercial and technical aspects) must try to think not only of those immediate points of concern, but whether there are wider matters which, for the clarity of all, should be written into the contract, to the exclusion of all else.

Early lessons

So far, it should be clear that in contractual dealings there are two golden rules. Firstly, be clear when words and actions are not intended to have any contractual effect. Secondly, when it is time to make a contract, write it all down in clear, complete and unambiguous language. But it has already been mentioned that most simple contracts do not have to be in writing at all. However, as a matter of professional necessity companies adopt a practice of committing all contracts to writing. This is for several good reasons. Firstly, the subject matter and rights and obligations of the parties may be extensive in description and definition. This naturally demands commitment to paper. Secondly, it is vital that both parties are clear and share the same understanding of the contract. Thirdly, as individuals move on, it is important that their successors can inherit a clear understanding. Fourthly, a written contract is a sound baseline for changes in requirements, rights and obligations that may arise and become contract amendments. Furthermore, in the event of a dispute during or after the completion of the contract a court will be better able to reach a decision based on written evidence. Finally, where many functions within the company will exchange correspondence with their opposite numbers, it is important to know which bits of paper actually constitute the contract.

The terms of a contract

Terms and conditions

The phrase 'terms and conditions' is commonly used but it is in some ways unhelpful. Some use it as a heading for the list of 'contractual' or 'legalistic' bits of a contract as though they are distinct from the interesting bits (for example, price and specification). This is nonsense. It is a condition of the contract that the specification is met. So, it is wrong to think of the contract as somehow having terms and conditions that are unrelated to the rest. Sometimes 'terms and conditions' are abbreviated to just 'the terms' or just 'the conditions'. Sometimes 'terms' means only those bits that have a time element such as a payment credit period. Contracts also contain 'undertakings'. Are these different from terms and conditions? The text will shortly show that the word 'conditions' does have a particular meaning. What is needed is just one word that will do as a generic heading for that list of the requirements, benefits and obligations of the parties to the contract that constitutes the entire contract. The word 'terms' will be used for this all-embracing purpose. Thus the terms of the contract embrace all the technical bits as well as the commercial aspects. As will be seen shortly, it is convenient from a practical point of view to consider the contract as constructed from these different elements, but this should not detract from the holistic view – there is but the one contract, which should be considered complete and whole in its own right.

Express and implied terms

Terms are either express or implied. Express terms are those that the parties themselves have established and usually put into writing. Implied terms are those terms that either a court will decide may be read into the contract, based on what the parties must have intended, or those that arise from a statute. An example of statutory implied terms is the term of satisfactory quality implied by the Sale of Goods Act. This Act and its implied terms of quality can cause a lot of difficulty in business contracts and will be considered in more detail in later sections.

Conditions and warranties

The terms of the contract are also sub-divided into conditions and warranties. Not all of the obligations created by a contract are of equal importance and this is recognized by the law, which has applied a special terminology to contractual terms to distinguish the vital or fundamental obligations from the less vital. The word 'condition' applies to the former and 'warranty' to the latter. 'Warranty' in this sense should not be confused with the common usage relating to a supplier's warranty (or guarantee) under which he will rectify problems discovered after delivery, which will be discussed in a later chapter. The difference between conditions and warranties has been described thus: 'A condition is a vital term which goes to the root of the contract. It is an obligation that goes directly to the substance of the contract, or is so essential to its very nature that its non-performance may be considered by the other party as a substantial failure to perform the contract at all. A warranty, on the other hand, is subsidiary to the main purpose, and there is no right in the injured party to repudiate the contract; there is only an action for damages. A warranty has been variously defined, but it may be said to be an obligation which, though it must be performed, is not so vital that a failure to perform it goes to the substance of the contract.'

The weakness of this simple distinction between conditions and warranties is that it presupposes that the parties have the desire and ability to make this distinction in their contract terms when the contract is made. In business contracts, this desire and ability may be absent, even if the parties think about the distinction at all. Consequently the law recognizes a third class of term that is called the 'innominate' term. This means that the term will be determined as either a condition or warranty depending upon the severity of the consequences of an actual breach (which may never happen), rather than the possible consequences as may have been contemplated when the contract was made.

As will shortly be seen, it is the injured party's remedies for breach that provides the vital definition of the difference between a condition and a warranty.

Representations

Prior to making their contract the buyer and seller make representations to each other that directly or indirectly lead them to a wish to do business. Such pre-contract representations if they are representations as to fact may be expressly incorporated in the contract and thus they become part and parcel of the contract promises. If they are not so incorporated they may still be of legal effect (unless expressly excluded from the contract). For example, if a buyer enters into a contract relying on a pre-contract representation (which is not incorporated in the contract) he may later be able to rescind the contract (see below) if the representation turns out not to be true.

Penalties

It has already been said that once in contract, performance relies upon the willingness of the two sides, failing which the courts will decide a remedy. The contract itself may provide a remedy but the remedy must not be of the nature of a penalty. A court would not enforce a penalty term. Whether a contract term is or is not a penalty is ultimately for a court to determine by reference to the substance of the term. A penalty cannot be dressed up as something else in the hope that it would not be found void.

Unfair contract terms

The purpose of contract law is to provide a set of rules, which if obeyed will ensure that the contract is enforceable. It is not designed to ensure that the contracting parties have a balanced deal – that is for each of them to decide. If one participant is in a stronger negotiating position, the deal is likely to prove in its outcome more beneficial to him than to the other party. Thus contract law exists to provide a framework of fair rules and not to ensure that the result of each game is more or less a draw. However, there is one major exception to this general principle. It has already been seen that a legally binding obligation can carry an unlimited financial liability for breach. Companies like to conduct their business at minimum risk and the prospect of unlimited liability contracts can make them shudder. So companies look for ways to limit their contractual liabilities. There are two ways of doing so. They can expressly exclude particular liabilities or they can expressly limit the financial exposure connected with liabilities that they cannot avoid altogether. These exclusions and limitations are subject to the Unfair Contract Terms Act (UCTA).

Liabilities excluded or limited

The liabilities that companies seek to exclude or limit are those relating to the following:

- Personal injury or death
- Breach of contract
- Performance as expected
- Complete performance

- Results of negligence

- That goods correspond with description or sample given

- That goods are of satisfactory quality

- That goods are fit for purpose

- That goods are unencumbered.

Liability for personal injury or death can never be excluded or limited in a contractual transaction. In business contracts all the other liabilities listed may be excluded or limited subject to a test of reasonableness and to notice of the exclusion having been given.

Reasonableness

The onus is on the party relying on the exclusion to show that it is reasonable. The reasonableness test is based on:

- The exclusion being fair and reasonable in the circumstances known or contemplated by the parties when the contract was made

- The relative bargaining positions

- The existence of any inducement

- Whether goods were manufactured, processed or adapted to order

- Whether the buyer had reasonable notice of the term.

If the liability were financially limited then also taken into account would be the resources available to meet the liability and the availability of insurance. It would be unfair of a company to exclude or limit a liability that it can easily meet from its resources or for which insurance cover is available.

Notice

For an exclusion to be effective then:

- Notice of the exclusion must have been given at the time the contract was made or the prior course of dealings or trade practice must show that the exclusion is standard practice

- Notice must be in a contractual document

- Reasonable notice must be given

- The exclusion must apply to that which was intended.

The UCTA was largely concerned with the absurd exclusions of liability that appeared in retailers' standard terms used for consumer transactions. The purpose was to set some fair rules that protected the consumer's interests. For example, it is accepted that consumers do not necessarily read or fully understand a standard term contract. It is rightly held that such failures should not harm the consumer's entitlement to a fair deal. In business contracts the parties are much more left to their own devices. However, in 1996 there was a case between St Albans District Council and International Computers Ltd (ICL). The case revolved around a contract term that purported to limit ICL's liability for the loss (of council tax revenue) suffered by the Council as a result of a defect in the computer system supplied by ICL. ICL did not deny the defect but relied upon the limitation to avoid paying the bulk of the Council's losses. ICL believed their position was secure because the Council was not dealing as a consumer and had negotiated the contract in full awareness of the limitation. The court did not agree with ICL and took into account a number of factors including ICL's substantial insurance cover. The result was in favour of the Council. The purpose in remarking upon this one case is that businesses should not assume safety in their exclusion or limitation terms. Since this case, it is important that legal advice is taken when drafting such terms.

Standard and negotiated terms

Where one or more parties regularly do business with one another there is advantage to all concerned in the use of standard terms; that is, a set of terms that buyer and seller will use for most, if not all, of their transactions. This saves considerable time in the drafting of contract documents and indeed in the physical bulk of the documents, as the standard terms can be included by reference. Not only that, but the contracting parties will understand and be confident in the custom and practice that grows up around the use of standard terms.

Standard terms are produced and used by government purchasing departments; by industry bodies (such as the Chartered Institute of Purchasing and Supply); by a sector of industry; and by individual companies, either as standard terms of sale or as standard terms of purchase.

If a trade body produces standard terms, the aim will be to make the terms reasonably well balanced between the interests of buyer and seller. Where one 'side' produces the terms only – whether a government department or a private company – then the terms will be one-sided! This risk must be borne in mind. There is no comfort at all to one side when the other side says 'don't worry, we'll use our standard terms'. The only other form of quasi-standard terms arises where the first one or two contracts between two parties are fully negotiated, but as subsequent contracts of a similar value and type are placed, the parties may agree to adopt the same set of terms that applied previously. This has the convenience of saving time and money, but there is a risk as no two contracts are quite alike and unthinking reliance on what went before may run the risk of changes in circumstances or law not being picked up as necessary in the express terms of the contract.

In the final analysis, contract terms can only be reduced to standards where buyer and/or seller see no advantage to the time-consuming activity of negotiating terms on each and every occasion that a transaction is contemplated. Also, some aspects are actually different every time a transaction is entered into and could thus never be reduced to a standard. For example, payment terms in industries where interim payments are permitted can vary on each contract and most companies will wish to negotiate these on a case-by-case basis. A key commercial skill with regard to negotiating contract terms is the trade-off analysis between genuine risk, practical solutions and legal niceties. For example, a term that permits the customer to cancel the contract for convenience might be perfectly acceptable legally, if the wording is correct, but commercially it might be a disaster unless an adequate period of notice is given. On the other hand a ludicrously brief period of notice might be acceptable if the risk of cancellation is highly remote.

If things go awry

The text has already shown that there are many pitfalls in getting to a binding contract. Nine situations have been given, any one of which can deny the existence of a contract. One of these situations (improper formation) itself has five criteria, failure in any one of which may cause the contract not to be formed. This already reveals a lot about the nature of contractual relationships. More is learned in considering the circumstances in which matters go awry.

Consent

Just as the parties are free to make their contract they are free to unmake it and to decide their own terms for so doing. This may be appropriate where circumstances have changed dramatically and both sides see no merit in continuing with their contract.

Convenience

Some contracts expressly allow the buyer (not usually the seller) to unilaterally and prematurely end the contract under a 'cancellation for convenience' arrangement. Such a right must be included in the express terms of the contract. A buyer who says that 'we can always cancel the contract' to put pressure on the seller is making an empty threat if he has no express right to cancel, provided that the seller is performing the contract properly.

Repudiation and breach

If one party to the contract expressly or impliedly announces to the other that he will not see the contract through, then he is said to be repudiating the contract. A failure to perform a contractual obligation is called breach of contract or contractual default. Breach may be actual, for example, where delivery is not made by the due date, or breach may be anticipated. The defaulting party may anticipate the breach by announcing its inability to perform, for example, by the seller telling the buyer that delivery will be late. The buyer, for example, may anticipate the breach by monitoring the progress of the seller and deducing that the seller will be late. If the seller anticipates his own breach he is repudiating the contract. If the buyer anticipates the seller's breach and takes pre-emptive action for breach before the seller is due to perform, then the seller can treat the contract as having been repudiated by the buyer.

Special circumstances

This book is primarily concerned with the normal course of business where contracts are made and the interest is in the risk and liabilities associated with the performance of the contract. This will be the subject of the next chapter. However, it would be wrong to entirely skip over other situations where the contractual position is not as the parties intended.

No contract

As the text has already remarked, the parties may proceed with their 'contract' only later to find that it is void for reasons of non-formation, public policy, of being an agreement to oust the jurisdiction of the court, restraint of trade, uncertainty, and a mistake. A 'contract' may be unenforceable if it is illegal.

Rescission

One side may undo the contract on the basis of a failed obligation that is outside of the contract. For example, if the purported contract followed a fraudulent pre-contract misrepresentation then the injured party may rescind the contract (unless he knows of the misrepresentation and takes some benefit from it).

Frustration

If a valid contract comes to a stop as a result of an event that arises after the contract was made then the contract may be dissolved for frustration. The event must be so significant and unexpected that it could not reasonably have been within the contemplation of the parties when the contract was made. This is the crucial point. Although both sides always aspire to low risk contracts, there are cases where significant risks must be carried.

Such risks may be allocated to one party or the other under the contract. If one such risk comes home to roost, then the party carrying that risk may not claim that the contract has been frustrated.

Legal remedies

If things do go awry then the law provides remedies. The parties may use the contract to restate, add to, or subcontract from their remedies, although the extent of addition or subtraction may be governed by the law (for example, see unfair terms earlier in this chapter). The terms of contract termination by consent are for the parties to decide. If the contract allows an express right for cancellation for convenience then the terms of cancellation are for the parties to set out in the contract. The main interest is in the remedies for breach, which are as follows:

Specific performance

The buyer's principle default is a failure to pay. For the seller the remedy is quite straightforward. He must sue payment of the contract price. The seller's principle default is to fail to get on with the job (to time or to specification). It would seem that the most obvious legal remedy for the buyer would be to get the court to enforce the contract. This the buyer may do by applying for a decree of specific performance. However, it is a discretionary matter for the courts to grant such a decree but the option is certainly there for the injured side to exercise. If the goods were readily available elsewhere, or if checking compliance with a decree of specific performance was impossible or required constant supervision by the courts, then a decree would not be granted. So where, for example, the goods are available elsewhere no decree would be issued, the contract would be considered terminated and if the goods bought elsewhere were of a higher price, then the buyer would have a right to damages from the defaulting supplier.

Termination

If the breach is a breach of a contract condition the injured party may terminate the contract. No right of termination arises if the breach is of a warranty only. This is the crucial difference between conditions and warranties. The absurdity here is that the consequences of breach of a condition might be trivial but the (lightly) injured party could terminate the contract, possibly to the severe detriment of the other side. Conversely the consequences of breach of a warranty may be very serious but the (badly) injured party has to continue with the contract. Thus the innominate term stands in the middle. However, this is not an automatic escape route for the defaulting party to avoid the risk of termination. If a contract term was clearly intended as a fundamental condition at the outset then a court is not likely to reclassify it after the event. It is in respect of those contract terms where the classification is not obvious in the first place that a court would apply the rules of innominate terms.

Damages

Breach of contract gives the injured party a right to damages, whether the breach is of a condition or of a warranty. Damages must reflect financial loss flowing directly from the breach. The loss may be actual (for example, unrecoverable, expenses) or anticipated (such as loss of expected profits). Such losses must have been within the reasonable contemplation of the parties when the contract was made. Simple contractual exclusions of 'consequential' damages are of little effect in business contracts as the courts find many categories of loss that flow directly from the breach, despite what the defaulting party may think. The losses must be real and not invented by the injured party.

Subject only to the tests of 'directly flowing' and 'within the contemplation of the parties' the scale of the damages that may be awarded for breach is unlimited. Such an unlimited sum is said to be unliquidated damages. It is open to the parties to agree in their contract a fixed, pre-estimate of the damages likely to flow from different categories of breach (delay in delivery being the most common example). Such fixed amounts are referred to as liquidated damages.

Special circumstances

The position regarding damages is somewhat different in the special circumstances mentioned above. If a contract is rescinded the aim of the law is to put matters back to square one, as though there had been no contract at all. If one side has suffered at the hands of the other then he may claim restitutional damages. If the contract is void or is unenforceable or has been dissolved through frustration, and if one side has gained at the expense of the other then the suffering party may claim a reasonable amount from the enriched party.

If a claim in respect of an allegedly void contract or in respect of a breach of contract is prosecuted in law, a case may be formulated under many branches of the law. As well as contract law, a claim may be made in tort, in equity, and in restitution and claims may be made for reliance damages and expectation damages. But such matters do not usually come to the fore where businesses choose to resolve their differences by negotiation. For the purposes of this book it is sufficient for the reader to understand the basic concept of direct damages flowing from breach and that such damages may be liquidated or unliquidated.

Breach and damages – who cares?

So what are the practical issues for the commercial manager? Is this not more esoteric stuff just to keep the commercial people and the lawyers employed? There are four points of interest:

Meeting the specification

Firstly, the commercial manager should remember that the bit (for example, specifications) of the contract in which he is most interested forms an integral part of the legal obligation. In some contracts, the specification may be so voluminous that, in simple terms, it makes up the bulk of the contract anyway. Unless the contract provides otherwise, the obligation is to meet all of the specification. It is most unlikely that a specification will be categorized to make it clear whether each individual requirement is fundamental or secondary. Therefore, assumptions about what is and what is not important are dangerous, as the penalty for failure can be different. Some contracts contain specifications that do categorize between requirements that are, for example, 'mandatory, desirable and non-essential'. In such cases it is still not obvious as to whether the middle category ('desirable' in this example) would be considered fundamental or secondary. It is thus most important to formulate contract specifications very carefully, not only as to their technical integrity, but also from the viewpoint of the legal consequences of failure. Some contracts provide for an allowable degree of variation from the specification (sometimes called 'concessions' or 'permits') perhaps with an automatic right for the buyer to demand a price reduction. Mechanisms such as these are useful tools to avoid the entanglement of a legal debate as to the nature of particular requirements.

Guessing wrong

The second area of concern relates to the extent to which the effect of failure may be foreseen. It has been known for a manager (or a company) to take a view that perhaps the customer will forgo a requirement (which is turning out to be difficult for the company to achieve) because, after all, the selling price to the customer (or the company's originally estimated cost) is low in value. The risk is that if the customer can show that the financial consequences to him are extensive and were known or were reasonably foreseeable by the company at the time the contract was made, then the company may be liable for the consequential costs to the customer.

Letting the 'cat out of the bag'

A third area of concern is the consequence of telling the customer (sometime after the contract was let) that the specification cannot be met or that the programme will be late. There is a laudable tendency for the manager to want to be perfectly open with the customer about such difficulties, but the risk is of contract termination as a result of 'anticipatory breach'. Thus the subject must be handled with judicious care.

Missing the hazard

The fourth point is related to the previous point. Late delivery may expose the supplier to the risk of paying 'liquidated damages'. This is usually a lesser penalty for the supplier than contract termination, but it is nevertheless painful. A non-commercial salesman, manager or supervisor working for the seller may not even be aware of this contractual arrangement and may inadvertently expose the company to this risk. The commercial manager working for the buyer may likewise in ignorance of the arrangement prejudice his company's rights to collect the liquidated damages from the late supplier.

The Sale of Goods Act

The Sale of Goods Act imposes duties on the seller. These duties are to:

- Pass goods title

- Deliver the goods

- Supply the goods at the right time

- Supply goods in the right quantity

- Supply goods of the right quality.

The Sale of Goods Act imposes duties on the buyer. These duties are to:

- Accept delivery of the goods

- Pay the agreed price.

The duty to supply goods of the right quality means that the goods meet the relevant express terms of the contract. Terms are also implied into contracts that goods:

- Correspond with their description

- Correspond with any samples given

- Are satisfactory

- Are fit for a particular purpose.

Business contracts should normally expressly deal with title, delivery, timeliness, quantity, quality and payment. The Sale of Goods Act merely states the position for consumer contracts and gives the fallback position for those business contracts that neglect to deal with these matters. The point of concern here is the implied terms of satisfactory quality and fitness for purpose. According to the Act, 'goods are of satisfactory quality if they meet the standard that a reasonable person would regard as satisfactory, taking account of any description of the goods, the price and any other relevant circumstances'. Quality takes into account 'fitness for all purposes for which goods of the kind in question are commonly supplied, appearance and finish, freedom from minor defects, safety and durability'. The implied term does not apply to any defect in quality specifically drawn to the buyer's attention before the contract is made or where the buyer examines the goods before the contract is made, but fails to notice the defect that the examination ought reasonably to have revealed. It is easy to see the application and merit of these implied terms in consumer transactions, but more difficult in business contracts where the express terms of the contract (for example, the specifications) may be drawn up in great detail, possibly with the buyer taking a proactive role. For this reason, it is open to the parties to a business contract to exclude the implied terms altogether. They must do this with an express exclusion in their contract; otherwise the implied terms are operative, regardless of the detail of the express terms.

Product liability

Product liability is concerned with the safety of goods. Between buyer and seller the seller has a strict liability to supply goods that are of the right quality. This means that if the buyer can show that the goods are defective, then the seller is liable for the damages flowing from such defect. These damages would extend to the cost of correcting the defect, recompense for damage to property caused by the defect and for claims arising from personal injury or death cause by the defective product. A claim for such damages would be a straightforward contractual claim by the buyer against the seller. The buyer could also claim under the tort of negligence if he believed that he could prove negligence. The buyer's better route is the contractual claim.

Where however the buyer wishes to claim against the manufacturer (where the manufacturer is not the seller) then the buyer has the harder task of showing negligence on the part of the manufacturer, showing that there is a so-called collateral contract between himself and the manufacturer or by instituting third party proceedings against the manufacturer. These common law rights are difficult to pursue and do not cover defects in the goods themselves, only damage, injury or death caused by the defects.

The legal remoteness of the buyer from the manufacturer makes it hard for the business buyer to secure a remedy, but for the consumer the matter is even more difficult. To correct this, Part 1 of the Consumer Protection Act creates a strict liability (meaning the injured party only has to prove that a product was defective and not that there was any negligence) on the producer provided that he supplies in the course of business or for profit. The producer is the actual producer of the product; or anyone holding himself out as the producer (for example, by adding his trademark to the producer's product) and anyone within the EU who imports the product from outside of the EU. The liability is for damages arising from injury or death and damage to property (being property for private use, occupation or consumption), but not for damage in the product itself or for pure economic loss. Whilst this book is not concerned with consumer transactions, the company further down the supply chain from the consumer may find itself caught by this liability.

Contract negotiation

Many business contracts are arrived at through the process of negotiation or at least some discussion between the parties. So it is necessary to look at what the law has to say about the process of negotiation.

Disclosure of information

The first principle is that in ordinary commercial relations (and unless there is a pre-existing contractual obligation to this effect) there is no obligation on the parties to disclose facts to one another. In some special circumstances there may be a duty of care in ensuring that when information is given, it is complete but in business contracts the parties are free to use their best skills and information to negotiate the best deal possible.

Bargaining power

The second principle deals with relative bargaining power. It is a fact of commercial life that the bargaining powers of the two sides to the potential contract will frequently be unequal but commercial pressure of that nature is usually legitimate. After all the weaker of the two sides is free to decide against entering into the contract.

Confidentiality

A third important principle is that the negotiating parties may owe each other the obligation to treat one another's information in confidence. Once a contract is agreed information exchanged must in any event be held in confidence. In the pre-contract stages it is as well to set up a binding confidentiality agreement (see Chapter 4). This may be particularly important where the negotiations fail to reach a conclusion and no contract is ever made.

Misrepresentation

In arriving at a contractual agreement there must be no fraud, coercion, duress, undue influence or misrepresentation. For most businesses it is misrepresentation that can cause practical difficulty. The text has already mentioned pre-contract representations. If these are recognized as mere 'puffery' (obvious exaggerations that simply grab attention) they have no effect at all. If they are of substance and are incorporated into the contract, they simply form part of the contract. If they are of substance but not so incorporated they may still have some legal effect. A representation must be factually correct, if not it is a misrepresentation. There are several forms:

- **Fraudulent**: A false representation made knowingly or without belief in its truth or recklessly careless whether it be true or false.

- **Innocent**: A misrepresentation in which there is no element of fault (that is, fraud or negligence).

- **Negligent**: A false statement made by a person who has no reasonable grounds for believing that statement to be true.

The remedies for misrepresentation may include rescission, termination and damages.

Thus for the commercial manager it can be seen that in participating in contract negotiations, there is no need to volunteer information if it helps the other party, bargaining power can be used to lever the maximum advantage, information must be kept in confidence and both unintended promises (representations) and false promises (misrepresentations) must be avoided.

The content of the contract

Having considered the legal principles on which a contract is formulated and having examined the legal constraints on negotiation (the practical side of negotiation will be covered in Chapter 5) the text will now examine the components of a contract that are essential from a practical perspective.

The 'what' (definition and specification)

It is vital that the goods are defined as absolutely as possible. In the simple case, the 'what' will be the part number, description and quantity, but it is also important to specify other things to be supplied – guides and spares for example. Where the 'goods' are particularly complicated, or where design and development or complex systems are involved then engineering standards, specifications, acceptance and handover arrangements are needed. Definitions of deliverable data must be given. Project control, monitoring and other services required must be specified.

The 'when' (timescale and timing of contract performance)

The contract should specify when and at what rate things should be delivered or services performed. The nature of the commitment (or otherwise) to meet timescales is crucial.

The 'where' (destination)

The contract should specify the destination to which the goods are to be supplied or the location where the services are to be performed. The contract may be required to be performed in several different locations and possibly in different countries.

The 'how' (method of delivery)

The contract must specify how the goods are to be delivered. Packaging, preservation, transport medium and allocation of carriage responsibilities must be specified.

The 'how much?' (price and payment)

The price for the job must be struck in the first place or, if not, then a proper mechanism must be recorded for the agreement of price. Careful attention must be given to the timing and triggers for payment. Details must be included for the procedure for invoicing. The contract must also state what rights, if any, the buyer has to recover payments made.

The 'what else?' (dependencies)

The contract may need to include certain responsibilities on the buyer, for example to provide facilities, data or goods; to inspect and accept the work of the contract. The contract must specify how contractual acceptance, including any testing, proving and trials are to be achieved.

The 'what the hell!' (the allocation of risk)

An absolutely fundamental role of any contract is to allocate risk as between the parties. Specific topics include: the risk of loss or damage to goods (pre and post delivery); the fitness for purpose of the end result; title in the goods; performance of the goods at acceptance and thereafter; liability to third parties; liability for the consequences of delay; liability for product safety; indemnities regarding accidental or knowing infringement of intellectual property rights; risk of damage to property; liabilities in the event of breach; the risk of contract cancellation or termination; the risk of delay through defaulting suppliers; exclusions; terms limiting liability; unlimited liability obligations; bonds and guarantees; cross indemnities; contract warranties. It is only when something goes awry and the contract is examined that the company first realizes (or remembers from when the contract was bid) what it has let itself in for. The reaction is often 'what the hell!'

Layout of a contract

The physical size of the contract documents almost always varies in proportion to the complexity and value of the job. The purchase of a standard product or service at a standard price may involve nothing more than the buyer's standard purchase order, comprising a single sheet of paper, the front side describing the item, delivery and price, the reverse side containing pre-printed terms of contract. The supplier may not necessarily agree with all these terms, but if, as a matter of practice, they have never given him a problem he may choose not to make an issue of it and risk losing a customer. However in a major contract it is essential that every word be carefully assembled into a coherent structure. There is no universal, standard layout of a contract, but the following is an outline, somewhat stylized, example.

Schedule of Requirements.

Contract Terms.
Annex 1: Specifications.

Part 1:   Performance specification

Part 2:   Test specification

Part 3:   Acceptance specification

Annex 2: Statement of Work.

Part 1:   Deliverable goods

Part 2:   Deliverable data

Part 3:   Programme plan

Annex 3: Payment schedule

Annex 4: Customer furnished material

A standard contract layout

The Schedule of Requirements is merely a helpful summary that introduces the contract. The contract in its entirety is defined by the contract terms. The contract terms will not only deal with the 'what the hell!' category of issues, but will also, through individual terms, deal with all the other subject matters from 'the what' to the 'what else'. Each such term may for convenience refer to annexes where more detail can be found, but the basic obligation to do whatever happens to be stated in each annex should be established in the contract terms. At the risk of labouring the point, the contract is not an unconnected collection of disparate material, but a single cohesive entity in which the pieces are bound together by the contract terms.

Contract requirements

One function of the contract is to say what the seller must do in performance of the contract. Such requirements, which may be set down in technical specifications or standards, must be incorporated properly into the contract. This may be done by physically including the requirements within the contract document so that they are present within the formal paperwork. Alternatively they may be 'incorporated by reference'. This means that they are simply called up in the contract document by reference. The important points are that the references are unique and precise identifiers and that the contract terms are clear that such requirements do indeed form part of the contract. A habit, which is to be deplored, is that of including at the start of the contract documents, or perhaps within a contract specification, a list of 'referenced documents'. Such habit leaves the list hanging in mid-air with the reader unsure as to whether the material is part of the contract requirement or is just useful background reading. There is no harm in using the contract to draw attention to useful background reading, but it must be clear that this is all that is intended. There must be absolute clarity on what is and what is not a contractual requirement.

Bringing the contract into effect

It has already been mentioned that a contract does not have to be physically signed by the parties. There must be an offer that is met with an acceptance. Offer and acceptance must be communicated, but in simple contracts, signatures as such, are not essential. Telexes, faxes and e-mail, as well as the spoken word can all suffice. It is however important that the parties do have a clear understanding as to what event signals that a contract has been made. Joint signatures of a formal contract document are a good method provided both sides know that prior to such event no contract has been made. However in practice a contract can be formed as a result of a sequence of correspondence in which case the parties should mutually record the correspondence that forms the contract.

Complete agreement

In cases where the formal contract document has resulted from extensive negotiation and much paperwork (for example where the contract document goes thorough many draft stages or where many aspects of the potential contract are clarified or expanded upon – whether orally or in writing – by one or both parties) it is good practice for the parties to include in the contract a 'complete agreement' (sometimes 'entire agreement') term which confirms that the full agreement is now incorporated in the formal contract document to the exclusion of everything that preceded it. This is good practice but requires great care by each of the parties (and especially so in the technical arena). This is because the buyer may have been persuaded to place the contract as a result of various pieces of information (representations) received from the seller and the buyer must ensure that any that are material to him are incorporated. Similarly the seller may have placed qualifications or caveats on some of his promises and he must ensure that these are captured in the contract if he is not to be caught out later. The alternative, which can often seem attractive, is not to have a complete agreement term thus opening the possibility that in a future dispute pre-contract information may be brought into account. This is a sloppy approach, unless one side plans to later rely upon a 'time bomb' ticking away in the earlier material, which is a cynical practice and quite unnecessary if good buyer/seller relationships are valued, and should be avoided.

Conditions precedent

Even where there is a formal contract document that is signed by both parties the contract (as a legally binding set of promises) does not necessarily have to come into effect upon signature. It is not unusual for a contract document to include 'conditions precedent'. These are terms that, if not fulfilled, prevent the contract from coming into force. An example is where the seller is not prepared to have the contract come into effect until he has received a specified amount by way of an advance payment. In such a case the parties will have arrived at their complete agreement and committed it to writing in their formal contract document, but the seller's obligations do not come into force until the advance payment (which may not be available in the buyer's budget by the time the contract has been signed) has been received by the seller.

Intentions to purchase and instructions to proceed

So far it has been supposed that there is time to put a full contract in place before work begins. In business it is not infrequently the case that, because of some urgency, or indeed for other reasons as well (for example the need to signal that other contenders for the contract are too late), the buyer would like the seller to proceed in advance of establishing a full contract. For reasons of his own, the seller may be prepared to go ahead without a full contract agreement where, for example, a later start would give him difficulty with availability of resources. In these circumstances the buyer may issue two different types of notice to the seller:

Intention to purchase

An intention to purchase (also known as a letter of intent) means exactly what it says – the buyer has an intention to purchase. The value of this to the supplier is only that it gives him a clear idea of what the buyer might want and perhaps gives him more confidence that a sale is close. An intention to purchase does not create a contract and the supplier, if he proceeds with work, does so at his own risk. The expression 'working at his own risk' means that the seller risks not recovering the cost of the work done in advance of a contract being placed. In specialist areas this work may be completely nugatory in so far as it may not even be of any use in meeting the requirements of other customers. On top of this the actual doing of the work will have diverted effort from real contracts where there are profits to be made. It cannot be stressed heavily enough that there are real dangers in doing what it is thought the customer wants rather than that for which he has actually contracted.

Instruction to proceed

This instruction is intended to create a binding relationship. Provided that the instruction and its response satisfy all the fundamentals a contract is created. This will be used where time does not permit the buyer to set out his full requirements but nevertheless sufficient of the contract terms can be specified. Wherever possible an instruction to proceed will be given in writing, but, as with oral contracts, the aim will be to formulate the full contract documents as quickly as possible.

It is perhaps a little risky to say that an intention to purchase does not form a contract and that an instruction to proceed is intended to form a contract. No matter how the communication is labelled, the real question is: does the communication amount to an offer of contract that is capable of being met with an unqualified acceptance? If it does, the seller has the option to accept or not. If it does not, then the seller cannot make a contract by purporting to accept the 'offer'.

Changing the contract

Amendments

Once the contract comes into effect it can only be changed under two types of arrangement. Firstly, there is nothing to stop the parties from changing their contract by mutual consent. Functionally, such an 'amendment' to contract has identical status to a contract itself. That is, before it can become a binding agreement there must be offer and acceptance, valuable consideration and intention to create legal relations. All the rules apply but in practice some aspects may be handled differently. For example, the contract amendment, being a contract in its own right, should identify all the terms that are to apply. However, in many cases the parties will wish the terms of the existing contract to apply, and rather than simply repeat them all, the wording of the contract amendment will close with a phrase such as 'all other terms remain unchanged'. As far as consideration is concerned, the wording of the contract may permit amendments to occur with the extra consideration to be arrived at later, but in a prescribed manner. For practical purposes the crucial point regarding amendments is that they must be accepted before they can become binding. It is important to be certain whether an amendment has been accepted or not. Confusion can be caused if either of the parties has the practice of distributing copies of amendments on the day of issue of the amendment (at this stage it is only a proposed amendment) rather than on the day of acceptance.

Changes

In the first arrangement, just described, the parties come together, as it were, outside of the contract to discuss a possible change and if they are then agreed, to cause the contract to be changed as described. The second arrangement is, as it were, within the contract itself. In such an arrangement the contract will provide for certain changes (perhaps the buyer has a right to demand a change to the specification or perhaps the seller has the right to deliver below specification within permitted tolerances) that can be introduced without a full contract amendment. This is a perfectly sound way to proceed provided the contract includes the details of the mechanism and in particular describes how revisions to price are to be handled. Such arrangements are quite common in contracts that have a high engineering content and the engineers control such changes under formal 'configuration control' procedures. But the contractual description of the process must be carefully drawn because such arrangements must satisfy all the rules for proper contract formation, just as with the first arrangement.

Risk

But the contractual aspects of contract changes are not just concerned with ensuring that the legal principles are satisfied. In the case of a contractual mechanism that allows changes to be introduced through a due process, there is the question of the commercial risk that buyer and seller may have to take by following the process. For example, in a contract where the buyer is allowed to direct the seller to meet a different specification it is frequently the case that the seller must change direction immediately (in order to meet the buyer's timeframe) leaving revisions to price, delivery schedule and payment terms until later. Thus the seller may suffer adverse effects on his cash flow while he waits for the commercial aspects of the change to catch up. If the seller will only work to an arrangement whereby he is not obliged to change direction until all the commercial aspects are settled then the buyer may find himself with the choice of settling the commercial aspects too quickly (to the seller's advantage) in order to meet his timeframe needs or delaying the implementation of the change whilst time is taken to deal properly with the commercial aspects. There are tried and trusted methods of dealing with these conflicts. For example, the change process may have different categories of change in which some (for example, those affecting safety) are adopted immediately whilst others are left on ice until the commercial issues have been cleared up. Alternatively the buyer may be given a time period in which he may verify and negotiate the commercial aspects, failing which he must agree the commercial changes proposed by the seller. For the commercial manager it is important that he is aware of the commercial aspects of the process such that he does not accidentally act against his company's best interests.

Authority

Whether a contract is altered by amendment or by change it is important that the parties are clear between them as to which of their respective representatives are authorized to deal with the formal adoption of proposed changes. This is best done within the terms of the contract and communicated to all concerned.

Checklist

- Companies have some freedom to choose and negotiate the applicable law for their contracts.

- A contract is a voluntary, mutual exchange of promises enforceable in law.

- Most business contracts are of the simple type and are best put in writing.

- Simple contracts require no signature.

- Care must be taken to ensure contracts are properly formed.

- Offer and acceptance must be communicated.

- Contracts must include valuable (future) consideration.

- Contracts may be made between companies.

- Contracts must be legal and possible.

- Care must be taken to avoid accidental commitments.

- It is dangerous to rely upon custom and practice.

- Terms may be expressed or implied in a contract.

- Terms are either conditions, which are fundamental, or warranties, which are subsidiary in effect.

- Pre-contract representations have important legal consequences.

- Penalty terms cannot be enforced.

- There are statutory restrictions on terms that exclude or limit liability.

- A contract may end through consent, convenience, repudiation, breach, rescission or frustration.

- A court may award a decree of specific performance but for most purposes the remedies for breach are damages and, if the breach is breach of a condition then the right to terminate also arises.

- The Sale of Goods Act imposes many duties on the seller and some on the buyer.

- Some of the Sale of Goods Act duties may be excluded in business contracts by an express contract term.

- Product liability law allows third party rights of action against producers of defective goods.

- In contract negotiations the parties have no general duty to disclose information to each other; they are reasonably free to make the best of their bargaining power; they should respect the confidentiality of each other's information; they should not make misrepresentations.

- The effective date of a contract may be delayed until conditions precedent have been satisfied.

- The parties may use intentions-to-purchase and instructions-to-proceed to effect an early start, but these are not without risk.

- A contract may be amended by mutual consent or changed by virtue of a mechanism set out in the contract.

Contract performance

Introduction

The phrase 'contract performance' means that each side completely discharges its obligations as set down in the contract. In the last chapter a thumbnail sketch of the contents of a contract was given and comprised the 'what', 'when', 'where', 'how', 'how much', 'what else' and 'what the hell'. Scattered through this description were a variety of important points that are fundamental to the achievement of contract performance and to what happens if things go wrong. This and the next chapter will explore these points using a structure that is familiar to commercial staff and should be familiar to the commercial manager. The structure is an example of a sequence of the contract terms. As mentioned in the previous chapter the terms must bind together all facets of the entire agreement even if some of the technical detail is separated into contract annexes. The structure is shown in the following table (overleaf):

	DEALS WITH
'Boiler plate'	Law, dispute resolution, definitions and order of precedence
Seller and buyer obligations	A description of work that each is required to do
Price	The price agreed for the job (which may be variable or non-variable) or a mechanism for fixing the price
Payment	Settlement of the contract by the buyer in return for the contract having been performed
Delivery	The point at which the main goal of the contract (for example the physical handover of goods) has been achieved
Passing of property	The transfer of legal title in the goods from seller to buyer
Passing of risk	The transfer of liability from seller to buyer for loss or damage to the goods
Acceptance	The point at which the buyer concurs that the contract has been performed forever extinguishing his right to reject
Rejection	The right of the buyer to reject goods which do not comply with the requirements of the contract
Time schedule for performance	The obligation of timeliness and the consequences of failure

Contract structure

In covering these topics over two chapters there was a temptation to find a split between topics of a technical nature and those of a commercial nature. This would have been quite wrong. As the text will show, these two categories are intertwined in almost every respect. Hence the order of play follows that of a typical contract.

'Boiler plate' terms

'Boiler plate' is somewhat of a derogatory expression since the subject matter is very important. It is simply a convenient heading for those terms, the main practical aim of which is to assist in clarity and to provide a basis for later sorting out ambiguity or dispute.

Applicable law

As stated in the previous chapter, the parties usually wish to state the law and jurisdiction that is to apply to the formation and performance of the contract.

Dispute resolution

The parties may specify arbitration or one of the alternative dispute resolution mechanisms. Such processes vary in their cost and time, but have the advantage of privacy over a court hearing. The parties may elect a jurisdiction for their chosen dispute resolution method other than the jurisdiction of the contract applicable law. This is because where buyer and seller are in different countries, the parties usually choose the law of one or the other of them to apply to the contract. In such circumstances, it can be of some comfort to elect a third, 'neutral' jurisdiction for dispute resolution.

Definitions

To avoid ambiguity it is common for the contract to give precise definitions of particular words and phrases, whether of a commercial or technical nature. A difference in interpretation, based on different expectations between buyer and seller, can cause much grief. It is much better to take the time before the contract is let to ensure that there is a common and recorded set of understandings and definitions of important words and phrases. It can be just as important to define everyday words, as the time and cost consequences of ambiguity can be unfortunate. One example will suffice to illustrate the point. The words 'shall' and 'will' are virtually interchangeable in everyday, spoken English. However, if in a contract the parties chose to use 'shall' to mean a requirement (of the specification) which must be met and be demonstrated (perhaps by testing) to have been met and 'will' to mean only that a requirement must be met, but need not to have been demonstrated, then it is easy to see that the difference between the two words may imply a significant difference in the amount of work to be done, and hence a difference in cost and time. If these words are not defined but have these meanings in the mind of one party but not the other, there is much scope for later disagreement.

Order of precedence

The idea here is that if a conflict is found (after the contract has been let) between aspects of the contract then the conflict will be resolved by reference to an order of precedence. This may say simply that the terms take precedence over the annexes or there may be a more detailed prescription giving precedence between particular terms and between elements of the detail included in annexes or in documents incorporated by reference. There are two schools of thought on the desirability of orders of precedence. Firstly, some think that there is no need for an order of precedence, because all conflicts should be ironed out at the contract drafting and review stage. Others believe in the imperfect world and would prefer to have an order of precedence, the alternative being to leave until later the resolution of any conflicts.

Seller and buyer obligations

Every term of a contract amounts to an obligation (to do or refrain from something or to carry a risk) on one side or the other. This section is concerned with the description of the work that the seller and buyer must do. In many contracts the buyer only has to accept the work and pay for it. In such a situation, this part of the contract only needs to describe the work that the seller must do. In more complex projects where seller and buyer are to work together then both sets of responsibilities need to be set out.

Specifications and statements of work

In all contracts, but especially in contracts having a substantial engineering content, it is necessary to define the seller's responsibilities. Where the objective is the delivery of a product the parties may elect to define the work by way of a technical specification that the product must meet or they may choose also to add further descriptive material, here called a 'statement of work'. The statement of work might describe the 'how' whereas the product specification should provide a taut description of the 'what'. Thus the statement of work might define activities (for example, design or manufacturing standards and methods, testing and proving regimes, sampling rates) that the seller must undertake. From a contractual viewpoint, the fun starts if the parties elect to include a specification and a statement of work. On the one hand, the buyer wants there to be an absolute obligation upon the seller to entirely meet the specification. However, as soon as he starts to 'interfere' with this principle by additionally stating the 'how', that obligation may become diluted. The seller may be able to say that provided he accomplished everything in the statement of work then the buyer should be happy, regardless of the exactitude with which the specification was met. On the other hand, the buyer may reasonably want to set parameters for the 'how' in order to build confidence that the end result will indeed meet the specification. In practice this pitfall can be avoided if the parties ensure that they mutually understand the purpose and relationship of the two documents and ensure that the contract expresses their true intentions clearly. This is an example where the commercial manager needs to be commercially aware when drawing up the documents.

Specification types – contractual implications

Now for the question of specifications, and more contractual fun. The first choice to be made is in the role of the specification. The specification might describe what the product is (for example in a technical specification), what it does (for example in a functional specification), how well it does it (for example in a performance specification), or what the end result is to be (for example in a requirement specification). Other specifications may be included; for example, an acceptance specification, which explains how the buyer confirms contractual acceptance. It is fundamental that the parties share an agreement and understanding of the type of specification(s) that they want to use.

The degree of freedom and responsibility that the seller has varies significantly depending upon the choice of specification type. If the contract is based on a technical specification then from a contractual viewpoint the seller has relatively little interest in what the buyer does with the product or how well it lives up to expectations. The seller must simply meet the specification. In comparative terms this amounts to the seller having little freedom in the execution of the work, but also little responsibility for the end result. On the other hand, if the contract is based on a requirement specification, the seller may have much more freedom to innovate, but he must meet the buyer's expectation in the end result. These distinctions between specifications thus have both a contractual and a practical impact. The parties must be clear on their mutual objectives in selecting the type of specification and in drafting the documents in detail. The buyer may try to have a hybrid specification or include one of each type. The former just leads to a muddle and the latter can lead to a totality of specification that can physically never be fully met. If there is to be more than one specification type, then it is as well to consider having an order of precedence (written into the contract) to allow the seller to resolve conflicts between the various specifications.

Fit for purpose

However, contractual life is not even this simple. If the seller thinks that a technical specification gets him off the hook of any interest in the end utility to the buyer he may be wrong. Unless the contract includes the right exclusions, the seller may be responsible for ensuring that the product is, in the buyer's eyes, 'fit for purpose'. But the buyer does not have it all his own way. The goods must be fit for the purpose for which such goods are commonly sold, but in many business contracts there is no such common purpose standard. The buyer must make the seller aware of the purpose(s) for which the goods are intended. This he must do at the time the contract is made (he cannot just change or make up his mind later). This is further demonstration of the need for the parties to be clear on their aims and to ensure that all parts of the contract – technical and commercial – are constructed so as to have mutual coherence and integrity. This is essential if both sides are to be fully aware of their risks.

Quantity

Where it is necessary to specify quantity, the contract must be clear on the size and form of batches that are acceptable.

Buyer obligations

Focus naturally falls on the buyer's primary obligation, which is to pay the contract price (see Payment, later in this chapter). He may have many other obligations, for example to:

- Inspect the work

- Witness tests

- Approve plans

- Sign documents

- Provide data

- Provide material for embodiment in the seller's work

- Lend equipment

- Provide facilities

- Provide resources

- Provide access to premises.

It is important that all such obligations are set down in the contract with the same clarity and completeness as any obligation on the seller. Where the buyer is to provide data, material, equipment, facilities, resources and access then proper definitions (and specifications where relevant), timescales and terms (for example, whether or not loan items are free of charge) must be stated. The seller may wish the buyer to warrant that such things are fit for purpose. He may want to specify that the buyer warrants that data will be complete, accurate and up-to-date.

Price

There are four aspects to price. These are: how a price is agreed; when a price is agreed; the type of price or pricing arrangement; and variations to price after the contract is made or after the price is initially agreed. The word 'pricing' is used to mean the process by which prices are agreed.

How prices are agreed

There are four normal means by which a price or prices can be agreed:

Advertisement

Where sellers make prices known through catalogues, sales and publicity material or through general advertisements in public media or specialized trade media.

Competitive tendering

Where sellers submit prices each in confidence to the buyer.

Single tendering

Where the buyer invites just one seller to submit prices.

Negotiation

Where the buyer and seller meet to agree prices through a process of discussion.

Proper contract formation requires that an offer has been made and has been met with an acceptance. Both offer and acceptance must be communicated. It is necessary to distinguish between an 'offer' (that is an offer that the offerer intends may be accepted by the offeree) and an 'invitation to treat' which by contrast means that the 'offerer' intends no more than discussion (that is, he positively does not intend an offer capable of acceptance). Thus it may be deduced that the advertisement route is not normally intended by the advertiser to constitute an offer capable of contractual acceptance, since the seller would presumably wish not to make contracts with buyers unknown. However legal precedence does not necessarily support such a deduction and if an advertiser wishes to avoid unintentional contracts he must ensure that the advertisement makes this clear. In comparison, tenders submitted by sellers, whether or not in competition are normally expected to be formulated as offers that are capable of acceptance and, again, if the seller does not intend this, he must say so. Any offer or any invitation to treat may be followed by negotiation, but as negotiations conclude it is important for one side or the other (it does not matter which) to reduce the results of negotiation to a formal offer, which the other side can then accept or reject.

It is natural to concentrate on price since, for example, an engineer managing a project budget will have great regard for his expenditure with suppliers, but it must be stressed that price is not agreed (regardless of the method) in isolation. Price is only one element of an offer. Price must relate to what is offered in both technical and commercial components. The offer of price must be clear as to the product, specification and quantity (the technical component) and as to commercial provisions such as payment arrangements, warranties, liabilities and, where relevant, intellectual property rights. Many of the commercial terms have an impact on cost and risk, and thus are essential to the completeness of any offer on price.

When prices are agreed

In order to satisfy the requirement of contract law, the price must be agreed at the time the contract is made or where this is not possible or is not desired there must instead be a stated mechanism, by which the price can be agreed later. If the contract is of this latter type, then in practice the price might be agreed during the course of the work or even after the work is finished.

Types of prices

Prices can be set by reference to future market prices. This is a useful approach for commodities such as oil. But more commonly the commercial manager is concerned with those types of contracts where the price is one of the following types:

Firm price

A price that is not variable.

Fixed price

A price the final value of which is fixed by reference to some variable parameter such as an inflation index or currency exchange rate.

Cost re-imbursement

A price based on the seller's actual costs plus a pre-determined amount or percentage by way of profit.

Incentive price

A price based upon the seller's achievement against predetermined targets of cost, time or technical performance.

Whatever the price type, buyer and seller are interested in the relationship between cost and risk. In a conventional arm's length relationship the seller will prefer a firm price where he perceives the risk to be small and the opportunity for profit great. Where the risk is high, he will prefer cost re-imbursement and hope that the buyer will have plenty of money to cover the inevitable expenditure that will be incurred purely as a result of the uncertainty in the contract. The buyer's perspective is the exact opposite. The greater the risk the more he will want a firm price arrangement so as to contain the risk, allocate it to the seller and avoid any liability to pay beyond his initial expectations. The cost incentive contract provides the compromise solution for high-risk work where neither side is willing or able to carry the entire cost risk. But whether firm price (seller risk), cost reimbursement (buyer risk) or cost incentive (shared risk) attention is focused on the degree of risk inherent in the technical complexity of the work. Two important elements of possible commercial risk relate to the effect of inflation (which is particularly important in high value, long-term contracts) and the effect of exchange rates (where there is high foreign currency expenditure). The effect of these two factors can be shifted to the buyer (or shared) in a fixed price contract. The same arrangements (described below) can also be adopted in a cost incentive contract.

Firm price

The definition given above says that a firm price is not variable. This is not strictly true. What it means is that when the price is struck it relates to a particular technical and commercial baseline. Thus if the buyer exercises any contractual rights to unilaterally modify the technical baseline (usually restricted to modifications to specification and quantity or possibly timeframe) then even a firm price is subject to variation. Contracts do not usually grant rights to unilaterally alter the commercial baseline. It may seem obvious that if the technical baseline changes then the price must change, but there are folk who misguidedly believe that once a firm price is agreed then the buyer can do what he likes in changing his requirements without any adjustment to the price.

Fixed price

Dealing with inflation

Contract terms that pass inflation risk to the buyer are usually described as 'Variation of Price' (VOP) or 'Contract Price Adjustment' (CPA). These generally work on the basis of a formula, for example:

$$Pa = Po \times \left(A + \frac{BLf}{Lo} + \frac{CMf}{Mo}\right)$$

Where:

Pa = Contract price as adjusted

Po = Original contract price

A = Non-variable element of price

B = Labour proportion of variable element

C = Material proportion of variable element

Lf = Labour index final

Lo = Labour index original

Mf = Material index final

Mo = Material index original

The original contract price is the contract price at a particular economics base. It may be the economics prevailing at the date of contract, the date of quotation, the date of invitation to tender or any other convenient point. The contract price as adjusted is the final value of the original price after the application of the formula albeit those interim adjustments can be made in long-term contracts. A, B and C add up to one. For example, if their values are respectively 0.1, 0.7 and 0.2 it means 10 per cent of the contract price is not variable, 70% is attributable to labour which is variable and 20% to material which is also variable (the labour and material proportions of the contract being 7:2). It is important to express it in this way so that it is the entire contract price (excluding the non-variable element) that is adjusted, including overheads and profit rather than just in respect of wages/salary/material cost changes. L and M refer to inflation indices published by Industry or the Government and selected for the relevant sector of industry. Lo and Mo are the indices as at the economics base date of Po. Lf and Mf are the value of the same indices prevailing at appropriate later dates. For example Mf may be at the mid point of material deliveries or invoices. Lf may be at, say, three months prior to due delivery reflecting the mid point of the manufacturing cycle.

In a fixed price contract the seller would prefer A to be zero conveying all the inflation risk (to the extent that movement in the chosen indices is likely to reflect actual potential changes in the particular company) to the buyer.

VOP/CPA terms tend to cover some or all of what are referred to as 'background' inflation, over which the company can exercise little control. Seeking long-term prices from suppliers can control material costs. Salary and wage costs can be controlled by everything from fear of redundancy to profit sharing schemes. However, buyers are generally wary of inflation terms that are linked to the seller's actual variation in wages, salaries and materials, as there is little incentive on the seller to exercise any control. An alternative method for passing the inflation risk to the buyer is for the seller to provide annual price lists for which the delivery price will be the price prevailing at date of order or at date of invoice.

Dealing with exchange rate risks

The seller can deal with exchange rate variation (ERV) risk in three ways. He can hedge his risk by buying forward his anticipated foreign currency expenditure. He can attempt to persuade the buyer to pay part of the contract price in the relevant foreign currency so that the risk lies fully with the buyer. Alternatively the buyer and seller may agree a contract provision that allows the price to change in line with certain movements in exchange rates. An example is given below:

$$Pa = Po \times \frac{(AER0 + B)}{ER1}$$

Where:

Pa = Price as adjusted for exchange rate variation

Po = Price at date of contract

A   = Variable element

B   = Fixed element

ER0 = Exchange rate at base date

ER1 = Exchange rate at date of variation

Rather like the VOP or CPA formula, ERV formulae tend to have a fixed element and a variable element. The greater the fixed element the greater the currency risk that is left with the seller. The exchange rate base date might be the date of tender or date of contract. The date of variation might be the date of delivery or invoice to the buyer. An ERV formula can protect the seller against all or part of the currency risk when a buyer pays in other than the seller's own national currency. It works by adjusting the contract price as the contract price currency fluctuates. However, an ERV formula can also be used where the buyer pays in the seller's national currency but where the seller has significant expenditure in a different currency. So in this case the formula works by adjusting the contract price for changes in the seller's costs caused by currency fluctuations in its overseas expenditure. In the formula given above the variable element (A) would be less than 1 reflecting the proportion of the contract price that is attributable to the overseas expenditure. ER1 would be the exchange rate at, say, the mid point of disbursement of the foreign currency.

Cost reimbursement

In essence a cost reimbursement contract is very simple. When the contract is finished the buyer pays all the seller's costs plus something for profit. The profit is usually predetermined either as a fixed fee or as a percentage of the actual costs incurred. These contracts are most useful where the technical risk is too high for the seller to carry, where the contract is simply of a fixed duration (for example, where the output cannot necessarily be defined, such as in a research contract) or where the seller is providing a service where there is no definable output, just an obligation to provide expert effort.

Incentive contracts

Incentives can be built into any contract with the purpose of motivating the seller to perform well (on cost, time or technical performance) to the benefit of both sides. In contracts of high technical uncertainty there is merit in the buyer and seller sharing the cost risk, particularly where the buyer can bring his own skill to bear and where the parties are desirous of a close working relationship. In a cost incentive contract the object is to work together in driving the seller's cost down, with savings being shared at the end. There are many different schemes and the following diagram illustrates the relationship between cost and profit to the seller of one such scheme.

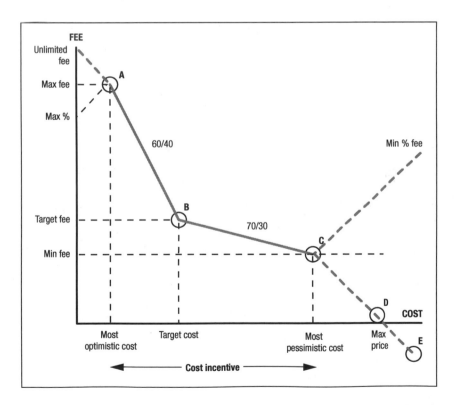

The relationship between cost and profit

The principles of the cost incentive scheme are:

Price agreement

The price is agreed after the contract is completed on the basis of costs incurred.

Target cost

The parties agree a target cost and a cost incentive range within which the actual costs are expected to fall. The target cost is a reasonable estimate assuming normal efficiency and typical problems.

Target fee

The parties agree a target fee that is the profit to be paid if the actual costs exactly equal the target cost. It is normally a percentage of the target cost.

Share ratios

The parties agree ratios in which they will share under spend or over spend against the target cost. The share ratios are negotiable. In the example they are 60/40 and 70/30 respectively. The buyer's share comes first.

Most optimistic cost

An estimate of the outturn cost that assumes improved efficiency and no problems.

Most pessimistic cost

An estimate of the out-turn cost that assumes degraded efficiency and major problems.

Final price

The final price for the contract is the actual costs incurred plus the target fee plus the agreed share of savings against the target or less the agreed share of overspends against the target. The profit is the target fee plus the seller's share of under spend or minus the seller's share of overspend.

If life were as simple as assuming that the actual costs will definitely fall within the cost incentive range then the scheme and the graph would only run from point A to point C. However, the parties must legislate for the possibility of costs emerging outside of the two extremes where they have a number of choices:

Profit limitations

At point A (in Figure 3), the scheme might permit the seller to continue to improve its fee at the same under spend share ratio if costs are lower than the most optimistic cost. This results in an unlimited fee opportunity. Alternatively the parties may agree to limit fees either in absolute or percentage terms. At point C the scheme might allow that for costs exceeding the most pessimistic cost the seller should suffer no further erosion of its fee and a minimum fee (in absolute or percentage terms) should apply.

Limiting the buyer's liability

On the other hand the buyer may demand an absolute limit on its liability and include a maximum price shown as point D.

Limiting the seller's liability

If a maximum price is operative point E does not exist as the seller's fee erodes at the rate of 100% from point C until it reaches point D, after which losses would accumulate at the rate of 100%. However, in such event the buyer may agree to limit the seller's liability for loss and introduce a point E, at which the curve changes shape to fix the loss in absolute or percentage terms.

This one graph shows that many variations can be negotiated not only beyond the normal boundary conditions at A and C but also between them in terms of the share ratios, target fee and cost incentive range. The great advantage of such schemes is that they are flexible and can be tailor made to individual circumstances, buyers and sellers.

In addition or as alternatives to cost incentives, the parties may agree incentives on the seller that are linked to timeliness or technical performance. These might be achieved by simple bonus schemes (extra money for extra performance, paid over and above a firm price, for example) or by inserting these additional incentives into a cost incentive scheme. The main difficulty for the buyer is in establishing firstly the range of time performance or technical performance that is beneficial to him (for example, there is no merit in paying a delivery bonus for earlier delivery if the buyer is going to be in no position to make use of the goods) and secondly in setting targets that are realistic. A bonus should not be earned too easily. On the other hand if the bonus can only be earned by extraordinary expenditure by the seller then there is little real incentive. Careful trade off analysis needs to be done by each side in order to ascertain the optimum combination of measures.

Variations to price

At the outset a contract should contain a technical component. This will be attached to the price in a firm price contract, to the base price in a fixed price contract or to the target cost (and maximum price if relevant) in a cost incentive contract. These 'anchors' must themselves be subject to change if the technical component is changed. In a cost reimbursement contract any change in cost as a result of a technical change automatically takes care of itself, unless such a contract includes an overall limit on the buyer's obligation, in which case even such limit must change if the technical component changes.

Payment

A central theme of this Guide is the importance of cash flow. In contractual matters it is essential that there is no room for any error in ensuring that payment is made when the seller expects. It is less of a concern to the buyer whose cash flow is improved by any unintended delay in paying the seller. Some companies have a (usually unwritten) policy of delaying payments to suppliers for this very reason. This is an inexcusable business practice. The very least that the seller can do is to ensure that the contract terms do not leave any doubt as to how and when payments will be made, as any ambiguity will be exploited by the unscrupulous buyer. The elements to be considered are the legal obligation to pay, the type of payment scheme, retentions, the currency of payment, delays to payment, penalties for late payment, the recoverability of payments, invoicing, the manner of payment, payment for changes and variations, and security of payment.

Legal obligation to pay

This is an obvious point, but once the contract is made, the buyer is legally obliged to pay provided the seller meets his obligations under the contract. The buyer must pay according to the terms of the contract. As will be seen in later topics, payment does not have to be linked directly to such things as delivery, the passing of title in the goods or acceptance. It is open to the parties to agree whatever arrangements they care to choose, but once the contract is made, paying the agreed price is a fundamental obligation on the buyer. The only legitimate reason for not paying is where the seller owes the buyer a debt. In this event the buyer is allowed to 'set off' his payment obligation against this debt. However, the buyer must have established that the debt is owed and the sum must be fixed and agreed. It is not unknown for a buyer to make a claim against the seller and set this off, whether or not the seller agrees with the claim. Whilst the commercial leverage is obvious, the buyer is not entitled to set himself up as judge and jury in such a manner.

Type of payment scheme

There are two basic approaches to the type of payment scheme. Firstly the buyer may simply pay upon (or following) delivery. This may be in one single payment or in a series of payments where there are several deliveries to be made. This gives the buyer greatest security and places the greatest incentive on the seller to perform. No deliveries, no money! However, on major contracts where the cost of financing work in progress is an issue or on contracts where the seller believes that the buyer must evidence his commitment beyond just placing the contract, it is open to the parties to agree a payment scheme that involves payments being made prior to delivery. Whilst there are no standard definitions of such advance payments the following serves to indicate the possibilities:

Down payment

This is where a proportion of the contract price is paid with or immediately following the contract having been made. The seller need not have done any work or expended any money. It is in effect a sign of good faith on the part of the buyer.

Progress payments

This is where payments are made as the work progresses, perhaps according to the rate of the seller's expenditure.

Stage payments

This is where proportions of the price are paid as stages of the work are achieved, measured perhaps in the elapse of time since contract award.

Milestone payments

This is where proportions of the price are paid as and when the seller successfully accomplishes predefined events.

A contract may have one or more of these types of scheme. If a contract is based on advance payments then the cash flow incentive on the seller to perform will be a function of the type of scheme. The seller has most advantage with a down payment and then time and materials payments as compared with milestone payments for which he must demonstrate concrete achievement in order to be paid.

Retentions

The word retention in the context of payment means that in a contract where there are to be advance payments, the buyer will wish to ensure that some, usually significant part of the contract price is not paid until the seller has fulfilled all his obligations. Retentions can be 'absolute' (for example, 10% of the price is not paid until the end) or 'running' (for example, 10% of every payment is withheld as the work progresses). Retentions are usually released on final delivery or may be partially withheld until the seller has discharged any warranty obligations. The degree of retention depends upon the bargaining power of buyer and seller at the contract negotiation stage and, because of the cost of money, the overall price to be paid.

Currency of payment

The contract must state the currency of payment including any arrangements for counter trade. Counter trade is where a contract is wholly or partly paid for in other goods rather than in money.

Delays to payment

Once the seller has established what he can be paid and when, he needs to consider what factors, apart from his own default, may delay cash changing hands. Factors in this respect are:

Paperwork

For example, assembling evidence that a milestone has been achieved.

Credit period

This is a time given in the contract that the buyer may let elapse before making payment. Buyers like to have a credit period in order to have sufficient time to check any supporting evidence and to process the paperwork. Thirty days is normally sufficient for this. Some buyers like to secure much longer credit periods, just to optimize their own cash flow. It is open to the parties to agree whatever credit period they choose.

Payment limits

Some buyers manage their budgets by imposing annual contractual limits on payment, whether or not the work is running to schedule.

Pay-when-paid

Some buyers manage their cash flow by not paying their suppliers until payments have been received from their customers. The law does frown upon pay-when-paid arrangements, but the seller may see some advantage if the qui pro quo is that he gains some influence over the conduct of business between the buyer and the buyer's customer. This is particularly so where the buyer/seller relationship is more than a simple arm's length deal. It is worth mentioning the effect of the Housing Grants, Construction and Regeneration Act 1996, which makes some, but not all, pay-when-paid clauses ineffective.

Discretionary delays

Some buyers like to reserve the right to withhold payments on the grounds of general dissatisfaction with the seller's contractual performance, whether or not the specific event to which payment is linked has occurred

Penalties for late payment

Provided the seller has performed to the contract and allowing for any buyer rights to delay or offset payment, the seller's right to payment is absolute. If the buyer does not pay, the seller has two alternatives. He may have chosen in the first place to make arrangements to secure payment from a third party (see further below) or he may charge the buyer interest. The arrangements for interest (accrual date and rate, payment arrangements) or other substantial remedy may be set out in detail in the contract. If no such details are included and in the absence of a provision denying any right to interest, the buyer is liable under statute[1] to pay interest on overdue payments measured from the expiry of the credit period. Where there is no credit period stated in the contract, the period is taken to be thirty days or where by custom and practice the buyer pays at the end of the month following the month in which delivery was made then interest accrues from the end of that period.

Recoverability of payments

By either paying on delivery or by holding retentions until satisfactory completion the buyer uses money to help secure performance from the seller. His second approach to security is to have a contractual provision that allows him to recover advance payments from the seller in the event of failure to perform. From the buyer's perspective this is quite reasonable. He is only interested in complete performance and has only made advance payments in good faith on account of the seller's promise of complete performance. It only makes sense that if the seller fails, the buyer should get his money back. The alternative is that he lets the defaulting seller keep the money, but sues him for damages (the amount of which may include the money paid out anyway) leaving the 'bad guy' with the

---

1 Prior to 1 November 2002 only small businesses (those employing less than 50 people) had this statutory right. This limitation was due to be removed on this date.

short-term advantage and the 'good guy' with a hole in his cash flow. Sellers frequently argue that once an advance payment is made it is never recoverable, because in the event of failure to perform, the buyer can resort to the law. Sellers also argue that the contract is capable of partial performance and therefore that part money for part work is a closed matter. This may be true for some types of contract. However for contracts where the end result is only ever accomplished when the sum of the parts is apparent (regardless of the value of the parts) the buyer must be careful to construct the contract so that it cannot be construed as permitting 'divisible performance'

Invoicing

With all the trauma of establishing that a payment is due, it would be easy to think of invoicing as the easy bit. And so it should be. The contract should specify all the details that are required (contract number, seller details, details of claim and invoice number) and the address to which the invoice must be sent (which is sometimes a different address to the buyer's address at which the contract was made) and details of how charges (for example taxes and duties) are to be shown. So far so good. The key issue is that the buyer is entitled to reject any invoice that is not correct in every last detail. Unless the contract requires otherwise, the buyer is under no obligation to advise the seller of an incorrect invoice or to do anything other than return the rejected invoice at the buyer's leisure. It is an unpardonable sin for a seller to miss a payment through an invoice error.

The manner of payment

Many business transactions still involve a paper trail culminating in a paper invoice, with its supporting paperwork, being paid by cheque. There is no reason why the whole process should not be done electronically with payment happening by the electronic transfer of funds. Either way, the contract should be clear on this point.

Changes and variations

For many reasons the invoice price may be different from the original contract price. The differences can come from a number of sources:

- Changes and variations to the work

- Variations due to currency fluctuation

- Changes due to inflation

- Changes due to market conditions

- Changes in the rates of VAT or other tax and charges.

In all cases the contract must be clear on how such matters are to be dealt with from a payment viewpoint. This could be by separate invoices on an as-and-when basis (which has the advantage to the seller that dealing with such matters separately avoids any risk of holding up a primary invoice), by adjustment to individual primary invoices or by one all-embracing invoice at the end of the contract.

Security of payment

It has been seen that the buyer can achieve some security with rights of retention and recoverability. The seller has a different type of problem. To the seller the main issue is getting the buyer to pay when payment is due within the terms of the contract.

Letters of credit

If the buyer is highly creditworthy then the seller need take no special approach. If the buyer is of strong financial standing, if he is local (in the sense that the seller can get at him), if he has a good payment reputation, if the seller has done good business with him before, then the seller may reasonably trust in the straightforward legal and contractual obligation upon the buyer to pay. If the seller has any reason to doubt the buyer's willingness or ability to pay then the seller will wish to bring a third party into the arrangements, one to whom the seller can look directly for payment. Such a third party is normally a bank or other financial institute or a parent company. The buyer is required to procure for the seller a letter of credit from that institution that allows the seller to present documentary evidence of delivery to the third party and on the basis of which the third party makes payment to the seller on behalf of the buyer. The best form of letter of credit (at least from the seller's viewpoint) is one that is 'confirmed' (that is the third party confirms the arrangement directly to the seller) and 'irrevocable' (which means that the buyer cannot take the unscrupulous step of cancelling the credit arrangement after the contract is made). There are other forms of credit arrangement, but the confirmed, irrevocable letter of credit has the merits of simplicity and fairness.

Retention of title

The seller may also consider a contract term under which he retains title to the goods, notwithstanding physical delivery to the buyer, until payment is made. This is not always so advantageous to the seller if the goods are of little resale value or if the goods are physically distant and difficult to recover.

Delivery and the passing of property and risk

In a contract for the sale of goods, delivery is concerned with a number of practical and very important issues. These are: the timing of delivery, the place, the means of transport from seller to buyer, the responsibility for the engagement of a carrier, requirements for preservation and packaging, delivery documentation (for example, advice notes, certificates of conformity, shipping documents, import and export licences), notices of intended despatch (in the absence of which the buyer may not be required to take delivery), the means of acknowledging receipt, the arrangements for inspection by the buyer and the procedures for acceptance or rejection by the buyer. Inspection, rejection and acceptance are covered below. For the other topics mentioned, the golden rule is to ensure that all of them are comprehensively covered within the contract. The doing of each of these things has a cost (which either buyer or seller must cover) and the failure to do any of these things will have cost and other implications for one or both parties. Failure to have these matters sorted out from the start will lead to confusion and acrimony later. They are all relatively straightforward in principle although errors may lurk in the detail.

Basic principles

However, beneath these practical matters lie some important legal and contractual issues. Firstly, the seller cannot sell the goods unless he is either the owner or the agent of the owner of the goods. For example, a buyer cannot acquire any legal entitlement to goods that have been stolen (although there are instances under the Sales of Goods Act when a buyer can acquire title from a non-owner). Secondly, the seller must have an unencumbered right to sell the goods. This means that, for example, no other party has any sort of prior claim (called a 'lien') on the goods. Such situation could arise either because the seller has not acquired an unencumbered right to sell on from his supplier or because the seller has another customer who has a claim to the goods under a separate contract. These are not just points of academic interest. Good commercial practice combined with conscious and careful choice of contract terms is essential if these points are not to interfere with the successful execution of the company's business.

Property and risk

There are two further points of contractual importance. Firstly, there is the question of legal title to the goods. In this section this is referred to as the passing of property. This means that from the moment the seller acquires material and allocates it to the particular contract through the period of his value adding processes to the physical delivery to the buyer and on into any period allowed for inspection, rejection, acceptance and payment the contract must be clear as to which of the parties has property in the goods. Secondly, over this same, extended time period, the contract must be clear on where lies the risk of loss or damage to the goods. The passing of risk from seller to buyer has many implications, not the least of which is the question of which of them carries the insurance responsibility.

In consumer transactions the Sale of Goods Act helpfully explains that 'unless otherwise agreed, the goods remain at the seller's risk until the property in them is transferred to the buyer, but when the property is then transferred to the buyer the goods are at the buyer's risk whether delivery has been made or not'. This reveals two interesting points. The first is that it is open to the parties to agree something different from that which the Act allows. Secondly, the construction of this sentence shows that the passing of property and risk are expected to be concurrent, but that such passing may be entirely divorced from the point of physical delivery. If these two points are put together, it can be seen that the parties are free to decide whatever they like in terms of the relationship between the passing of risk, the passing of property and physical delivery.

In business contracts the passing of property and risk are frequently divorced. In a contract in which the buyer agrees to pay advance payments (for example a down payment with contract signature or stage payments as work progresses) then he may seek a 'vesting' term in the contract. This provides that property passes to him in material and work in progress well before delivery is due under the contract. At the other extreme, the seller may wish to retain property until final payment has been received. This is called a 'retention of title' provision. The reason is fairly obvious. If the buyer, having received the goods, does not pay, then the seller can legitimately recover the goods, given that the property in them still rests with him. In practice such a remedy may be of little use, if the goods have been consumed or altered in some way by the buyer or have moved onto a destination where recovery is impracticable. In such circumstances the seller's better bet is to interest himself in means of ensuring payment.

Consequences of rejection

A further matter is the question of what happens about property and risk if the buyer rejects the goods. Life can become complicated here. If the goods are fairly rejected by the buyer, then he may wish both property and risk to revert to the seller. In this case the contract provisions must say so and provisions be included for the passing of property and risk to the buyer in replacement and repaired goods. The seller may wish to include a term that allows the reversion of property and risk to depend upon the outcome of a contractual appeal against the rejection. In any event the reversion of property may not be accompanied by the reversion of risk if the goods do not physically move, since the party in possession has the better opportunity to take care of the goods. In contractual negotiations this is all good knockabout stuff, but securing resolution on all such matters is part of sound commercial risk management.

Incoterms

To reduce the time spent on the knockabout, companies may prefer to use a standard approach to the passing of risk. The International Chamber of Commerce 'Incoterms' provides a range of approaches from which the parties may choose:

Ex-Works (Ex W or EXW)

This means the seller's only responsibility is to make the goods available at the seller's premises, i.e. the works or factory. The seller is not responsible for loading the goods on the vehicle provided by the buyer unless otherwise agreed. The buyer bears the full costs and risk involved in bringing the goods from there to the desired destination. Ex works represents the minimum obligation of the seller.

Free Carrier (FCA or FRC)

This term has been designed to meet the requirements of multi-modal transport, such as container or roll-on, roll-off traffic by trailers and ferries. It is based on the same principle as FOB (see below) except the seller fulfils its obligations when the goods are delivered to the custody of the carrier at the named point. If no precise point can be named at the time of the contract, the parties should refer to the place where the carrier should take the goods into its charge. The risk of loss or damage to the goods is transferred from seller to buyer at that time and not at the ship's rail. The term 'carrier' means any person by whom or in whose name a contract of carriage by road, rail, air, sea, or a combination of modes has been made. When a seller has been furnished with a bill of lading, waybill or carrier's receipt, the seller duly fulfils its obligation by presenting such a document issued by a carrier.

Free on Rail or Free on Truck (FOR or FOT)

Both refer to goods being carried by rail and should only be used when the goods are carried by rail. The risk of loss or damage is transferred when the goods are loaded onto the rail.

Free Alongside Ship (FAS)

This requires the seller to deliver the goods alongside the ship on the quay. From that point on, the buyer bears all costs and risks of loss and damage to the goods. Unlike FOB, FAS requires the buyer to clear the goods for export and pay the cost of loading the goods.

Free on Board (FOB)

This means the goods are placed on board the ship by the seller at a port of shipment named in the contract. The risk of loss or damage to the goods is transferred to the buyer when the goods pass the ship's rail (i.e. off the dock and placed on the ship). The seller pays the cost of loading the goods.

FOB Airport (FOA)

This term is very similar to the ordinary FOB term. The seller fulfils its obligation by delivering the goods to the air carrier at the airport of departure. The risk of loss is transferred from the seller to the buyer at such time.

Cost and Freight (C&F)

This requires the seller to pay the costs and freight necessary to bring the goods to the named destination, but the risk of loss or damage to the goods, as well as any cost increases, are transferred from the seller to the buyer when the goods pass the ship's rail in the port of shipment. Insurance is the buyer's responsibility.

Cost, Insurance and Freight (CIF)

This is C&F with the additional requirement that the seller procure transport insurance against the risk of loss or damage to goods. The seller must contract with the insurer and pay the insurance premium.

Freight/Carriage Paid To (CPT or DPC)

This term means the seller pays the freight for the carriage of the goods to the named destination. The risk of loss or damage to the goods and any cost increases transfers from the seller to the buyer when the goods have been delivered to the custody of the first carrier, and not at the ship's rail. Accordingly, 'freight/carriage paid to' can be used for all modes of transportation, including container or roll-on roll-off traffic by trailers and ferries. When the seller is required to furnish a bill of lading, waybill, or carrier receipt, the seller duly fulfils its obligation by presenting such a document issued by the person contracted with for carriage to the main destination.

Freight/Carriage and Insurance Paid To (CIP)

This is the same as 'freight/carriage paid to' but with the additional requirement that the seller has to procure transport insurance against the risk of loss or damage to the goods during the carriage. The seller contracts with the insurer and pays the insurance premium.

Ex Ship (EXS)

This means the seller shall make the goods available to the buyer on board the ship at the destination named in the contract. The seller bears the full cost and risk involved in bringing the goods there. The buyer must pay the cost of unloading the goods and any customs duties.

Ex Quay (EXQ)

This means the seller has agreed to make the goods available to the buyer on the quay or the wharf at the destination named in the contract. The seller bears the full cost and risks in delivering the goods to that point including unloading. There are two variations of ex quay contracts: 'ex quay duty paid' and 'ex quay duty on buyer's account'. In the first, the seller pays the duty. In the second, the seller also pays the duty, but the buyer must reimburse the seller.

Delivered at Frontier (DAF)

This means that the seller's obligations are fulfilled when the goods have arrived at the frontier but before the customs border of the country named in the contract. The term is primarily used when goods are carried by rail or truck. The seller bears the full cost and risk in delivering the goods up to this point, but the buyer must arrange and pay for the goods to clear customs.

Delivery/Duty Paid (DDP)

This represents the seller's maximum obligation. The term 'DDP' is generally followed by words indicating the buyer's premises. It notes that the seller bears all risks and all costs until the goods are delivered. This term can be used irrespective of the mode of transport. If the parties wish to make clear that the seller is not responsible for certain costs, additional words should be added (for example, 'delivered duty paid exclusive of VAT and/or taxes').

Delivery Duty Unpaid (DDU)

Under these terms, the seller fulfils his obligation to deliver when the goods have been available to the buyer uncleared for import at the point or place of the named destination. The seller bears all costs and risks involved in bringing the goods to the point or place of the named destination. There is no obligation for import clearance.

This list serves to show not only how many different options there are on passing of risk, but also the key differences that are buried in the detail.

Acceptance and rejection

One of the most significant milestones in any contract is the point of contractual acceptance. This means that the goods have been tendered to the buyer in performance of the contract. The seller is saying to the buyer that these goods are fully in accordance with the specifications and are now ready for the buyer's beneficial use. The buyer must decide to accept or reject the goods. This is a crucial moment. If the buyer accepts, then the primary goal of the contract is performed and the buyer forever loses his right to terminate the contract for the seller's default. If any defects are found after acceptance then the buyer must go after the seller under an express or implied warranty.

Methods of acceptance

There are four common mechanisms used in business contracts by which acceptance is conveyed.

Buyer confirmation

Firstly, acceptance may happen when the buyer says that he has accepted the goods. This is good news for the buyer and bad news for the seller. Such an arrangement is open ended in time and thus highly unsatisfactory to the seller.

Expiry of right to reject

Acceptance may occur upon the expiry of any period for rejection stated in the contract, except where the buyer has exercised his right of rejection within such period. This approach always invites the same tussle in contract negotiations. The seller offers a period of five minutes, the buyer demands a hundred years and a compromise is eventually reached.

Buyer behaviour

Acceptance can be given when the buyer takes the goods into use or otherwise behaves in a way that is inconsistent with his not having accepted the goods, for example, by incorporating them in other goods that have been sold on.

Acceptance procedures

The fourth method is to record in the contract detailed arrangements for the granting of acceptance. These may involve extensive testing (witnessed by the buyer or certified by the seller), stressing, proving and demonstration of the goods. There may be detailed acceptance test specifications, plans and schedules. The drawing up of the details requires a lot of thought and care. The tests must fairly examine the goods, but must not be so extensive as to be excessive in cost or time. The buyer then gives contractual acceptance when the acceptance arrangements have been completed. In complex contracts, it may be necessary to take the pragmatic view that acceptance testing will reveal some problem areas. It is not unusual to extend the arrangements to allow categories of 'failure', classified perhaps between 'major' meaning the problem must be fixed immediately, 'minor' meaning the problem must be fixed, but can wait until later or 'trivial' meaning that no remedial action is ever required. This is all perfectly okay, provided that the contract contains the arrangements and those topics such as the method of classification, the definition of each classification and the resultant actions and responsibilities are included.

Inspection

Whichever of the four methods of acceptance is chosen, the underlying principle is that the buyer is reserving some time and some means to inspect the work before he gives acceptance. Even in consumer transactions the buyer is entitled to a period in which to satisfy himself that the goods are in accordance with the contract (never sign for goods at the front door without writing 'received, not accepted' or 'received, not inspected'!), but in business contracts inspection may be a much bigger deal. To inspect on delivery or under detailed acceptance arrangements is all right, but some buyers insist on having rights of inspection prior to delivery being tendered. The positive side of this is that when things are going well, pre-delivery inspection gives the buyer confidence. On the other hand, if the buyer is going to have a contractual right to pre-delivery inspection then he must give thought as to what happens if the inspection reveals problems. He may want to reserve the right to reject the goods before delivery (saving himself cost and time later) or he may want the right to terminate the contract for anticipatory breach. For the seller, the threat of such sanctions even before he tenders the goods for delivery can seem harsh since there may be every chance that the problem can be ironed out before delivery is due.

Checklist

- Take time and care with definitions and orders of precedence in a contract.

- Be clear on the contractual role of different types of specification.

- Make sure that the contract delineates buyer responsibilities in as much detail as seller responsibilities.

- Understand and be consistent in the use of 'firm' price and 'fixed' price.

- Cost reimbursement and cost incentive contracts have a useful role where risk is great.

- Use VOP/CPA and ERV terms to share risk in inflation and in exchange rates.

- Use down payments, progress payments, stage payments and milestones payments to reduce the cost of financing work in progress.

- The buyer can use retentions, credit periods, pay-when-paid terms, recovery rights, set-off, payment limits and discretionary rights as means of controlling his cash flow and as means to use cash as an incentive on the seller to perform.

- The seller may have statutory or contractual rights to interest on late payments.

- The seller can use letters of credit and retention of title terms to protect his right to payment.

- Ensure that the contract prescribes in detail the invoicing arrangements.

- The seller must invoice precisely in accordance with the contract in order to be certain of payment.

- Make sure the contract says how payment for changes will be made.

- Make sure the contract specifies the currency of payment and if electronic transfer of funds is permitted.

- In business contracts the parties are free to decide how title to goods and the risk of loss or damage pass from seller to buyer.

- Acceptance is the single most important contractual milestone. Once acceptance is given the buyer cannot reject the goods or declare the contract repudiated by the seller. Make sure acceptance is covered in detail.

Commercial
relationships

Introduction

The theme of this book is that the commercial manager should understand and strive in the achievement of the company's commercial goals of profits, cash flow and growth. The vehicles for this include the protection and exploitation of intellectual property and the negotiation of good contracts. An overriding objective is to do business at the lowest possible risk. The last two chapters have gone to some length to explain how a contract works in practice and to illustrate just how much the contract is a device for allocating and avoiding risk. Contract negotiations crystallize the battle for risk avoidance and if problems arise during contract performance then one or both sides may try to hide behind the contract. With such a fraught, antagonistic basis for a legal relationship it is a wonder at all that companies ever manage to do business on larger projects (on smaller transactions risks are often ignored or, if considered at all, treated as having negligible effect). But working together is essential if the commercial goals are to be realized, particularly as the marketplace is increasingly international. In this chapter we will consider some of the more common ways in which companies work together and will draw out the distinctions between antagonistic and co-operative dealings.

Competition law

Perhaps surprisingly, the first thing to consider is whether the law has anything to say about the freedom with which companies may work together. It does have plenty to say, under what is known as competition law or anti-trust or anti-competitive law. The underlying principle is simple to state. It is a matter of public policy that businesses should not conduct themselves in such a way that the freedom of the market is degraded to the detriment of the public interest. As long ago as 1776, Adam Smith wrote that, 'people of the same trade seldom meet together, even for merriment and diversion, but the conversation ends in a conspiracy against the public, or in some contrivance to raise prices'. A little harsh maybe, but the law seeks to control such behaviour.

Penalties

Businesses who break competition law face the possibility of raids on their premises (to gather evidence), seizure of documents and fines of up to ten per cent of turnover. The disruption to business whilst proceedings are going on can be very damaging and a fine at this level can be fatal. The penalties are severe and rightly so. Both written agreements and mere behaviour can offend the regulations. The regulations catch private companies, public companies, sole traders, partnerships and associations such as trade unions. However, business units within a corporate structure are not likely to be caught.

Prohibitions

The law prohibits practices that have an appreciable effect on competition, for example bilateral or multilateral agreements that:

- Fix prices or other trading terms
- Limit or control production, markets, technical development or investment
- Share markets
- Share sources of supply

- Make contracts subject to unrelated terms

- Apply different trading terms to equivalent transactions so as to disadvantage certain parties.

The law not only has something to say about inter company co-operation that may adversely affect competition, but also about companies that seek to unfairly exploit a dominant market position. Thus the regulations also prohibit unilateral practices by a business enjoying a dominant position (usually more than 40% of market share) such as:

- Imposing unfair prices

- Limiting production, markets or technical development to the prejudice of consumers

- Applying different trading terms to equivalent transactions so as to disadvantage certain parties

- Attaching unrelated supplementary terms to contracts.

Exclusions and exemptions

Where companies work together there are a number of exclusions and exemptions (in 'individual', 'block' and 'parallel' varieties) from the regulations, of which three are probably of most interest to the reader of this Guide. Firstly, commercial agreements that do not have an appreciable effect on competition are not caught by the regulations. Secondly, 'vertical' agreements are excluded. A vertical agreement is one made between two businesses at different levels in the supply chain and includes supply agreements, purchase agreements, some distribution agreements, some franchising agreements, agency agreements, subcontracting agreements and licences for intellectual property rights. However, whilst a vertical agreement does not of itself get caught, the details of the agreement (for example, price fixing) may offend the regulations. Thirdly, a commercial agreement may be exempted if it:

- Contributes to improving production or distribution, or to promoting technical or economic progress; and

- Allows consumers a fair share in the benefit; and

- Is indispensable to the attainment of those objectives; and

- Does not eliminate competition in a substantial part of the products concerned.

A business view

Anti-competitive practices whether written, unwritten, or by action or inaction breach the regulations and serious consequences may ensue. And yet many businesses that genuinely have no untoward intentions regarding the marketplace find the law perplexing. In some situations the prohibitions seem positively perverse. For example, companies often seek 'exclusive' commercial agreements regarding a joint endeavour to bid for a major contract. The business logic seems impeccable. The strength of the combined effort may far exceed that which either can mount alone and the cost of working with more than one associate may be prohibitive. On the face of it, an exclusive agreement is nevertheless in breach of the rules. However, from a practical perspective the test in such a situation may be put thus. If competition is not significantly influenced (for example, there are other companies or consortia that are competent to bid) and the result of a winning combined effort is passed on to the public in some way, then the commercial agreement may not be caught. There are two key points to be made. Firstly, there are legitimate and sound reasons to allow ostensibly anti-competitive agreements and thus businesses should not be put off by the law. The second and most important point is that the agreement should be in writing and drafted by expert legal staff, who will also consider the benefits of voluntarily disclosing the agreement to the relevant authorities.

Confidentiality

It is a common first step in establishing a proposed commercial relationship to set up a confidentiality agreement, also known as a non-disclosure agreement (NDA). Where once companies may have relied upon some protection from implied obligations of confidentiality or just plain, old-fashioned trust, it is now more normal to put in place a written agreement. This has a number of advantages. It forces the parties to think about the issues. It requires them to take positive steps to protect information and, in the extreme, it provides a basis for legal action, although in many cases the provisions of the agreement may be unenforceable. Either way, it is no bad thing for companies to have to consider the issues carefully at the outset of their potential relationship. There may be several reasons for companies to exchange information. It may be in pursuance of a contractual obligation to another party or it may be for some mutual benefit, perhaps where the companies are working together to bid for a contract. Confidentiality agreements cannot be used to conceal anti-competitive practices such as price fixing or market rigging.

Not all prospective commercial relationships demand such close attention to the protection of confidentiality. If a buyer wants to solicit prices from suppliers he may do so without the need for any particular confidentiality. Where a supplier wants to offer or promote his goods or services there is no need for special measures. It is in those relationships where specific, valuable information is to be provided or exchanged that a confidentiality agreement is most necessary. Such information is not restricted to technical information. Information about bidding intentions may be of value to the buyer and hence in that situation he may want a confidentiality agreement with his suppliers before any discussions take place about products and prices. It is because of the need to consider confidentiality in the earliest stages of an enterprise that the confidentiality agreement is the first commercial agreement described in this chapter.

Typically a confidentiality agreement will have the following features:

Definition of information

The word 'information' will be given a full definition to include some or all of: information in writing, information disclosed orally, printed material, software and information disclosed by way of models, demonstrations and presentations.

Confidential information

Depending on the circumstances, the parties will decide whether they wish all information exchanged to be considered confidential or just specific material, in which event it will need to be marked or identified in some way. This decision will in part be based on the volume of information to be exchanged. It is tempting to simply classify all information as being confidential, but this has major practical disadvantages. Firstly, it is unlikely that all information is actually confidential. Secondly, keeping track of not only what information comes into the common domain, but also the identity of the originator is simply impossible. In such circumstances, attempts to classify all information as confidential are virtually useless and certainly a court of law would have little interest in such an arrangement.

Proper use

A statement will be included as to the proper use to which the information can be put. This must be carefully defined otherwise misuse would be impossible to establish. It is sometimes tempting to list prohibited uses, but this suffers from the drawback that the list may not be exhaustive. It is better to say what can be done, and thus automatically exclude everything else.

Protection and marking

It is important to say what must be done to physically protect each other's information. For companies of similar character each side agreeing to treat the other's information in like manner to the treatment of its own may achieve this. There may be obligations only to divulge information on a need-to-know basis. The companies may choose to appoint named individuals who will be the sole points of contact for exchange of confidential information. All confidential information must be marked to highlight its confidential nature. Relying on company standard copyright legends may not be sufficient and it is as well for the parties to agree other restrictive legends such as 'in-confidence'. Information exchanged orally presents a real problem. At best, meetings must be declared (at the start), as being in confidence and it may be worthwhile to make a note afterwards as to what confidential information was actually exchanged. But the practical difficulties are considerable, especially where exchange becomes dialogue with new ideas being jointly formulated, making the distinction between old and new impossible to establish. The Freedom of Information Act 2000 should be consulted for details of legislation in this area.

Exclusions

In some circumstances, information cannot fall under the confidentiality agreement. It is conventional to state these exclusions, so as to avoid any doubt. The exclusions are:

- Information already known to the other side at the date of the confidentiality agreement

- Information that is available to the public at large

- Information received from a third party where the third party was entitled to divulge that information.

Intellectual property rights

The agreement will normally state that the receiving party acquires no intellectual property rights in information provided by the other party. Any grant of rights would come later under a contract or licence agreement.

Termination

Like any commercial agreement, there will be a statement as to what events bring about the termination of the confidentiality agreement. Examples are: breach by one side giving the other the option to terminate; the achievement of the purpose of the agreement (winning a contract perhaps); the purpose of the agreement having disappeared (the cancellation of a potential contract is an example). Whether or not the agreement is ended, the parties may agree to carry on protecting exchanged information for several years, but not indefinitely – most confidential information has a definite shelf life and indefinite protection is not a practicable proposition other than perhaps for a small volume of information. Ultimately any written material will be destroyed or returned to the originating side.

Confidentiality agreements are a useful device for the protection of commercially valuable information, even if recourse to law is not always a practicable possibility. In some instances, where commercial information is especially valuable, companies may desire that individuals who work for the other party sign individual confidentiality undertakings. The logic of wishing to reinforce the value of information to individuals who may receive and use such information seems impeccable. In practice, many companies will not agree to require their employees to enter into such agreements and many individuals would refuse anyway. The legal recourse of a party whose confidential information has been misused is against the other party. That party may wish to take action (disciplinary or legal) against the employee who may be in breach of his employment contract. Employment contracts frequently contain obligations on the employee not only to treat his employer's information as confidential, but also to likewise treat information received from other companies in the course of his employment. This seems a fair chain of recourse. However, the danger for the disclosing party is that the employee of the other party may leave that company's employment and take and misuse the confidential information elsewhere. The burden of proof, which lies with the injured party, is difficult and there may be recourse at law anyway, whether or not there is an individual confidentiality undertaking. Suffice it to say that the protection of confidential information is easy to discuss, but much less easy to achieve once inter-company co-operation has been decided. As William Congreve said, 'I know that's a secret, for it's whispered everywhere'!

Suppliers and subcontractors

There are no common or legal definitions to distinguish suppliers and subcontractors. As ever, labels do not really matter. It is the substance of the transaction that counts. However, it is convenient to think of suppliers as those who provide standard items at catalogue prices according to standard terms of contract and subcontractors as those who provide customized work at negotiated prices according to contract terms which are negotiated and that may be reflective of the end customer's contract. Terminologically a supplier receives a 'purchase order' and a subcontractor receives a 'subcontract', but these too can be misleading labels. Suppliers' items might be partly customized, the prices might be negotiated to some extent (for example, best customer or volume discounts) and the standard terms might be the seller's or the buyer's dependent upon a number of things (for example, custom and practice and relative bargaining positions). Furthermore, a purchase order can be of much greater value (for example, high quantity of high cost items) than a subcontract (for example, providing one small area of specialism) but be less important because the items are readily available elsewhere. Conversely a small value purchase order for an item on a project critical path can assume much greater importance than a major subcontract, the activities of which have some 'float' in the project plan.

Purchasing, procurement, buying and outsourcing

These four expressions mean different things to different people, but there are no standard definitions. Sometimes 'purchasing' means the buying of fairly minor items such as stationery. Sometimes 'procurement' means buying on a major scale. Sometimes 'buying' means buying raw materials and parts. Sometimes 'outsourcing' means the acquisition of services conventionally undertaken in-house. These words and the meanings given are often interchanged. For the purposes of this chapter the text will standardize on 'procurement'. But regardless of labels, the underlying point is that companies must decide on what they will do themselves and what they will acquire from the outside. These are known as 'make/buy' decisions. It matters little whether the subject matter is raw materials for external orders, internally consumed services or any other commodity.

Procurement – benefits and risks

For a company, a first question is always the extent to which it wishes or needs to procure work, perhaps to reduce cost, improve efficiency, bring in skills, or to compensate for under capacity. Sometimes, procurement is unavoidable. An internal service may be proving too costly or difficult to maintain. A customer may demand the use of sources external to the company in order to achieve industrial participation by preferred sources or in favoured territories.

Make/buy decision process

But where the company has freedom of choice then still the question must be asked, does the company want to take the risk at all? It might be less risky but more costly to undertake all the work of a contract in-house. A cost/benefit analysis must be done before a decision is made. The make/buy decision process can be summarized as follows:

- Initial cost/benefit analysis: establishing the desirability of external sourcing

- Market survey: determining if products or services are available of the right type, quality, quantity and specification

- Outline strategy: deciding the 'shape' of the scheme

- Market testing: determining the interest and responsiveness of the market

- Cost/benefit decision: taking the plunge in principle

- Final strategy: deciding the details

- Implementation: taking the plunge

- Review: checking that predicted benefits are being realized and refining the scheme as necessary.

Procurement strategy

Commercially, there are three main questions in formulating a procurement strategy. These are:

1. the method of selecting a supplier

2. the method of pricing and

3. the contract strategy.

Examples of options are shown below.

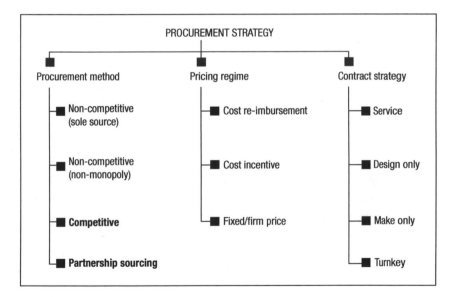

Formulating a procurement strategy

Procurement method

For these purposes non-competitive (sole source or non-monopoly) and competitive selection are assumed to lead to an arm's length relationship. An arm's length relationship means that the parties' interests are narrowly limited to their contract. Provided the seller supplies and the buyer pays, that is all there is to it. If things go wrong, the parties' main interest will be in using the contract to sort things out. Partnership sourcing may be competitive or non-competitive, but it leads to a closer working relationship between buyer and seller, although it is nevertheless a situation in which the buyer is the dominant party.

Pricing regime

The alternative approaches to pricing are as defined in Chapter 3.

Contract strategy

Contract strategy allows several choices. 'Service only' means, for example, acquiring the services of a designer whose liability is limited to the quality of the service and not to the performance of the end result. 'Design only' means, for example, that the supplier is liable for the quality of the design – that is, if the design does not meet the specification he will change the design at his own cost, although he will normally try to avoid any liability for the consequences of a poor design (for example, rework of production items). 'Make only' means that the supplier is liable for the quality of the produced product – that is, if there are manufacturing defects he will correct the defects at his own cost, although he will try to avoid any liability for design defects, particularly if the design is not his own. 'Turnkey' means a contract in which the supplier has responsibility for design and production (or construction) and possibly also installation and commissioning, in which the buyer takes no risk or responsibility until the final stage (whatever that may be) is complete.

Buyer control against risk

Taking these three principles in turn it is possible to visualize where the balance of advantage lies in the connection between buyer control of the supplier and the level of risk that the buyer delegates to the supplier.

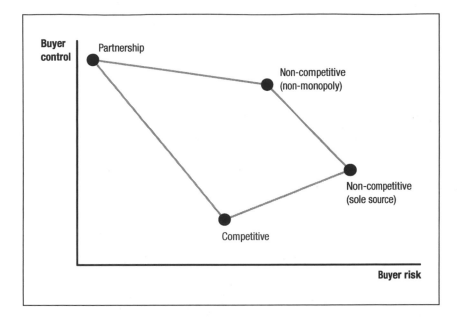

Procurement method – buyer control against risk

This illustrates the wisdom of partnership sourcing against competitive arm's length buying. In partnership sourcing the buyer has greater control through communication, openness and cooperation which are the principles of that philosophy. In competitive arm's length procurement control is much more limited as the nature of the transaction militates against it. This is particularly so as in the former, companies have a small number of partnership sources where in the latter a large number of suppliers may be the norm. In partnership sourcing there is time to talk to and influence the supplier, in competitive arm's length there is not. However, partnership sourcing does not mean that the buyer has reduced his supplier risk to zero. Apart from the fact that things can and do go wrong no matter what the nature of the transaction, partnership sourcing in itself is not a perfect answer. Partnerships in supply, just as in all other partnerships, can suffer from complacency and over familiarity. The aim must to be to ensure that the commercial objectives of the two sides to the bargain are as much in harmony as possible and partnership sourcing is certainly an improvement over the tough but simple alternative of arm's length contracting where the respective objectives can easily come into conflict. Sound partnership sourcing however retains a competitive element either as a 'threat' that the work could go elsewhere when the order is due to be renewed or by maintaining two or more partnership sources for the same products.

The generally much less desirable alternative to both partnership sourcing and arm's length competitive procurement is the selection of a non-competitive supplier. The term 'non-competitive' in this sense is used to mean selected without competition. Non-competitive sourcing is used where there is only a single source of supply, or urgency precludes the time taken by competitive selection or where constructing the basis for a competition is too difficult or impracticable. Whatever the reason, the end result for the buyer is the same. Less control and more risk as the supplier, who essentially enjoys a captive customer, is not motivated to heed the wishes of the buyer or to perform in such a way as to minimize buyer risk. After all if things do not work out quite right, the buyer has little alternative but to stick with the supplier until things come good. This is perhaps too black-and-white a picture. The advantage of a non-competitive supplier is that he may feel much more motivated to provide a long-term commitment to support the buyer's needs and it is in his interests to grow his business with this particular captive buyer which, in the final analysis, is still best achieved by delivering quality products on time at good prices and responding to the buyer's needs.

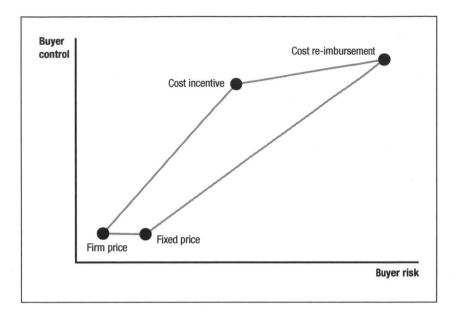

Pricing regime – buyer control against risk

This illustration shows that the choice of pricing regime also has no perfect solution. The buyer must make the choice as to which pricing regime best suits the particular circumstances. A firm price often most suits the buyer as it offers him maximum protection against cost increases no matter what the cause, whether the cause is simply the effect of inflation or whether the cause is poor estimating by the supplier in the first place. On the other hand if the work is so incapable of proper estimation it could be as well for the buyer to swallow the bitter pill of a cost re-imbursement arrangement (subject perhaps to a maximum price) with his supplier than to face an endless stream of claims for price increases resulting from changes in the requirement.

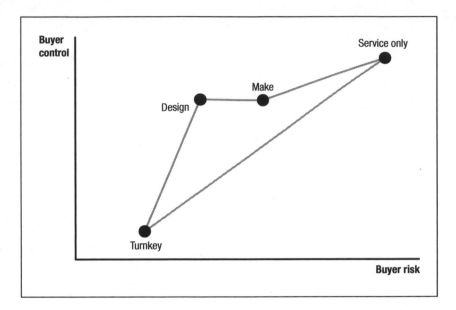

Contract strategy – buyer control against risk

Similarly, with contract strategy the buyer must make his choice as to the degree of control he seeks to exercise over the supplier and the risk he is prepared to take. It may be that the buyer considers that, overall, risk to his project is minimized by retaining maximum control of suppliers by procuring only a service, or by letting segments of the work at a time (for example, feasibility, project definition, design, make). However, in doing so he has in the contractual sense retained also a degree of risk of failure. It is his decision to use or not to use the advice of a consultant (acquired under a service order). It is his decision that the design is mature enough to proceed to the make phase. The turnkey approach, in which the supplier is responsible for everything, has the effect, in that contractual sense, of passing risk to the supplier. So the choice must be made between maximum control, which equals retaining the contractual risk, and minimum control, which equals delegating the risk.

These diagrams are not definitive. It is possible to mount arguments that would significantly alter the shape of the illustrations. But the central point is unassailable. If the make/buy decision is to buy, then the connection between buyer control and buyer risk depends upon the procurement strategy. A decision to buy usually ends one set of problems but reveals a new set. The selection of the right strategy to achieve the best balance of control and risk is essential to overall commercial success.

So, does the buyer want to take the risk at all? The advantages of procurement not only provide the opportunity to share or delegate risk but also there is the chance to gain additional skills and experience in working with outsiders in areas for which the buyer has little knowledge. Additionally, the buyer and supplier in partnership may well be qualified in terms of resources, capacity and skills base to bid for work for which neither by itself would be qualified or otherwise likely to be in a strong position. On the down-side, procurement means working with a supplier who may be geographically remote, who may have different priorities from those of the buyer and who is not susceptible to local management action by the buyer (in the same way that the buyer's internal activities are subject to control) in the event of problems. All of these things do cause the buyer a burden of management (of suppliers), which can be costly and on any serious scale at all requires a dedicated, expert resource. Putting work out can mean providing jobs for suppliers at the expense of the buyer's own personnel. Finally, no matter how good the contract provisions, a supplier can suffer a catastrophic failure causing serious problems for the buyer.

Prime contractors and subcontractors

A traditional form of commercial relationship is one in which the customer hands over (under contract) complete responsibility for a project to a prime contractor who, in turn, delegates (under contract) significant responsibilities to subcontractors. Each subcontractor may have his own subcontractors and suppliers. In this structure the supply chain may be quite deep. Prime contractors are used for large-scale, particularly turnkey, projects.

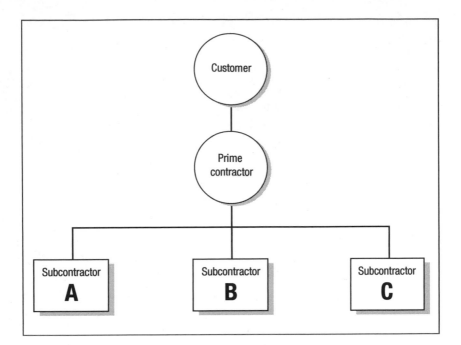

Prime contractors and subcontractors

The customer may know what he wants and may have the money but he may not possess the necessary resources, technical skills or management skills to undertake the entire procurement by himself. In placing one 'prime' contract he avoids the cost and effort of co-ordinating several contracts with many companies. On the other hand, he has put all his eggs into the one basket and takes the risk, notwithstanding any legal or contractual remedies available to him, that his chosen prime contractor is capable of taking on the responsibility of the full task. Typically the responsibilities that a prime contractor may assume are: overall design; placing and administering of subcontracts; 'delivery'; programme planning and co-ordination; financial management.

Design responsibilities

For the customer the principle question is to what extent it is desirable or necessary for him to be involved in the design process when the major responsibility has devolved to the chosen prime contractor. On the one hand, provided the overall aim is well defined, the method of arriving at the overall aim may not matter. On the other hand, the customer may wish to remain involved as an added safeguard in ensuring the technical integrity of the design and to ensure that, whilst the prime contractor is producing the lowest-cost design, it is not at the expense of other features such as ease of maintenance. If the customer wishes, for whatever reason, to remain involved it is necessary to consider the nature of the involvement. This may range from retaining the option to attend design-review meetings to requiring to review and approve all technical and other specifications of whatever level as and when they emerge. In this latter event the prime contractor will seek a contractual commitment from the customer that he will review and approve such documents within set periods of time. In the event of disagreement over technical issues the customer may wish to reserve to himself the final decision. This may lead the prime contractor to look for contractual protection against decisions of the customer with which he disagrees.

This puts the customer in an awkward position in so far as he cannot disagree in principle with his chosen prime contractor's need for protection against imposed technical direction, but conversely he is the customer and is entitled to get what he wants. Anything more than superficial involvement by the customer tends to pervert the purpose of appointing a prime contractor in the first place. However, if the prime contractor is not 100% certain of his own technical competence – which may quite easily be the case where major subcontractors of specialist technical discipline are involved – then the possibility of the customer retaining detailed involvement and therefore some responsibility can seem quite attractive. The customer will be alert to this dilution of the prime contractor's responsibility and will usually negotiate a contract term to the effect that the prime-contractor's responsibility is not diminished by any act or approval of the customer unless specifically agreed in writing. This is not that unreasonable as, even where the customer reviews specifications, the prime contractor must have greater, more detailed technical knowledge and competence. Without a safeguard the prime contractor could offer for approval a specification, which, with his detailed knowledge, he knows to be deficient and yet he knows that the customer does not have the ability to notice the deficiency. Therefore, the prime contractor should be responsible for the deficiency unless he has specifically drawn it to the customer's attention and received written acceptance of it.

Subcontracting

The customer may specify that certain subcontractors are to be used for particular elements of the work, or the use of subcontractors may be inevitable because of the nature of the work (for example, where the prime contractor does not possess all the necessary skills in-house), or where the size of the job is beyond the limitations of the prime contractor's own resources. Where subcontractors are used the customer saves himself considerable time and effort in passing responsibility for the negotiation, placing and subsequent administration of subcontracts. Commercially, the most significant point here is that the customer is giving the prime contractor contractual responsibility and liability for the elements of work that are to be subcontracted. In return for this the prime contractor is entitled to earn profit on the prices charged to him by the subcontractors. This is distinct from the situation in which the customer pays the prime contractor a management fee to negotiate and administer subcontracts that in practice are placed directly between the customer and the subcontractor. In these circumstances the prime contractor is arguably only acting as an agent and is not a prime contractor at all.

The prime contractor will aim to base the subcontract on three types of provisions. Firstly, the inclusion of contract terms which the customer requires to be included in all subcontracts. For example, an obligation to permit the customer access for inspection purposes. Secondly, the inclusion of contract terms which are not required to be flowed down from the prime contract but which nevertheless it is prudent so to do; for example, cancellation-for-convenience. If this is in the prime contract but not in the subcontract and the customer cancelled the prime contract for convenience the prime contractor would be in breach of contract with his subcontractor if he failed to continue with the subcontract. Thirdly, the inclusion of contract terms that are designed to afford the prime contractor some protection against risks inherent in the prime contract. For example, liquidated damages. If the achievement of a major prime-contract milestone and payment is largely dependent upon the progress made by a subcontractor then it is commercially wise to include liquidated damages against the consequences of being prevented by the subcontractor's default from making achievements under the prime contract.

Thus the drafting and negotiation of subcontracts presumes the existence of a fully negotiated prime contract. Where this is not the case the prime contractor will have to judge what subcontract terms are likely to be necessary in line with the foregoing. In some instances the negotiation of the prime contract and the subcontracts will be concurrent activities. The prime-contractor's aim in negotiation is to be in a minimum-risk situation by leaving as much risk as possible with the customer and by passing risk down to the subcontractors. All parties are intent on minimizing their own risk, and as the man in the middle the prime contractor is possibly best placed to be the more successful in this regard. However, one thought which the prime contractor will have at the back of his mind is that on another day on another job he may find himself as a subcontractor. 'Do as you would be done by' is a good maxim in this respect.

Delivery

In accepting contractual responsibility for the entire end goal the prime contractor really starts to earn his money. In this context 'delivery' means achieving full contractual performance in accordance with the provisions of the prime contract. This could include manufacture, integration, testing, installation, commissioning and handover (which may include a period in which satisfactory operation has to be seen). It is in these stages that the prime contractor (and the customer) really begins to find out if the design and if the subcontracting strategy has been successful. If there are problems the prime contractor's first instinct is to look for sub-system faults, which may be the liability of subcontractors, or for deficiencies in the specification, which may be the customer's liability. Failing these two escape routes he has no choice but to spend his own money until the job is complete according to the prime contract.

Planning and co-ordination

Planning and co-ordinating the efforts of several hundred people or more, spread throughout many companies and possibly located in more than one country, is no mean task. All the companies involved have the same objectives – maximum profit, minimum risk. The prime contractor's job is to manage and control activities to bring about the efficient and timely achievement of the tasks in hand.

Financial management

The type of contract dictates the degree of financial management that is required by the customer and the amount of financial information that is to be visible to him. If the contract is firm price at the outset, resulting from effective competition, then the amount and type of financial information to be passed to the customer is minimal. In such a contract the prime contractor may provide no more than a forecast of invoicing, if indeed this requirement is not already satisfied by the inclusion of a stage-payment scheme with defined dates and invoice amounts. At the other extreme, if the contract is one under which the contractor and his subcontractors will be reimbursed their actual costs, then the financial information to be provided can be substantial and the need for financial management quite explicit. In a firm price contract sound financial management is implicit. The existence of a firm price pressurizes all the contractors to progress quickly at minimum cost. For a cost reimbursement-type contract the prime contractor will be required to provide a highly detailed cost plan identifying estimated costs against contract-line items, major tasks and work packages, all of which must sit within the framework of a cohesive work breakdown structure. Expenditure will be monitored on a quarterly or monthly basis by means of financial reports that must indicate actual spending against forecasts made in the cost plan. The prime contractor will operate the same arrangements between himself and his subcontractors, and the customer may have some visibility of subcontract cost plans and reports. The customer may demand a number of reports and forecasts such as earned value analysis.

The prime contractor's risk

If the customer gives contractual acceptance at each of the delivery waypoints (and possibly also gives acceptance at the completion of design) then the prime contractor's risk is reduced. If no acceptance is given until satisfactory handover then the prime contractor's risk is at maximum.

In subcontracting work – particularly if he is saddled with subcontractors nominated by the customer – the prime contractor is taking a major risk. The direct control and management of the work is removed from him and in the event that a subcontractor fails to perform there is no direct remedial action that he can take. Work is being undertaken geographically distanced from his own site and in any event the subcontractor's priorities are not likely to match his own. The prime contractor's performance under contract is at risk because it depends on the performance of the subcontractor. Furthermore, in some examples the subcontracted element may be bigger in financial and value terms than the prime contractor's own intramural contribution and yet as between himself and the end customer he takes the entire risk in the performance of the whole.

Whilst prime contracting is a valuable commercial relationship, it is nevertheless in its frequent form based on nothing more than arm's length buyer/seller contracting, albeit on a grand scale. This can cause discontent all around. The customer may feel that his prime contractor is arrogant (an easy trap for the prime contractor, because he may be more expert than the customer), the prime contractor may feel that the customer just treats him like 'any old' supplier and that subcontractors are difficult (once subcontracts are placed, there is usually no alternative but for the prime contractor to continue with the subcontractor, effectively ceding significant barraging power to the subcontractor). And subcontractors complain about the high handedness of prime contractors. These observations lead nicely into an exploration of alternative forms of commercial relationships.

Partnerships and partnering

Partnership

A partnership is a 'relationship which subsists between persons carrying on a business in common with a view to profit'. This is a legal definition of a legal term. On the face of it, any relationship between two (or more) businesses where the aim is co-operation in the expectation of profit would fall within this definition. However, partnership law has some particular principles that mean most commercial co-operation does not amount to the formation of a partnership. One important distinction is that a partnership is not a separate legal entity distinct from its partners, whereas a company is a legal entity separate from its shareholders and directors.

One vital result of this distinction is that in a partnership the partners are liable for the losses of the partnership and are entitled to its profits. Company shareholders and directors are not normally so bound or entitled. This is a crucial point. A business operated as a company does not want to interfere with this allocation of duties and benefits. Therefore, most companies do not want to form partnerships in the legal sense of the word. Inter-company co-operation is thus usually constructed under some different arrangement. The phrase 'partnership sourcing' (which is a common enough expression and has been used earlier in the text) is thus misleading, because, normally, no partnership is formed. In this sense 'partnership' is used loosely to mean co-operative.

Partnering

For the avoidance of confusion, this section will generally refer to co-operative working as 'partnering'. The somewhat ugly word 'alliancing' means the same thing, although a distinction is sometimes made on the basis of the treatment of costs and risk, which the text will explore a little further on. There are no legal or other definitions of these and similar words. The participants of partnering are referred to as the 'parties' as in any other commercial relationship or more specifically as 'team mates'.

However, as with many other legal principles, the law does not concern itself with what companies care to label their activities, but only with the substance of their arrangements. If a partnering deal is so structured as to come within the legal meaning of a partnership, then a partnership it is and the relevant law applies, regardless of the intentions or reactions of the participants.

'Partnership sourcing' as described earlier is mostly used where the buyer is dominant and wishes to reduce his supplier base to a smaller number of companies with whom he can work on a co-operative basis. Some businesses have achieved apparently astonishing success, reducing the number of suppliers from thousands to hundreds or tens. The nature of the relationship, albeit based on a conventional contract, is one in which buyer and seller believe that working together to overcome problems (for example, technical, timeframe and economic) is in net terms more beneficial than resorting to the contract and adopting adversarial behaviour.

The seller has the courage to bring problems to the attention of the buyer at the earliest stage, confident that the buyer's reaction will be positive. The buyer may invest in new technology at the seller's premises in order to bring mutual gain. The buyer will let the seller have advance notice of his requirements. Such arrangements are convenient where the buyer has many possible sources of supply, where the products are relatively off-the-shelf and where each supplier's contribution is relatively small (albeit vital in some instances) in comparison to the buyer's operation.

However, on major projects the industrial participants may be of comparable influence (that is, there is no single dominant party), the synergy of their combination may be unique, one or all may be effectively sole sources in their own domains and, possibly, none may want to carry the entire commercial risk. In such situations, partnering becomes an attractive option. The principle of partnering considered in the context of proximity to the end customer can be seen in comparison with arm's length contracting and partnership sourcing in the following diagram.

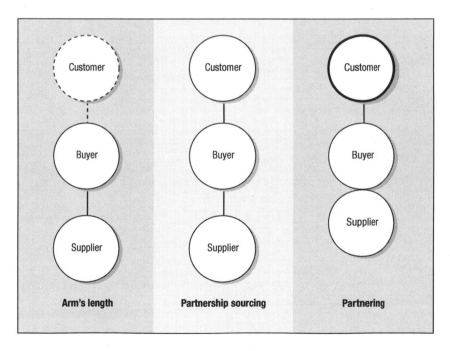

Commercial relationships compared

The progression can be seen as the level of importance of satisfying the end customer. In an arm's length relationship the supplier is little concerned with the end customer. His vision is narrow and limited to completing his order. In partnership sourcing the supplier has a wider vision and understands that his endeavours will help the buyer to perform well but his main focus is still in satisfying the terms of his order from the buyer. In partnering the end customer looms larger and the supplier focus has shifted towards contributing to the performance of the end customer order.

Overt and covert partnering

There are two main ways for the parties to organize themselves in order to achieve a partnering arrangement, as shown in the following diagram.

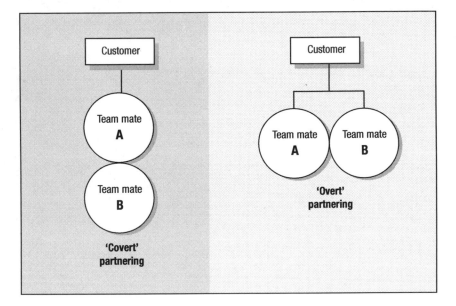

Partnering relationships

The words covert and overt mean nothing more than the degree to which the customer has direct contact with team mate B. In covert partnering the parties would conduct themselves as follows:

- A would negotiate with the customer.

- A would provide B with sight of all or part of the draft contracts and invite comments.

- The contract between A and B may require B to participate in the performance of the contract between A and the customer or of a particular part only (for example, a specification).

In overt partnering the approach is somewhat different:

- A and B would jointly negotiate with the customer.

- A and B would jointly review and comment on the draft contract.

- The performance of the contract would rest with them both.

However, in both cases there must be a contract between A and B and the contract between the customer and A would be accepted and signed by A but with the prior agreement of B. The arrangements between A and B might be such that A is obliged to offer a contract to B (and B is obliged to accept) concurrently with signature of the contract between the customer and company A.

A potential pitfall for the parties in both covert and overt partnering is that a clear definition is still required as to the parts of the work which each will do. Once that is done it tends to drag the relationship back towards a conventional arm's length deal under which a failure by one party could lead to a claim against it by the other party in respect of delay and additional costs. To avoid this the parties may decide in their partnering agreement to agree to waive all such claims against each other. This certainly motivates them to work together as though they were a single company but it is a very big decision for each to make and hence the reference to the degree of mutual trust. The good thing about a conventional contract is that it is fairly straightforward to establish liability and remedy if things go wrong. It is less than easy to legislate for the difficult times when the whole premise is mutual success. Rather like those who seek a divorce settlement agreement as part of the contract of marriage the very act of talking about possible problems can introduce uncertainty in the first place. However, this threat of loss of confidence, like any other risk, is there to be overcome and is not in itself a reason not to proceed.

Consortia and joint venture companies

The overt and covert partnering arrangements might more simply be referred to as consortium arrangements. A consortium is a partnering arrangement that governs the manner of co-operation but does not interfere with the normal contract hierarchy. An alternative for the team mates is to form a new, joint venture company and create a different contract hierarchy as shown below:

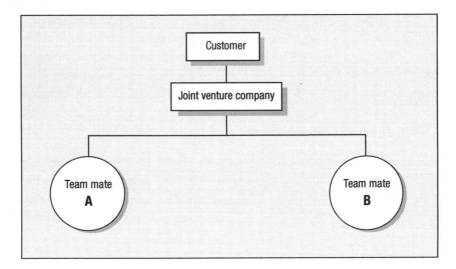

Joint venture relationships

The joint venture company may be provided with sufficient resources that it is able to undertake all its operations independently from the parents. Alternatively it may undertake a more limited range of activities and procure the rest by placing subcontracts with its parent companies as shown in the diagram. The joint venture company may also place subcontracts with suppliers other than its parents.

A joint venture company represents a much more strategic and permanent arrangement between the team mates. It implies a very high level of co-operation and sharing of information, facilities and resources. It demands that each team mate will (within defined limits) let go of the reigns and let the joint venture company develop its own identity and culture. It should benefit from the strengths (marketing, reputation, finances, skills) of its parents but have the freedom (within limits) to operate outside of the corporate mechanisms of the parents. This is easier said than done. Although the rules are changing, a parent that owns more than 50% of the shares in the joint venture company can consolidate the company's financial results through its own accounts. This can cause the majority shareholder to treat the company as a subsidiary, which has the danger that the company cannot operate with appropriate degrees of freedom and may cause upset with the other team mate. Joint venture companies work best where the venture relates to many products in many markets. For single projects, there may be severe conflict between the team mates (each trying to exert significant influence over the joint venture company's operation) and between the team mates and the management of the joint venture company. This is particularly so where the team mates are normally competitors and where the joint venture company management may wish to have the company compete with the parents. The end customer may have reservations about dealing with a new joint venture company and may demand guarantees from the parents. This is particularly so as one advantage and purpose for the team mates in a joint venture company, as opposed to a consortium, is that the company will be set up on a limited liability basis, thus insulating the parents from the possible losses of the company.

Preliminary agreements

Heads of agreement

Once the potential parties have held exploratory discussions and decided in principle that they wish to work together, then an initial statement of intentions is committed to writing. This may be labelled in whatever manner the parties choose, but 'heads of agreement' is the most common term. It is intended as a management level statement of the main aims and principles of the proposed co-operation. It is normal practice to restrict the heads of agreement to a single side of paper. This forces the parties to crystallize their intentions in simple, but clear fashion. The heads of agreement will cover the main principles only, for example the form of relationship (partnering, prime contractor/subcontractor, joint venture company etc.), who will lead, the purpose of the relationship and an initial division of responsibilities which is usually called 'work share'. Work share may be allocated by percentage, by percentage of value or by domain expertise.

In concluding a heads of agreement, it is accepted that very many things, some potentially very contentious, remain to be agreed. But it is an important first step and the process of moving to the next steps will be a useful test of the strength of the relationship that is intended.

Memorandum of understanding and memorandum of agreement

The next step is to formulate a memorandum of understanding or memorandum of agreement. The former expression may be felt to be less substantial than the latter, but in practice the two expressions are interchangeable. It is the substance of the material that matters. Either form of memorandum is usually concluded after a small elapse of time from the heads of agreement. The aim is to flesh out to some extent the principles already agreed. The character of these memoranda is also in the nature of management statements. It is unusual for heads of agreement or such memoranda to be intended as legally binding obligations. This is for a number of reasons. Firstly, the mode of expression of the principles may be susceptible of little legal interpretation. What the managing directors of the parties may sign as a statement of their understanding may leave the legal mind quite baffled! Secondly, by their very nature many of the principles may amount to no more than vague 'agreements to agree', which cannot be enforced in law. Thirdly, for the parties to intend their agreement to be legally binding, they really have to consider and prescribe the consequences of breach. At these preliminary stages, this is not usually something that the parties wish to consider. Finally, there may be good reasons that inhibit the creation of a legally binding agreement. For example, for a major enterprise, the representatives dealing with the prospect may need higher-level approval (in some cases board level approval may be necessary), which cannot be secured until more of the details of the proposed deal (and in particular a full financial appraisal) have been worked out.

It must also be recognized that at these preliminary stages, either party may decide to pull out completely if, for example, the working out of further details reveals a less sound business case or indeed if the withdrawing party sees a better opportunity with another potential participant. In such situations the remaining party may be able to use the preliminary agreement (and the behaviour of the withdrawing party) as the basis for a legal claim for financial damages from the withdrawing party. For this reason, even a preliminary agreement may need to expressly state that the agreement is not only not intended to be legally binding, but also that each party forgoes any claim against the other if the other elects not to proceed.

Full agreement

Partnering, alliancing, teaming, consorting, joint venturing

There is no legal necessity for the preliminary agreements, but they are useful stepping-stones where time permits. Each preliminary agreement may include a target date by which the next agreement should be put into place. The final such deadline is the date for concluding the full agreement. Again, it matters little what the parties may label their full agreement for it is the substance that counts. Common expressions are 'partnering agreement', alliance agreement', 'teaming agreement', 'consortium agreement' and 'joint venture agreement'. The full agreement must leave no principles unresolved and the entire content should be expressed in sufficient detail so as to minimize the scope for ambiguity, misunderstanding or differences of interpretation. The main topics of the full agreement are covered below.

Exclusivity

If the full agreement is not to be exclusive it means that each party remains free to work with other companies on the same enterprise. At the bidding stage of a contract this would allow a party to back several horses at the same time; money and resources permitting. Such an arrangement may suit both parties, in which case a non-exclusive agreement is fine. However, it is frequently the case that one party may have severe reservations about non-exclusivity. It may feel that the enterprise is only worth addressing because of the unique combination of its talents and those of its intended team mate. It may feel that the risk to its intellectual property rights is too great. It is one thing to allow release of its special knowledge to a chosen team mate, but quite another matter to risk seepage of that knowledge to other, probably unknown, parties. It may consider that the particular co-operation may lead to wider joint interests and that such would be compromised by non-exclusivity. All such concerns are perfectly legitimate. Exclusivity could be left unwritten and merely taken on trust, but this is unsatisfactory because of the legal position already described. It is much better for the parties to decide if they prefer exclusivity and if so to take legal advice on the legality of the proposed arrangement and also in the drawing up of detailed provisions.

Purpose

There will need to be a clear and unambiguous description of the purpose of the partnering. Frequently team mates are established in the same or closely adjacent industrial domains. It is important that neither side is unclear on the scope of the partnering. This may not be too difficult if the scope is limited to, say, the bidding for and execution of one contract. But if, for example, the scope relates to one project (rather than one contract) then the parties need to be clear on whether they remain as team mates for all phases and contracts for the one project. If this is their decision, then they must consider if the relationship between them should change as the project phases unfold.

Legal and contractual relationship

The full agreement will state that the parties remain independent companies and that no legal partnership or other statutory entity is formed by their co-operation. The provisions of the partnering agreement have to be carefully constructed in order to avoid the agreement being construed as a legal partnership. The exception is where the parties intend to create a joint venture company.

The arrangements will also state whether the parties are to operate as prime contractor and subcontractor or in some other way. It is somewhat of a moot point. Unless the arrangement brings into being a new company (being a separate legal entity distinct from the parties) it is most likely that one of the parties will take the contract from the customer and then be obliged to place certain work with the other party under subcontract. This is the practical solution anyway and permits customers their usual preference of dealing contractually with one legal entity only. However, the partnering arrangements may provide for a switch of roles between the parties for different stages of a multi-contract project. The arrangements may describe the party that is in a contractual relationship with the end customer as the 'lead contractor' and the other party may be the 'principle subcontractor'. This latter expression will distinguish between the party to the partnering arrangements and other subcontractors with whom either of the parties may have to deal. The contract with the end customer may be referred to as the 'head contract'.

Partnering arrangements sometimes state that subcontracts are, as compared with the head contract, to be on 'equivalent terms', 'back-to-back terms' or on terms 'no more onerous than'. This aim for equivalency is an understandable objective of partnering, but the sentiment needs to be carefully considered. It is not as simple as it sounds. The principle subcontractor wishes to ensure that the lead contractor does not seek to impose greater burdens than he is carrying in the head contract. On the other hand, contractual risk increases towards the top of the supply chain. Therefore it is likely that in the normal course of events (that is, in a non-partnering environment) the main contractor has greater risk than a subcontractor. Thus it is important that in partnering the parties understand that a back-to-back approach to subcontracting between the lead contractor and the principle subcontractor means that the principle subcontractor is not only assured of having the good bits of the head contract included in the subcontract, but also that he must carry his fair and equivalent share of risk in the performance of the head contract (normally his risk is in the performance of the subcontract only). This simple proposition of equivalency in the partnering arrangement thus leads to the need for the provisions of the principle subcontract to be especially constructed.

Work share

By the time that the full partnering agreement is being put in place the work share needs to have been worked out in some detail. This part of the negotiation can be fraught with difficulty. If the parties come from complementary, non-overlapping industrial domains then work share allocation may fall out quite naturally. Although, if a natural distribution of work share when seen from a technology viewpoint leads to a significant imbalance from a financial perspective, then the minor party may seek allocation of additional work (from the other party's domain) in order to balance the financial perspective. This seems only fair if the risk in the head contract is to be shared evenly. But from any other viewpoint danger lurks. Allocating work in an unfamiliar domain imports additional risk. Assistance from the domain expert may only be grudgingly given for fear of loss of market position or compromise to intellectual property rights. If the parties are from the same or overlapping domains then allocation of work share is even more difficult as each will want the best bits for himself. In these situations the parties must remember that their decision to partner was based on the belief that co-operation would lead to their common good and that individually their prospects were weaker. Compromise is almost always essential to achieve the common good. It is however much easier to say this than to achieve it.

Early resolution of work share is also important because contract specifications and statements of work will need to be drawn up. It is not uncommon for this work to be going on in parallel with the finalization of the partnering agreement, for example where a bid is being prepared for a customer. Delay in resolving work share may threaten the timeliness or quality of the bid.

Costing, pricing and financing

The parties must decide how to formulate a selling price to the end customer. In the simple case where the parties decide that they will deal with one another on a firm or fixed price basis then three main issues arise. Firstly, they may need to agree costing rates (for example, labour rates) and pricing factors (for example, allowances for overheads, risk and profit). Secondly, they must agree on the extent to which each will reveal to the other details of particular estimates, supplier prices and other raw costs. These two needs will reveal the extent of trust between the parties. Sharing such information is essential if the lowest cost, most robust and accurate figures are to be jointly produced. However such information is usually considered to be of the utmost commercial sensitivity with each party having strong and legitimate concerns about revealing information that may damage its competitive position on other work. Thirdly, the sharing of information on rates and factors may reveal that one party is significantly more expensive in certain types of work than the other. This disparity can add further spice to the debate over work share.

These problems are fairly routine. However, arguing over costs and prices is not really in tune with partnering and nor does a simple firm price contractual arrangement between the parties do very much to establish genuine sharing of risk and opportunity in the enterprise. So, the parties may elect for a different arrangement. They may choose to base the principal subcontracts on a target cost incentive fee (TCIF) scheme (see Chapter 3). Such schemes do genuinely share profit and loss (described as under spend or over spend against the target cost) but the drawback is that they share in, as it were, one direction only – up the supply chain. Savings or overspends at the seller level are shared with the buyer, but savings or overspends by the buyer are not shared with the seller. This is because the standard TCIF scheme is merely a process for fixing the price for the subcontract. Thus to achieve partnering the subcontract TCIF scheme would have to be constructed so as to make an allowance for the outturn position of the head contract. It is quite possible to do this, but there are some constructional difficulties, for example, adjusting the subcontract price as a result of the lead contractor's performance at the head contract level (a matter over which the principle subcontractor has no overall influence – but see subsequent topic on management) could be construed as a penalty and thus not be enforceable.

An alternative approach (sometimes called 'alliancing') is to treat each of the parties as a cost centre in a virtual company. Thus the price to the end customer is formulated together and both parties have the same understanding of the estimated total costs and allowances for risk and profit. They have a prescribed agreement on how total profits (including any unspent risk allowance) or losses may be shared. At the project conclusion, each party is paid (from customer receipts) his actual costs plus or minus his share of profits or losses. The advantage with this is that both sides have a complete and vested interest in the success of the entire enterprise, notwithstanding that there is still a contractual relationship established by the principle subcontract. The objective in this – and this is the huge leap forward in partnering – is that each is concerned with helping fix the other's problems. In a single company, arguments of fault and blame between cost centre managers are at best interesting, but ultimately futile (unless used to bring about process improvements). The company has a problem and it must be fixed. In the virtual company the same principle is true. In conventional contractual arrangements it is always good if the other guy is in trouble as it diverts attention from your own problems and can even be exploited to parochial advantage. In the alliancing deal, if the other guy is in trouble, he is eating into your share of the profit opportunity and thus you are motivated to help, not exploit. This way of thinking can be a huge and difficult leap of faith. Companies where the culture is to cynically exploit the other guy's problems and to lean on the contract for commercial advantage find the prospect daunting. To give the lawyers apoplexy, the parties are essentially saying that they will only ever work for success and that, for example, the normal remedies that the buyer has (in law or in contract) – for example the right to terminate for default or to claim liquidated damages – will consciously be set aside.

An alliancing deal is not easy to strike. There may be cultural problems to solve. Reluctance over sharing costing, pricing and technical information does not easily evaporate. The structure must be carefully considered to ensure that the virtual company is not construed as a partnership or as a real company. The choice of partnering arrangement will depend upon the nature of the enterprise. For a single, large, higher risk project alliancing is a good solution and worth the time and effort. For a co-operative effort aimed at many orders from many customers for fairly straightforward products a more conventional pricing structure is fine.

The partnering agreement must also deal with all the financing costs, which include the effort in setting up the deal, investments and recovery, shared facilities, co-located teams and publicity.

Management

It is possible that the primary purpose of the partnering agreement is to cover exclusivity and work share with the outcome being a conventional prime contractor/subcontractor relationship. However where the purpose is more intimate and, in particular, where the purpose is to achieve common commercial success and genuine sharing of risk, then the parties will want an equal say in the conduct of the enterprise, notwithstanding that contractually the parties will conclude a principle subcontract. The normal approach is to establish a joint committee (usually called the 'steering committee' or 'executive committee' or similar) that acts as a single management team to set policy, give guidance and resolve disputes. For larger projects there may be a (small) hierarchy of committees dealing with different levels of problem.

Duration

There are two main choices for the duration of the partnering agreement. Firstly, the agreement may automatically terminate as soon as its primary goal is achieved (for example, the winning of a contract), then be followed by a normal contractual relationship (for example prime contractor and subcontractor). Alternatively the agreement may subsist for a longer time and thus over arch individual contracts. The latter is appropriate where, for example, the joint management arrangement needs to subsist for the lifetime of the enterprise. In this situation care needs to be taken to ensure that the partnering agreement is not in conflict with any contractual arrangements. The parties may agree at any time to cease the partnering or they may give it an initial fixed period duration, sufficient to see if their goals are likely to be realized.

Termination and other nasties

Although the text has distinguished between the partnering agreement and contractual arrangements (meaning the principle subcontract or standard subcontracts) the fact is that the partnering agreement is also, strictly speaking, a contractual arrangement. At the stage of their full agreement, the parties will want the deal to be legally enforceable and in which event it is necessary to deal with all the usual contractual pleasantries of termination, indemnities, guarantees etc.

Special provisions

If the partnering is to involve the establishment of a new joint venture company then additional provisions are needed to cover: constitution of the company, registered office, shareholdings, appointment of directors, financing and accounting, tax, change of ownership, winding up and the agreement of the company's memorandum of agreement and articles of association.

The preliminary agreements and the full agreement may be preceded by other agreements (for example a confidentiality agreement). They may need other agreements to be drawn up in parallel (for example a licence to cover the use of each other's technology) or they may express an intention for further agreements to be drawn up later (for example a marketing agreement to cover downstream exploitation of the co-operation).

Ancillary agreements

The text so far has taken the partnering to be between just two parties. There is no reason for there not to be several parties. The advantage in several team mates is in the assembly of an ever more capable conglomerate and for each of the parties, the spreading of risk. The main disadvantage is the extra time and effort needed to negotiate all the necessary agreements – the time and effort increases with the square of the number of participants. There are also many practical difficulties. For example, if the joint steering committee has two members from each of six companies in three continents, then the simple job of assembling the committee for meetings becomes a Herculean task. Video conferences can alleviate the problem but on many occasions there is no substitute for face-to-face encounters.

Multi-party agreements

It is our old friends intellectual property rights and the protection of confidential information that can create some of the worst difficulties in a multi-party agreement. Companies A, B and C may be happy to work in the same team, but A may not agree to his information being disclosed to C. B may not want his information disclosed to A or C. And this is just a three-way deal. The management of confidential information in such a situation can be a nightmare. For the company acting as team leader and lead contractor this can create a real blockage to progress. The situation can be exacerbated as more companies are later added to the deal. Each addition requires the subject of confidential information to be reconsidered by each of the parties. Administratively the confidentiality obligations become impossible and legally all protection is lost when the engineers get in amongst each other's information with scant regard for the commercial position. In these multi-party situations the team mates must be very pragmatic. They must remember that there may be some loss of protection of confidential information in return for the benefit of the partnering deal. This means that each must be open minded about the release of information across the team and insist on tight protection only for the most sacred information.

A multi-way partnering deal does not have to be encapsulated in a single partnering agreement to which all team mates are a party. The lead contractor may choose to have separate agreements with each member. This has the advantage that each negotiation is possibly easier having only two parties to satisfy. The disadvantages are that the lead contractor must make sure that all the agreements have the necessary read across of provisions in order to make the whole deal function. Also, individual agreements can cause suspicion within the team, unless each agreement is available for the scrutiny of all – in which event, there seems little point in having separate agreements.

Licences

Intellectual property can be bought and sold. However it is much more common for it to be licensed. The owner of the intellectual property retains the ownership, but grants restricted rights of use to the licensee. Whilst competition law does much to prevent restrictive practices, intellectual property law grants quite specific monopoly rights. Thus licences that exploit intellectual property are often restrictive in nature. It is nevertheless as well for legal advice to be sought in checking the terms of any restrictive licence provisions. A licence may be the only legal relationship between licensor and licensee. An incoming licence can provide a company with access to valuable new technology without the expense or time of developing similar technology in-house. This can provide access to new markets and bring about company growth at relatively little trouble. A company may also make money out of outgoing licences, in which the company licences its own technology to other companies for commercial exploitation in return for fees and royalties. This is a useful strategy where, for example, the company has no further wish to market and sell the product in which the technology resides on its own account. It is also useful where the licensee has access to markets where the licensor has no access. This may be where the licensor has no marketing presence in the relevant territories; where the costs of marketing would be prohibitive; where politics or culture inhibit direct marketing; or where the customer demands local manufacture under licence to an indigenous supplier.

A licence may also be necessary when the parties are entwined through a partnering agreement, a joint venture company or even a routine subcontract. Because licence drafting is a specialized task, it is sometimes better to produce the licence as an ancillary agreement to the main commercial agreement.

Either way, the main issues normally covered in licences are as follows:

Definition of the licensed technology

It is important that the licensed technology is well defined so that licensor and licensee know where they stand. If the definition is vague then the licensor may overstep the intended grant of rights bringing the parties into dispute at some later stage.

Definition of licensed territories

It is usual for a licence to state the geographical territories in which the licence is effective. This may be because the licensor wants to protect territories in which he is successful and open up only those territories in which he has enjoyed little or no access.

Exclusivity and soleness

The licensor may elect to licence as many licensees as he can find. For the licensee this may be undesirable if the effect is to create competitors in his marketplaces. If the licence is to be restricted, then it is usually either 'exclusive' (meaning no-one else including the licensor can exploit the technology in the given territories) or 'sole' (meaning the licensee and the licensor can exploit the technology).

Duration

A licence may have a fixed duration. This would suit the licensor because if under an exclusive licence the licensee fails to make significant sales, leaving the licensor with little revenue, then the licensor may wish to find another licensee. The licensee will normally want a licence 'in perpetuity' allowing him the freedom to exploit the licence when costs allow and the opportunity is right.

Revocability

The licensor will normally want the right to revoke the licence in the event that the licensee fails to achieve sales targets or if a better deal presents itself. The licensee will wish the licence to be irrevocable.

Scope and data

The licence will specify the scope of the licensee's rights in the technology, for example: market, sell, manufacture, modify, repair, and maintain. This will necessitate stating the rights in the licensed intellectual property, for example: the right to copy, modify and use any technical data. This in turn means that the licence must specify the scope and definition of the technical data to be provided by the licensor, for example: drawings, handbooks, specifications and software (object code, source code and documentation).

Sublicences

The licence will state the extent, if any, to which the licensee may grant further sublicences to other parties. This may be to mutual advantage since all exploitation will bring revenues to the original licensor. The licensor may not however wish to allow any sublicensing without his prior agreement – again so that he may retain control over his markets.

Fees and royalties

The licensor may want an upfront fee payment. This is a zero risk reward for the licensor and hence is attractive. However it may be based on predicted sales by the licensee and the actual sales might turn out to be higher, leaving the licensor with a lower (albeit safe) revenue. Alternatively, the licensor's revenue may be based on royalties linked to the sales actually achieved by the licensee. There may be a combination of fees and royalties. A single once-off fee has the advantage of needing no administration. Royalties require the licensee to make returns to the licensor and to allow certain rights of access for verification purposes. This creates an administrative burden and cost for the licensor.

Technical support

The licence may oblige the licensor to provide the licensee with technical support. This may be free of charge for an initial start up period (particularly if there has been an upfront fee) followed by a time and materials based charge for further help.

Grant back

Many licences require the licensee to grant back to the licensor rights in any improvements in the technology achieved by the licensor. This grant back may be free or subject to royalties (or a reduction on the main royalty structure).

Indemnities

The licensee usually requires an indemnity from the licensor to the effect that the licensor will hold the licensee harmless from third party claims of intellectual property infringement by the licensee. This seems entirely fair, as the licensee must take it in good faith that the licensor owns the intellectual property in the first place and is free to grant licences. There is very little chance for the licensee to check this himself (with the possible exception of patents or registered designs – if he has the time and money to do so). The licensor has a different view. He will wish an indemnity from the licensee on the grounds that, notwithstanding the provisions of the licence, the licensor has no actual control over what the licensee does with the technology. The usual answer is to thrash out a counter indemnity provision that deals with both concerns.

Termination

As with most commercial agreements the licence will cover the events that can bring about the demise of the licence. The normal coverage is for a fundamental breach of the licence provisions, allowing the injured party the option to terminate.

It's a 'people thing'!

This chapter has considered competition law, confidentiality, arm's length dealings, purchasing, procurement, buying, outsourcing, prime contracting, subcontracting, partnership sourcing, partnership, partnering, alliancing, teaming, consorting, joint venturing and licensing. All these topics are concerned with the ways in which companies can construct commercial relationships. But the most important feature of any (non-trivial) business relationship is the relationship between the people. If the people relationship is poor then you can have more commercial agreements than you can shake a stick at, but it will make no difference – the result will be failure. The commercial agreements must exist both to record what the deal is about (for example to ease communication with others) and as an 'insurance policy' if things really do go wrong. The prudent householder may take many practical precautions to protect his investment – fire alarms, smoke alarms, burglar alarms, locks and security systems – but he is foolish to believe that the risk is so diminished that there is no need for insurance. But to rely solely on the insurance policy is equally foolhardy. Thus it is with business. The commercial agreements must be in place, but the people relationship will bring success.

Checklist

- Beware of competition law.

- Consider confidentiality at an early stage.

- Base make/buy decisions on a cost/benefit analysis.

- Prime contracting is only arm's length dealing on a grand scale.

- Beware of the difference between a legal partnership and partnership sourcing and partnering.

- Consider both overt and covert partnering arrangements.

- Forming a joint venture company is a special form of partnering.

- A heads of agreement and a memorandum of understanding or memorandum of agreement normally precede partnering.

- The full partnering agreement will take some time to negotiate but is the bedrock of the future relationship.

- Multi-party agreements can be very time consuming to establish.

- Licences are the key commercial tools for exploiting intellectual property rights.

- Personal relationships are the key to success.

Negotiation

Introduction

The *Oxford English Dictionary* defines the word 'negotiate' as 'try to reach agreement or compromise by discussion with others'. The word originates in the 17th century and derives from the Latin word 'negotiat' meaning 'done in the course of business'. So negotiation has a flavour of 'trying', which means that failure must be contemplated as well as success. It talks of 'agreement or compromise'. In modern business negotiations the difference between agreeing and compromising is significant. An agreement implies a settlement where each side has an acceptable deal that may have been based upon bargaining, in which one parameter is traded for another. Compromise means, for example, splitting the difference on a single parameter such as price, the desire being to get to a quick agreement without too much of a fuss. Negotiation also involves discussion, which means oral dialogue – no-one ever negotiated in writing, although written exchanges can be a useful device in the overall negotiation process. And the context is business.

In business there are many things requiring negotiation and any supervisor or manager may typically be involved in discussions on the detail of technical specifications, programmes, manufacturing plans and the like. There are occasions when a variety of staff are needed to support commercial negotiations, and where this is the case this role, and the manner in which it is played, is most important.

Many books and manuals have been written on the art and skills of negotiation. The reader is commended to these invaluable works as they provide instruction in many aspects, such as: venue, timing, positional versus principled argument, role-playing, hard man/soft man, humour, stonewalling, the 'walkout', bluff and aggression. The purpose of this chapter, however, is not to repeat what can be read elsewhere in specialist volumes but to draw out key points which experience shows are fundamental and in which the manager can best make his or her contribution to the overall commercial success.

Who are the negotiators?

Many companies appoint individuals to act as authorized negotiators, but in many instances others undertake negotiations quite consciously, for example the manager or salesman who is agreeing the specification with the customer or supplier. Unauthorized negotiations may take place accidentally because one side assumes that the person on the other side has the ostensible authority of his employer. It may be that the parties understand that no commitment is given until a written contract is fully agreed and signed or that no-one has the authority to vary the contract other than by an agreed, written amendment, but the truth is that actual and anticipated contractual positions are flavoured or compromised by any and all discussions by any staff. The practical conclusion is that everyone is a negotiator!

What is negotiation?

In business, every contact with the external world of customers, suppliers or other agencies is a negotiation. This seems a bit broad, but think of it like this. Every external discussion leaves the company's position unchanged, worse or better. With this simple philosophy in mind, it can be seen that not only is everyone a negotiator, but every discussion is a negotiation. Even business social events are negotiations. The aim of each employee must be to say and do those things that will improve the company's position. The deliberately broad definition of negotiation is intended to serve as a re-enforcement of the importance of the succeeding material.

Prior events

The commercial manager should note that almost invariably negotiations are preceded by events that are recorded or by propositions that are argued in writing. Care should always be taken in what is put in writing, and in other than routine matters, advice should be sought on what to say and how to say it. Unintentionally or unconsciously giving a commitment or yielding a principle that subsequently proves to be vital has caught out many a manager.

It is usually the case that a negotiation is preceded by a chain of events, meetings and correspondence, most of which at the time may seem to be routine. However, since earlier events are bound to feature in the negotiation, everybody having contact with the other side must keep at the front of his mind the potential benefit or potential damage that specific statements, promises and actions may have in the future. In particular, if the other side has said or done something of value then it is important to get it confirmed in writing. If the company side has said or done something of value, write to the other side to confirm it and seek his written acknowledgement.

The value of documentary evidence – formal correspondence, minutes of meetings, e-mails and notes of telephone calls – cannot be overstated.

Events leading up to the negotiation can in themselves have a material impact on success. For example, within a proposal that had been sent to the customer was a particular assumption forming a key part of the offer, albeit described in fairly innocuous terms. The customer picked it up and queried it with the company's engineer. The engineer formed his own view that it was trivial and led the customer to believe that it was of no consequence at all. As a deliberate, well-thought-out tactic, this possibly could have been a legitimate ploy. In the actual circumstances the engineer allowed the customer to believe that the point was not seriously made. When the negotiation meeting commenced the company then had an uphill struggle to convince the customer that it was indeed serious. The moral of this story is to be found in a further general rule describing the engineer's role in a commercial negotiation: The engineer must work in close contact with his commercial negotiator in preparing the ground with the opposition. This truism applies whether or not the engineer is actually to be present at the negotiation.

Using the analogy of the chess game, the negotiation itself may be likened to the 'end game'. Too frequently, negotiation is seen as the start of a process that will conclude with an agreement. This is quite wrong. Negotiation comes at the end of a series of events. It is the end of a process. Extending the analogy to the levels at which chess is played, two variations can be seen: Play can be at the beginners level, in which the two players move their pieces almost at random until by chance an opportunity for checkmate arises and the end-game is only then conceived. In the advanced level, the end game is planned from the outset and each move by the opponent is countered by moves that aim to restore progress towards the end game. In business the equivalent to the 'beginners level' is a situation in which events are following a normal and natural course, a crisis or problem then emerges and a negotiation then takes place to effect resolution. The equivalent to the 'advanced level' is a situation in which it is estimated from the outset that a negotiation will be necessary before agreement is reached, and thus all events over which control can be exercised must be pre-planned to achieve progress towards the desired end. Just as in advanced chess, the side which can then see the greatest number of moves ahead and predict the opposition's counter moves is the more likely to succeed. Where the company is involved in an 'advanced' game the importance of the engineer liasing closely with his commercial department cannot be overstressed.

Purpose and importance

The negotiation might relate to:

- A pre-contract issue

- The process of agreeing a contract or partnering agreement

- A difference of interpretation during contract performance

- A failure by the other party affecting contract performance

- A third-party act affecting contract performance

- An event affecting the contract but not previously contemplated and therefore not legislated for within the contract

- A dispute over completion or acceptance of the work

- A post-contract claim.

Whatever the issue, buyer and seller potentially have at stake profit, cash flow, growth, reputation, nugatory work, diversion of effort, and delay.

Thus, and not surprisingly, the two parties each may have as much to lose or win as the other. Bluntly put, one side's profit is the other's loss – although this is an over-simplistic view of what transpires in negotiation. Nevertheless the point is well made that each party is faced in the extreme with success or disaster. That is to say, when all the normal processes by which progress is achieved and agreements made have been exhausted, the parties must meet face-to-face to negotiate. Letters, routine meetings, minutes, and phone calls have all failed and it is down to the negotiators to thrash out a deal. Indeed, it is a well-established rule of thumb and good practice to follow that, if a single round of correspondence has failed to resolve a problem once it has become an issue, then a negotiation should be the next step. Further rounds of formal correspondence are likely to cause only entrenchment of the respective positions and thus inhibit a satisfactory agreement as both sides feel bound not to yield principles that the written correspondence record as being immutable.

Serious matters

Whilst care must be taken, these comments are not intended to caution the commercial manager not to put things in writing to the other party. Indeed, in any commercial negotiation – and in extreme in front of a court of law – the volume and accuracy of documentary material is important and may be crucial. In general, factual information is most important (dates of meetings, events, records of phone calls) but opinion and speculation should be avoided. In particular, the following should not be discussed without considered prior thought:

- Costs and prices

- Cash flow and payment arrangements

- Programme schedule and delivery dates

- Liability for delay, mistakes and accidents

- Liability for poor technical performance

- Ownership of intellectual property.

For each of these bullet points, one example of simple but fundamental errors can be given.

Unauthorized information

A manager, supervisor or member of a sales team may be asked informally by a customer representative for an informal budgetary estimate. The individual does a quick calculation (using labour rates guessed or discovered without checking their applicability) and gives his contact the information requested. When the formal request for quotation arrives the figures are then properly formulated and turn out to be much higher, perhaps due to the use of correct rates, the addition of factors (overheads, financing charges, contingency and profit) that had escaped the individual's thoughts. By this time the damage is done. The customer may only have budgeted for the amount informally advised, thus jeopardizing the order. The customer will be suspicious of the seller's 'rip-off' prices and the supplier's reputation will also be sullied. For this reason, many companies rightly have an absolutely rigid, unequivocal rule that cost and price information is never to be given by any route other than a formal route that ensures thorough review and company approval.

Devaluing a done deal

'Yes, we can give you a down payment' a buyer tells a supplier. At best this will prejudice future negotiations. At worst it may give the supplier a free 'extra'. If the price had already been negotiated on the basis of payment on completion (meaning the price includes an allowance for financing costs) then the award of an advance payment simply improves the seller's profit with no gain for the buyer.

Exposure to penalties

As with the informal request for price information, so too with the informal request for timeframe information. A salesman wants to delight the customer and gives his estimate of best timescale. This ignores the proper planning process, the dependency on the order intake date, the availability of resources and the scheduling with other work. Unaware that legal 'penalties' flow from late delivery the salesman gives a date that if translated into a commitment then exposes unnecessarily the threat of those penalties or if the company is unable to confirm the date indicated then, again, reputation suffers.

Admissions of liability

'Yes, it's our fault that we're late' is another killer blow to commercial negotiations. In the previous chapter an analogy was made between a contract and an insurance policy. Car insurers always insist that motorists make no admission of liability – the matter being for the insurer to decide. The analogy holds good here. The cause of the delay may be from within the company, but contractually there may be no liability. The contract may provide *force majeure* relief for the seller, the contract may exclude timeliness from the essence of the contract and any delay may be attributable to the acts or omissions of the buyer. Until these matters are reviewed, no statement on blame or liability should be given. This is not untoward business practice, but merely ensuring that the company's risk is always kept to a minimum.

Accidental additions of liability

'We agree the product is not fit for purpose and we'll put it right' says the supplier. The expression 'fit for purpose' is legal dynamite and should not be bandied about. Such loose talk may import a Sale of Goods liability where none had previously existed because of an express exclusion in the contract. Even if used in a non-legal sense the supplier may be creating a liability additional to the contract provisions. If the contract is constructed such that the seller's duty is limited to meeting a specification prescribed by the buyer then the seller's duty may be discharged provided the specification is met, whether or not the product 'works'. Again, this is not sharp practice. The price for the job and the decision to take the job on will have been based upon the seller's understanding of the risk and associated liabilities. It is not for the engineer to interfere in this balance after the event. The seller rightly wants the customer to be delighted and so does the company. But the negotiation for additional work must start from the position established under the contract and not from any other perspective.

Throwing away valuable assets

'You (the customer) are paying so of course the design is yours, how many copies of the drawings would you like'. By now it should be clear that ownership of intellectual property and the entitlement to rights does not necessarily follow a simple 'who pays owns' principle. The buyer may be delighted to be given more than his entitlement, but such cavalier disregard for such an essential subject damages the seller's property and harms his future prospects.

Preparation

Almost all successful negotiations are based upon thorough preparation. Too often the date for the negotiation is fixed as the first available date in people's diaries. If it is the first available date then impliedly the days leading up to the agreed date are already planned to be occupied by other non-related events. In those circumstances preparation for the negotiation has to be squeezed in amongst many other things. Similarly, if the preparatory meeting is left to the last minute then it may be too late to gather information or consult other people where these needs are only identified in the pre-meeting discussions.

Rule: Allow sufficient time

It is the responsibility of the intended leader of the negotiation to arrange the pre-meeting. It is the responsibility of the commercial manager to make the time available to support and attend the pre-meeting. The pre-meeting must be seen by all participants as absolutely crucial. It is the meeting at which the plan for the negotiation will be thrashed out and it is madness for participants to the negotiations not to meet beforehand. It is wrong to think that the participants have all the necessary information in their heads, that they can simply meet on the day and that a successful negotiation will ensue.

Rule: The preparatory meeting is crucial

The primary objective of the pre-meeting is to establish the negotiation plan. However, equally vital is the gathering and assimilation of information. It is in this area that the commercial manager can make his greatest contribution to the preparation stage. The lead negotiator must have to hand all related information so that he can analyze what is useful to him, what is useful to the other side and what can be discarded. Notice that for this purpose he needs *related* information rather than just *relevant* information. That is to say, irrelevant information may have its place in the negotiation by way of red herrings, diversionary tactics, and time-wasting tangents. Although it sounds senseless, the hardest part of the process is in thinking what is related to the issue in question. At the pre-meeting the lead negotiator will already have a number of questions for the other participants to answer or investigate and report upon. However, the commercial manager may have been involved with the other side for a considerable period of time and have been involved in many meetings, reports, discussions, presentations, and demonstrations. Amongst the enormous mass of information that this represents the individual must recollect and volunteer almost everything that comes to mind. He should never conceal anything that he or the company has said or done or anything that the other side has said or done which weakens his own side's position. If weaknesses are identified the negotiation plan can accommodate counter-measures to be deployed if and when the other side attacks the weaknesses. The pre-meeting is also the opportune time to identify the people and personalities on the opposition team.

Rule: Identify both sides' objectives

It is essential that before any negotiation takes place there is a full analysis of both sides' objectives. A simple list of things to be sorted out is not sufficient. For one thing, each side may have a different list. Listing objectives is not the same as agreeing an agenda for the negotiation as both sides may well leave critical issues off the formal agenda, as a tactical ploy. Thus, identifying all potential issues is a key part of the analysis. The analysis must identify both sides desired 'gains' and both sides 'yields'. There must be an overall appreciation of how these four lists can be balanced.

The negotiation plan

Montgomery said, 'planning is everything but nothing ever goes according to plan'. This wonderful statement encapsulates the principle that no matter how thorough the preparation, how good the rehearsal, how comprehensive the plan, there will inevitably be unexpected and unpredictable events, questions, issues and difficulties to deal with. Nevertheless, the existence of a plan with its goals and objectives gives a stable framework from which to diverge and a framework for reconvergence once the unexpected has been dealt with.

Rule: There must be a plan

A negotiation without a plan is like erecting a skyscraper without any drawings. You can assemble a random set of materials, throw some foundations down, put up a few walls and take it from there – making it up as you go along. This might work. More likely, the whole edifice will tumble down before the task is complete. Some people have a natural talent for negotiation and can wheel-and-deal without much preparation or any plan. In serious business matters, structure and process is crucial as a framework within which the flair of the natural negotiator may operate. But a plan there must be. If the negotiation is straightforward or if undertaken by a lone individual then an unwritten plan may suffice. For complex or team negotiations a written plan is essential. The plan can deal with matters such as location, timing, tactics and role-playing but it should also include a categorization of both sides' objectives.

Rule: Categorize company objectives

Objectives may be categorized using a table of the following type:

	OPPOSITION'S POSITION		
COMPANY OBJECTIVES	Impossible	Difficult	Easy
Must have			
Nice to have			
Bonuses			

Company objectives

Rule: Categorize opposition's objectives

The opposition's objectives may be categorized likewise:

COMPANY OBJECTIVES	COMPANY'S POSITION		
	Impossible	Difficult	Easy
Must have			
Nice to have			
Bonuses			

The opposition's objectives

If there are objectives in the 'must have' but 'impossible to attain' segment then the purpose of the negotiation must be re-examined and if necessary redefined. Possibly the purpose devolves, on the other hand, to simply maintaining (or opening) dialogue, or, on the other, to commencing a series of negotiations.

Rule: Be realistic

It is the task of the commercial manager to ensure that technical objectives are viable and to help the lead negotiator understand the true position. For example, if the commercial manager tells the lead negotiator that the opposition's delivery time must be halved and yet it is known that component lead times make this impossible, then trouble is being needlessly invited, particularly if the company's side is made to look foolish for apparently not knowing a common fact. Similarly, if an objective of the other side is that the power output of your product must be increased by 15% then do not let the lead negotiator believe he can agree 10% when the product is already operating beyond its performance envelope.

Rule: Thoroughly brief the lead negotiator

On this question of advice to the lead negotiator, it is the responsibility of the commercial manager, and indeed any other individuals involved in the preparation of, or involved in, the negotiation, to brief the lead negotiator thoroughly and honestly. For example, in connection with cost or time estimates the commercial manager should not keep a 'bit of contingency' to himself. The lead negotiator must know the complete and real picture if he is to successfully prosecute the deal. In this example, if everyone quietly adds a bit of contingency for himself then the figures and the objective can become quite ludicrous.

Rule: Structure the negotiation

The plan must have an intended structure for the negotiation. If the discussions proceed to your plan then the chances of success are improved. The structure should include the following topics:

- Opening position
- Order of play
- Manner of tabling issues
- Timing of offers/counter offers
- Information to be tabled.

The plan should also cover the timing and mechanics for breaking for lunch, time-outs, and other pauses in the progress. These are not minor issues. Many a deadlock has been broken by a timely break for lunch or for separate reflection by each of the parties.

Rule: Allocate specific functions to each member of the negotiation team

Most importantly, the negotiating team must have clearly defined roles and contributions to make. Each member must be fully briefed on his own specialist subject and on the generality of the negotiation plan.

Follow the leader

Experience shows that in the vast majority of negotiations the actual process of negotiation occurs between just two people – one on each side – regardless of the respective team sizes. This is hardly surprising since the negotiation may be likened to a game of chess. It would be ludicrous to think of a chess game being played equally well by a team as by a single person. The single person controls the tactics within an overall strategy, sacrifices pieces or positions and captures pieces or territory as part of an overall game plan. The golden rule must be that the negotiation is the responsibility of the leader and all other participants are there to support him.

Rule: Listen well and be sensitive

To effectively support the leader commercial staff must develop listening skills so that they are sensitive to the line being pursued by the leader, to its probable purpose and such that they are alert and prepared to lend supporting argument if invited to do so by the leader.

Rule: Stick to the plan

One of the worst things that can happen to the leader is for one of his team accidentally or, even worse, intentionally, in the heat of the moment, to usurp the leader's role. If the problem is bad then the seriousness is increased tenfold if the usurper or indeed a supporter deviates from the agreed negotiation plan. At best this will cause confusion and at worst is a recipe for disaster.

Rule: Recognize when the leader is deviating from the plan

However, as Montgomery said, nothing ever goes according to plan. The leader must orchestrate diversions from the plan and the team, if they have been listening well and have been sensitive to the general trend in the negotiation, will see how and to what extent the plan is being abandoned. The leader will be conscious of the need to let the team know his thinking and will find a way of bringing everyone up to speed, even if it means calling a time-out.

Rule: Do not throw in new information

A further action to be avoided is the tabling openly at the negotiation of 'new' information. It is not unnatural as the discussion proceeds for an individual to recall additional data, to see a new slant on certain things or indeed to have been given further information after the pre-meeting but before the negotiation. Whatever the reason, the worst thing he can do is to table it, leaving the leader with the awful prospect of trying to recover a self-inflicted wound to the foot. If there is new information to consider it should be communicated to the leader. Again, it is preferable to have a time-out rather than potentially destroy the painstakingly achieved progress through ill-timed presentation of extra information.

Rule: Do not drop the team in it

Regardless of the leader/supporter functionality, the team is nevertheless there as a team representing the company. The opposition should see it as being united and of a common view. It destroys the credibility of the entire enterprise if the team appears to be divided, or not equally briefed or, in the very worst extreme, antagonistic to one another. For example, if an individual should say to the leader 'actually I disagree with you there' then the negotiation will almost certainly plummet. It is an unforgivable mistake, which the opposition should ruthlessly exploit. There may very well be disagreement but it should not be made public, and if the engineer believes the leader has got it seriously wrong he must find a discreet (but rapid) means of letting the leader know.

Questions and information

In many cases the commercial negotiator shows a certain reluctance to take along an expert in support of the negotiation. This reluctance flows from a great fear that the expert will hinder, not help, through his not unnatural wish to answer questions. If there are technical issues to resolve then the presence of the expert may be unavoidable. From the point of view of the lead negotiator there is a great danger that the expert will then rush off in his eagerness to display his deep understanding and knowledge of the subject to answer all the wrong questions from the other side. All of us have the basic intellectual desire to demonstrate that we can answer the question. In a negotiation the other side will be seeking to put questions on areas in which they perceive your position to be weak. To answer such questions fully and frankly is to pull the proverbial rug from beneath one's feet. Far better, within reason, to feign ignorance, promise to check later or find some other way to avoid giving a direct answer.

Rule: Avoid answering awkward questions

It is good defensive thinking to believe that the opposition only asks those questions that are intended to expose a weak position on the company side or that will otherwise give the opposition an advantage. In negotiation, no one asks questions that are deliberately designed to allow the other side to improve its position. It is somewhat hard-nosed to believe that all questions are running torpedoes that the opposition hope will strike home, but it is helpful to bear the danger in mind. Always engage brain before mouth! Negotiators should not be shy of using all the techniques in the politician's tool kit. In response to awkward questions, reply with another question, change the subject, and attack the opposition. If this does not work, wander off and stare out of the window, go for a pee, spill coffee, anything but walk into a trap.

Rule: Be economical in answering questions

Another facet in answering questions – where it is in the company's interest so to do – is to be economical with the response. From a legal viewpoint there are significant risks in lying your way out, as you and the company may be guilty of fraud, attempted fraud, or misrepresentation. Lying is not acceptable and in any event is not necessary. Economy with the truth is not free of these risks but the general objective must be to answer questions with the minimum of information. As ever, it is a question of putting the company's position in the best possible way. A short and succinct answer can be much better than comprehensiveness if there is potential weakness in the argument. It is for the other side to probe and not to be put off. It is not the company's job to help. Flexibility is the watchword though. There are occasions when the best response is to provide an overwhelming response in which it is difficult for the other side to see the wood from the trees. These 'games' are all grist to the mill and both sides play.

Rule: Do not stray into areas in which you are not the expert

Even worse than answering awkward questions is answering questions in areas where you have no expert knowledge. Although the aim of this book is to broaden your knowledge into wider commercial fields you should still, by and large, leave the answering of the commercial questions to the lead negotiator. The leader has enough problems with which to deal with without having to keep his own side under control and without having to interrupt his own people to prevent them going off on the wrong subject.

Rule: Do not volunteer information

There is good information and bad information when it comes to the actual negotiation. Beforehand, all information is good, even if in itself it is bad news, but once at the meeting one of the worst statements the engineer can make is one that begins with the words 'I don't know if this helps or not'. Almost certainly, if he does not know, the chances are that whatever he is going to say will help the other side. In any event he is giving his own side no more time than the opposition to consider the information and its implications.

Rule: Do not lose sight of the objective(s)

One of the golden rules in any negotiation is not to lose sight of the objectives. It can be all too easy to get carried away and perhaps submerged in vast volumes of information, intellectual debates and arguments, but the objective must be kept in sight and it should be pursued relentlessly.

Rule: Do not argue the other side's case

Finally, it should not be forgotten that the other side will have good points, and in the extreme the opposition may actually be in the right and you in the wrong. This is no reason, though, to go agreeing with him. Similarly, you must resist the temptation to support the opposition's case, which at worst can have you actually appearing to change sides.

Rough and tumble

A sportsman/sportswoman may spend years preparing for a major event such as the Olympics. Training will have been hard and the preparation exhaustive. The competitor must look forward to a tough cauldron, but once there he must not only give of his best but must also remember to enjoy the actual moment. So too are the characteristics of negotiation.

Rule: Do not forget it's tough

A feature of the negotiation that often comes as something of a surprise is the apparent attitude of the opposition and the atmosphere in which the negotiation is conducted. Whatever the subject of the negotiation, it is likely to have cropped up as an issue following a considerable period of friendly relations. For example, where a contract has been running smoothly for some time, the relationship between the parties will have been amicable. Routine progress meetings and reviews will have passed off with the two sides congratulating themselves on their close co-operation and the friendly manner in which the business is conducted. Suddenly there is an issue to resolve which normal activities and correspondence have failed to settle. A negotiation is necessary and the other side appears in a far more aggressive, difficult and formal manner than previously. This is not really surprising and indeed one's own side will be in a similar mode. It should therefore be seen as a normal part of negotiation and, whilst excessive aggression or rigidity is rarely a recipe for success, it should not be found off-putting.

Rule: Don't forget to have fun

Even though the negotiation should be expected to be tough it is a very stimulating and potentially rewarding activity. By and large the best negotiators are those who not only have the technical and personal skills to carry it off successfully but also enjoy it for its own sake. Similarly, you should see your participation in the same light and hopefully expect not only to make your contribution but also to take some degree of personal satisfaction from it.

Win/win

The final fundamental is the concept of the good deal. That is a deal, which both sides find satisfactory. Both wish to 'win'. It is unusual to be negotiating with another party where there has been no previous business, nor any likelihood of further transactions in the future. Thus, if an overall balance of good relations is to be maintained, both sides must leave the table content, more or less, with their half of the bargain. The negotiation must not be seen as a pitched battle from which there must emerge a clear victor and a clear loser. It is the job of the lead negotiator as the negotiation draws to a conclusion to decide if overall, he is being offered an acceptable deal. Amongst many other things, in making his decision he will take into account the consequences of not making an agreement on the day. The consequences may include delayed payment, late delivery, lost profit, and indeed he must also consider the chances of improving upon the offer if he decides to wait for a further negotiation at some later date. You should be aware that these deliberations are running through the mind of the leader and he should support the decision whatever it may be. These considerations apply equally to both sides.

That 'people thing'

No matter how much preparation, planning and analysis is done, no matter how many techniques have been learned, no matter how skilled the negotiators, the one most important ingredient in negotiation is the relationship not only between team members but also between the representatives of the two sides. Personal contact and bonding are everything. The most impossible situation is one in which the negotiator must make a telephone call (because of urgency) to someone they have never met or spoken with in an effort to broker some deal. It is much better for negotiations not to take place until there has been time for the build up of a personal relationship. Trust in the other person is essential. Understanding of the other side's position is essential. These two maxims seem incompatible with the rules of negotiation stated earlier. In respect of the first maxim, the point is this. Both sides will know that the other will use recognized negotiation techniques to set out the position in the best possible light and to prosecute the objectives most vigorously. So much is given. What is unacceptable is to break trust. If an agreement is given it must be honoured. If factual information is proffered it must be reliable. Understanding the other side's position and needs is also crucial. Understanding something does not mean agreeing with it, but without understanding, the mind may be too closed in the search for an acceptable solution. Trust and understanding come from time spent in personal contact between the opposing sides. Negotiations may become heated and the corporate bodies may be at each other's virtual throats, but the negotiators must be able to prosecute the party line, but walk away on friendly terms. Trust is everything.

Examples

To illustrate the operation of some of these principles there follows some actual examples where the commercial negotiation was scuppered, jeopardized or hindered by well-intentioned team members failing to observe the self-preservation rules.

Example one

In this example the customer wished to place a contract for the supply, installation and commissioning of electronic equipment. The scope of the work was not fully defined and some actual development work would also be necessary. The key features of the customer's needs were that the requirement could only be satisfied by a single supplier and that delivery on time was absolutely crucial. The supplier was in a very good position to negotiate a favourable contract. He decided that in the particular circumstances his optimum method for exploiting the opportunity in terms of increased profitability was to negotiate a bonus scheme for timely delivery rather than, for example, attempting to charge high prices. The negotiation plan was thrashed out and centred on two key principles. Firstly, that the supplier would formally table a programme of work and delivery dates which clearly showed that under a conventional contract the customer's vital date would be missed. Secondly, outline details would be proposed for a cash bonus scheme that would indicate a higher probability of meeting the vital date.

The supplier's negotiation team would be led by the commercial manager with the project manager in support. A preparatory meeting was held and the role of the project manager was defined as being to provide technical arguments and reasons to explain why the work was difficult, why delivery could not be brought forward under a conventional contract, and the special measures that could be taken if a bonus scheme were to apply. Crucial to the success of the strategy would be resistance to pressure from the customer to improve delivery with no bonus scheme.

The negotiation meeting commenced and, exactly as predicted in the premeeting, the customer's angle was the importance of timely delivery, his wish to place a contract quickly and his difficulty in acquiring authority to include a bonus scheme. The supplier stuck to his line until in desperation the customer said: 'Look, if we place a conventional contract with you, can you advance the delivery plan you've offered?' The supplier's project manager leapt in with words equivalent to 'of course'. The supplier had thereby pulled the rug from beneath his own feet and his position, so carefully developed, collapsed. It is not difficult to see the mistakes of the supplier's project manager. These were that he did not stick to the plan, he did not follow the leader, he lost sight of the objective, he gave a straight answer to an awkward question and he yielded to the emotional 'cry-for-help' pressure, forgetting the 'it's tough' rule.

Example two

The company had arranged a meeting with three other companies to negotiate the essential features of a teaming agreement. The features were the scope of work, volume of effort and applicable prices – these three variables being interdependent. The nature of the overall job was such that each of the four companies would wish to secure a wide scope of work, a sizeable volume of effort and, not surprisingly, high prices. The lead company needed to settle a compromise of these twelve variables between the four organizations within an overall ceiling value.

A preparatory meeting was held although the project manager was unavailable. The agreed tactic was to concentrate on the arguments which would be put forward by the other three, each in defending its own position, and to leave the company's own contribution to last in the probability that it would go through almost on the nod. The negotiation started well, with close adherence to the plan. However, the company could not escape having its own contribution interrogated. Choosing his words carefully the lead negotiator asked his project manager to describe the technical nature of the work (as opposed to asking him to defend the level of effort proposed). The project manager replied by saying that the leader was probably not yet aware of some paper in the system that conveyed a large reduction in the company's planned amount of effort. Whilst this may have been true, it nevertheless, undermined the company's position at a stroke. In this example the mistakes made were: the project manager did not attend the pre-meeting, there was no chance at all of everybody sticking to the plan, the project manager did not listen properly and he threw in new information.

Example three

The supplier and customer had been involved in a long running argument over whether the supplier's proposed design met the requirements of the contract. The customer had steadfastly maintained that the design was not sufficient and that the supplier must change the design at his own cost. The supplier was in a diametrically opposed position. It had proved impossible to resolve the issue on purely technical grounds as these aspects were extremely complex and the issue hinged on differing interpretation and differing expert opinion on the two sides. Whilst arbitration and recourse to the courts was open to the two sides, it was in neither's interest to follow such a course of action. To do so would have meant the customer tolerating unacceptable delays in delivery – there being no practicable alternative method available to him. The supplier would have been starved of cash flow for an extensive period of time.

In an attempt to move forward, the supplier and the customer had agreed without prejudice to the position of each that the supplier should put forward a change to the design and a price quotation for the additional work. It was quickly agreed that the change was desirable and that it would correct the perceived weakness in the design. This did not settle the question of who should pay. The customer called the supplier to a meeting at the customer's premises, which were geographically considerably distant from those of the supplier. The commercial manager and project manager had a pre-meeting at which it was agreed that if the customer was not preparing to alter his stance he would have communicated the fact by telephone or in writing. Thus it was a good sign that the customer sought a face-to-face meeting, particularly in view of the distance involved, as the customer was known not to waste people's time capriciously. The plan for the meeting was that a compromise on possible splitting of the costs would be acceptable, albeit that it would be a hard slog fought for inch by inch.

The prediction about the meeting proved to be accurate and the customer repeatedly came down heavily with his much stated view that he carried no liability whatsoever for additional costs. Nevertheless, slowly but surely progress was made towards a compromise settlement until, in nothing short of exasperation, the supplier's project manager blurted out the question, 'if you're not liable, and you won't pay, why have you called us to this meeting'. Although not catastrophic, this put at risk the progress so far made and almost invited the customer to bring the shutters down and entertain no further discussion. The project manager did not stick to the plan, did not follow the leader and forgot that negotiations are tough.

Example four

The supplier had arranged a meeting with the customer to discuss a potential order for a range of products, which the customer had bought previously from the supplier. The nature of the work was relatively involved and included elements to be supplied by several major subcontractors. There were many issues to be discussed, including the question of where certain risks were to be carried. The supplier's aim was to establish the principle that as, between himself and the customer, he, the supplier, carried the risk. This was an important point, as the price to be agreed would be linked to, amongst other things, the level of risk inherent in the job. At the pre-meeting it was agreed that the project engineer would support the commercial manager and answer only those questions that the commercial manager put directly to him.

At the meeting with the customer the supplier put forward the various relevant arguments to sustain the principle that he was proposing. As a natural part of the process the commercial manager gave examples of how in practice a real problem would fall to his account since he carried the risk. At the worst possible moment the project engineer interrupted to say that in the examples given, that was not how the problems had been dealt with in previous contracts. The interruption was in part made in frustration, through his not understanding the significance of the apparently irrelevant principles. This statement caused the negotiation to take five steps backwards from the point of view of the supplier. The project engineer had not stuck to the plan, his intervention 'dropped the team in it', he strayed from his topics, he did not follow the leader and he had completely lost sight of the objectives.

These examples are based upon actual events and are not exaggerated for effect. Apparently trivial or helpful comments, no matter how well intentioned, can destroy a carefully constructed negotiation. From the lead negotiator's point of view these major or even minor disasters present immediate problems. He must recover the ground lost with the other side, explain away his own side's comments, avoid an argument developing on his own side and maintain his own side's professionalism. This is a difficult juggling act to pull off in the heat of the negotiation.

Example five

The purpose of the negotiation was to reach a preliminary set of agreements in principle with respect to a very important partnering agreement. The negotiations were to be led by an engineer holding a most senior position in the company. Although not a natural negotiator, the lead was ceded to this individual in deference to his position. This engineer gave little time to prepare, despite the importance of the prospective deal. His time saving technique was to rapidly (in practice, hastily) formulate the company's minimum position (that is, the worst deal that it could accept) and to open the negotiations with a take-it-or-leave it offer at the minimum position (and he described it as such) – because he was in such a hurry. Now it is a time-honoured practice that no one opens with his or her minimum position. Arguably in an ideal world such a practice would be useful and would save much time. But it does not work; the other side always assumes that an opening offer from the opponent can be improved. In this instance, the company opened with its minimum position (which genuinely was its minimum position), the other side took no notice of how the offer was characterized and picked away at it, offered nothing tangible in return and slowly but surely drew the engineer into agreeing a worse position. This was a negotiating and business disaster, the ramifications of which damaged the company for years. None of the above rules were followed.

Checklist

- Negotiate for a good bargain, not a compromise.

- Everyone is a negotiator.

- All discussions with the outside world are negotiations.

- Take care in the conduct of business: a negotiation may be prejudiced (or the prospects of success enhanced) by all prior events.

- In negotiation, play at the advanced level. Do not play at the beginners' level.

- A lot is at stake in a negotiation, from money to reputation.

- Do not give away unauthorized commercial information.

- Do not upset or devalue 'done deals'.

- Take care not to expose unnecessary penalties.

- Don't admit liability.

- Don't accidentally increase the company's liabilities.

- Don't give away valuable intellectual assets.

- Preparation is everything – allow sufficient time and get the people committed.

- Analyze and categorize the company's and the opposition's objectives.

- Have a plan.

- Be realistic.

- Brief the leader.

- Structure the negotiation and allocate specific functions to each member of the negotiation team.

- Follow the leader.

- Listen well, stick to the plan but recognize when the leader is deviating from the plan.

- Don't throw in new information and don't drop the team in it.

- Don't answer awkward questions and be economical with any answers.

- Don't stray into areas in which you are not the expert.

- Don't volunteer information.

- Don't lose sight of the objective.

- Don't argue the other side's case.

- Don't forget it's tough, but have fun.

- It may seem like a battle, but it's only business – remember win/win.

- Remember the importance of personal relationships.

Part two

COMMERCIAL RISK MANAGEMENT

Principles of commercial risk management

Taking a risk

A gambler is someone who takes a risk. He makes a reasoned calculation of the risk of losing and weighs that against the possible reward of winning and the investment required. Everyone is a gambler and every business is a gamble. People assess the risk of bad weather before starting to paint the house or go on a picnic. Banks take a risk in deciding to whom they should lend money. Life Assurance companies take a risk in offering policy cover. These are simple examples where the risk is obvious. It might rain, the mortgagee might default on his loan, the life assured might die prematurely. And yet in each case the risk taker does more than identify the risk. He also assesses its probability and its impact. Was the weather forecast good or bad? If it rains what will I lose (spoilt paint, annual leave etc)? Before we lend this money we must assess the credit-worthiness of the customer, if he defaults how much does the bank lose? Before we assure this person's life we must carry out a medical examination; if he dies prematurely what is the outlay compared with Premiums received?

What is more, the risk taker not only assesses probability and impact, he also looks at mitigation and holds a fall-back plan in reserve. The house painter waits for the summer when the weather should be safer, decides on quick drying paint and, if it does rain, to put up his feet and watch TV cricket from Australia instead. The bank mitigates its risk by limiting the size of the loan and its fall-back plan is to repossess the property if the mortgagee defaults. The Life Assurance company mitigates its risk by not assuring people over 55 and its fall-back plan is to avoid paying out by relying on an exclusion clause in the policy. Thus it can be seen that taking a risk should mean:

a)   Identifying sources of risk.

b)   Assessing the probability of those risks arising.

c)   Assessing their potential impact.

d)   Adopting mitigation techniques.

e)   Identifying a fall-back plan.

However, it is frequently the case that either this process is not completed or not done thoroughly. The house painter thinks about the weather but not about falling off the ladder or that half way through the job the EC might declare the type of paint chosen as illegal! If he does think of these things he may dismiss them as too remote or academic, which may indeed be the appropriate response provided the risks have been properly analyzed. So risks come in three basic varieties:

a)   Obvious or obscure.

b)   High or low probability.

c)   Large or small impact.

The bank can choose between not lending the money, lending it and relying on the mortgagee to repay, or lending it and requiring the mortgagee to pay for an upfront insurance policy in favour of the bank (not the mortgagee), essentially indemnifying it against non-payment. Thus, in risk management three alternatives present themselves:

a)   Avoid the risk (eg do not lend the money).

b)   Take the risk (eg the mortgagee is credit-worthy).

c)   Pass the risk (eg to the insurance company).

The bank can on an individual case basis avoid the risk by not lending the money. It cannot do that universally because it is in business, in part, to lend money. Risk avoidance is therefore not an option that is always available. Frequently the choice is between taking the risk, passing it on or a combination of the two. This could be defined as the Risk Bearing or sharing dilemma. In this context sharing the risk means passing on any proportion of the risk from 1-100 per cent. One hundred per cent is hardly sharing but in the real world the hundred per cent option is hypothetical as it is virtually impossible to completely eliminate a risk by passing it to someone else. '

Commercial risk management

So far, so good. What application does this have to businesses not obviously in the field of risk taking? Banks, assurance companies, insurance companies, venture capitalists, are all obviously in the risk business. Many other companies do not consider themselves in the business of risk. They see themselves as offering their customers:

- Value for money
- Quality
- Reputation
- Reliability and safety
- Engineering skills
- Design excellence
- Capacity
- After sales service

all of which could be summarized as quality product delivered on time at attractive prices. Indeed, this is the meat of company 'glossies' and other advertising material. This is fair enough, particularly when aimed at consumers. However, this section of the book is not about consumer sales, nor is it about selling techniques. It is about risk in commercial transactions. In commercial transactions risk is being bought and sold and it is this principle which is at the very heart of the book. To put this into some sort of framework, consider the objectives of the company (see the following diagram).

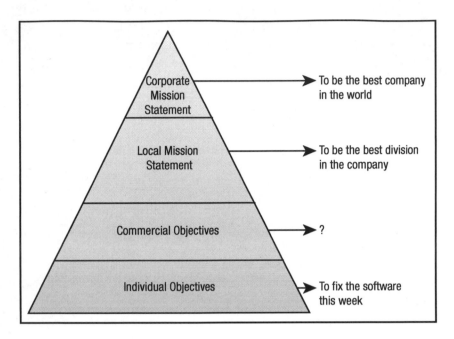

Hierarchy of Objectives

This illustrates that a link must be found between top level 'mission statements' which, while of great importance in overall goal setting terms, tend to be a little nebulous and the concrete, specific tasks which individuals carry out. The linkage can be found in a set of commercial objectives (Figure see below) which are common to all profit making concerns.

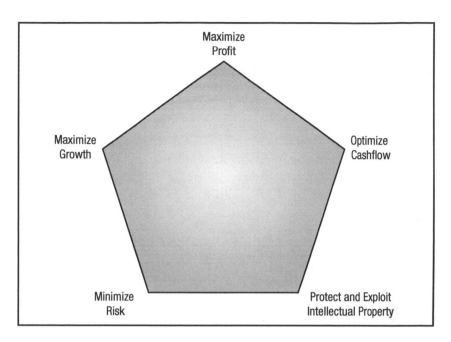

Maximize
Profit

Maximize
Growth

Optimize
Cashflow

Minimize
Risk

Protect and Exploit
Intellectual Property

Commercial Objectives

If all company employees, whether at the top or bottom of the organization, concentrate on maximizing profit, maximizing growth, optimizing cash flow, protecting intellectual property (the single most valuable asset of most companies) and minimizing risk, then all will be well. This book concentrates on the risk element of the equation. It is appropriate to refer to an equation because often the five commercial objectives are linked, appear to be in conflict or mutually exclusive in terms of the objectives of a contract negotiation. For example, lower prices achieved by reducing profit might improve growth but at the expense of the 'bottom line'. Accepting contracts without a proper review of the terms might accelerate order intake but will increase risk to the business. Excessive protectionism over intellectual property rights might prejudice orders from those customers who have a legitimate need to gain certain licences or other rights from the company. Thus the five elements must be kept sensibly in balance.

So a priority is the minimization of risk. If a typical project is imagined of not insignificant value, to be executed over perhaps months or years and involving a lot of people and a mass of technology, then traditionally risk is considered from the purely technical viewpoint (will the software work?), and from the purely programme perspective (can we build it inside three years?). Traditionally risk analysis techniques are used to identify these technical and programme risks which are then managed using sound project management procedures. This book aims to show that these risks have a contractual dimension as well as a project management dimension. It will also be shown that there are other inherent risks (eg supplier risks and third party risks) which are quite separate from the technical and programme risks. So Commercial Risk Management can be defined as the management from a contractual viewpoint of all the risks inherent in carrying out a project.

Of course it is important to be sure that whatever the intended commercial transaction, it is legal in the first place. The law will not enforce illegal contracts, but since it must be assumed that readers of this book are unlikely to be dealers in unlawful drugs or procurers of criminal acts, the question must be asked as to where lies the risk of illegality in 'normal' business transactions. There is a considerable body of legalization with which businesses have to comply ranging from employment law to VAT regulations. However, matters such as these affect the running of the business and usually have no immediate impact on particular contracts. The risk area regarding specific contracts or markets is in competition law. As an essential part of good commercial risk management it is important that contractual agreements such as sales orders, purchase orders, consortium agreements and the like contain only those restrictive provisions which are permissible within the UK and EC law and regulations.

The risk pendulum

In any commercial transaction it is inevitable that all the implicit risks will be borne by one party or the other. It may take a court of law after the event to determine on which side of the barrier an implied risk lay but surely enough all the risks lie somewhere. Perhaps in an ideal world the risk pendulum would lie perfectly balanced between the two sides (see diagram below).

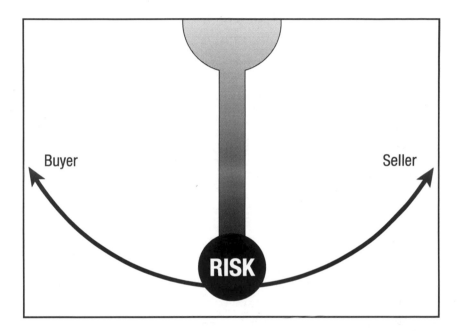

The Risk Pendulum

However, in reality the position of the pendulum largely depends upon the bargaining position of the two sides. Theoretically it should be decided purely on the basis of which side can best cope with or absorb the risk. For example, in a contract in which a UK company is buying from a US supplier the question will arise as to whether payment of the contract price should be in Sterling or Dollars. Another way of looking at this is to say that either buyer or seller must take the risk of adverse movement in the Sterling/Dollar exchange rate. Each will prefer its own national currency. If the US company also makes purchases from the UK in Sterling he is in the best position to avoid the currency risk by using Sterling earned in one transaction to fund another transaction. He is logically in the better position. On the other hand, if the US company wishes to be paid in Dollars, it will get its way if the UK company has no alternative source of the product.

This swing of the pendulum on the basis of bargaining power is well illustrated by the change in defence procurement policies brought about by the UK Government between the 1970s and the 1990s. In the earlier period defence procurement was characterized by:

a) Cost-plus contracts.

b) Procurement decisions based on paper studies.

c) Little competition.

d) Serious delays.

e) Under-performance against specification.

f) No recourse or remedy against contractors.

The nature of the procurement policy and the type of contracts placed left all risk with the Government. Cost-plus contracts, whereby contract prices were agreed at the end of the contract based on reimbursement of actual costs incurred plus a fixed percentage rate of profit, provided no incentive for companies to contain costs. All expenditure beyond the estimated costs fell to the Government's account. The then project life cycle (feasibility, project definition, development, production, support) frequently had major commitment to development decided upon no more than paper reports emerging from project definition. Thus, the technical risk inherent in development lay with the Government for having decided to proceed to that phase. For major systems and weapons there was little competition as the Government awarded contracts to the major UK defence companies on, it was said, a 'buggins turn' basis. This effectively tied the Government to the chosen company no matter how good or bad its performance. In being so tied the Government had little choice but to accept late delivery and little choice but to accept under-performance against the specification. If the equipment under-performed, was late in delivery and exhibited poor reliability in service, then the Government had virtually no remedy against the company because the development contracts under the cost-plus arrangements were 'non-risk' to the company and, in any event, it was policy to support in-service equipment by placing further contracts with the original designer/manufacturer. Under that regime all financial, commercial, technical, performance and delivery risk lay with the Government. The new policies turned this on its head under an overarching philosophy of putting risk with the company. Many techniques were adopted and against the previous characteristics the following devices were deployed:

Old	New
Cost-plus prices	Firm prices
Decisions based on paper	Decisions based on technology demonstration
Little competition	Only competition
Serious delays	Penalties for delay
Under performance	Rolling liabilities
No remedies	Contractual and legal rights

In a short space of time the risk pendulum swung from its extreme position with the Government to an equally extreme position with the industry. Many companies were badly damaged, particularly in those projects involving a high degree of software development, by finding that firm price, high risk contracts bid in competition against exacting specifications and tight timeframes were impossible to complete on time and within budget.

Here lies a golden rule of successful commercial risk management. As the Government found, it is sound policy in principle to ensure that contractual and legal risk lies with the other side. It is good practice to construct contracts so as to maximize the commercial incentive on the other side to do well. However, these approaches do not necessarily in themselves eliminate risk to project success. It is comforting to know that when disaster has descended someone else is liable for the consequences, but it does not actually prevent the consequences from being suffered.

In any complex contract it is as well for both parties to work together for mutual success even within the confines of a proper contractual relationship. It is unwise to feel contented merely by having achieved a massive swing of the pendulum. The 'tautest' contract can fix liability, it cannot guarantee quality and timely performance.

Nevertheless, the experience in the defence industry shows that the pendulum can be made to swing more by bargaining power than by logic. Logically the Government was better able to survive large project cost increases than companies with much more limited assets but the vastly superior bargaining power of the Government meant that the risk was transferred.

Risk bearing, risk sharing

Conventionally, a contract is defined as:

'A legally binding exchange of promises.'

For example, the seller promises to deliver the goods and pass title. The buyer promises to pay the agreed price. Non-conventionally, a contract could be defined as:

'The vehicle by which the risks inherent in the transaction are allocated as between buyer and seller.'

For example, the seller agrees to carry the risk of loss or damage to the goods until delivery. The buyer agrees to carry the risk that the goods will or will not meet his purpose.

It is sometimes said that the contract serves no practical purpose. If everything goes well the contract stays in the filing cabinet gathering dust. If things go wrong the contract is of no use since it does not legislate for the particular problem that has arisen. This is short-sighted in so far as most contracts probably lie somewhere between those two extremes and, in any event, if the non-conventional definition proposed above is accepted, then it is to the contract that the parties must turn as a starting point in establishing ownership of, and liability for, the risk which has given rise to the problem.

So, in the sense that the contract provides the vehicle for allocating risk, what then in simple terms is this risk? The risk is that the contract did not turn out as the parties intended (see following diagram).

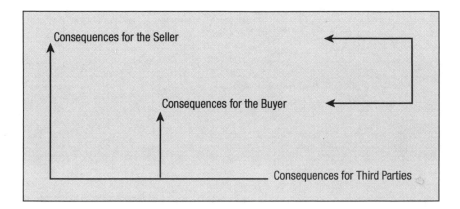

Contract Failure

If things do not work out the buyer and seller may have liabilities to each other. Either or both may have liabilities to affected third parties. Again, in simple terms the parties' expectations were quite straightforward (see following diagram).

Seller Expected	Buyer Expected	The 'World Expected'
• To get paid	• Performance on time	
• To transfer title and risk	• Performance to spec	
• The Buyer to take delivery and accept the goods	• Performance to quality	• Not to be interfered with
• To complete the job within budget	• To acquire title	
• To be left alone	• To be left alone	

The Parties' Expectations

The one common expectation between buyer, seller and the rest of the world is that each should be left alone or not interfered with as a result of the transaction between buyer and seller. The buyer expected to receive the goods and be happy with them. The seller expected to be paid by a contented customer. This private arrangement was not expected to come to the notice of the world. However, the car manufacturer who buys defective brake components and innocently sells them on to a motorist whose new car crashes, causing injury, will find himself in all sorts of problems. Nevertheless, it is the contract between buyer and seller that provides the principal medium for establishing where the liability lies. In the example just given, the car manufacturer and injured third parties may have action in negligence against the brake component supplier but, as between manufacturer and supplier, the strongest claim against the supplier could be based upon breach of contract (eg breach of express terms, such as the goods not meeting their specification or of a warranty that they are free of hazard and defect), or upon breach of implied undertakings as to satisfactory quality or fitness for purpose. This could be the strongest case depending inevitably on the specific contract terms and in particular on the effect on any so-called exclusion clauses, a point which will be covered later in this chapter. The contract allocates risk between the parties. But before drafting and negotiating the contract the parties need to be clear on the nature of the relationship which they seek to establish between them. The relationship should be considered on the basis of risk, value and duration (see following diagram).

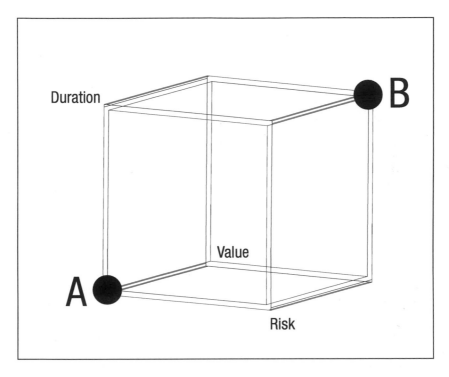

Contract Characteristics

Where the transaction is in a zone close to point A in Figure 1.6, then a simple 'arm's length' relationship is appropriate. As the type of transaction moves towards point B, then some form of partnership is usually more suited to the circumstances. Where there is low risk in a short duration, low value transaction, simple contracts are acceptable. Any combination of high risk, high value or long duration demands more considered thought.

When a company decides to procure rather than undertake all the project activities itself it must consider three essential elements:

Procurement Type

- Non-competitive (sole source)
- Non-competitive (non-monopoly)
- Partnership sourcing
- Competitive arm's-length

Pricing Regime

- Cost reimbursement
- Cost incentive
- Fixed price
- Firm price

Contract Strategy

- Service only
- Design only
- Make only
- Turnkey

Let's look at the question of the nature of the commercial relationship at a more fundamental level. Earlier in this chapter the golden rule of commercial risk management was discussed. This might be summarized as:

'There is more to minimizing project risk than ensuring that the contractual risk pendulum has swung away from you.'

While in large part the theme and motive of this chapter is to show how to swing the contractual risk pendulum away, it would be an incomplete picture if the analysis were left there. In the cut and thrust of contract negotiations buyer and seller are both trying to push the pendulum towards the other, and it can be a demanding intellectual leap for them to consider alternative arrangements based on sharing rather than bearing risk.

Partnership sourcing and partnership contracting

There are two main varieties of arrangement between buyer and seller that can be used depending upon the nature of the activity. Both are based on the principle of partnership. Both assume that partnership reduces project risk while not interfering with the allocation of contractual risk, albeit that 'in the spirit of partnership', contractual remedies may consciously be set aside in the event of a problem so as best to preserve the broader benefits of that partnership. The two varieties are partnership sourcing and partnership contracting. These partnerships are not partnerships in the strict legal sense, rather they are concepts for promoting cooperation and openness.

Partnership sourcing is convenient when buyer and seller are quite remote. A car factory may adopt partnership sourcing to achieve a number of aims. The benefits may include a smaller number of suppliers, reduced overhead burden, improved quality, timelier delivery, commitment to problem solving and responsiveness to evolving needs. However, the automotive component supplier and Joe Public buying his new car through a dealer are remote in the sense that they do not expect to come into frequent contact with each other. In comparison with the end product, a car (a single high value item), the supplier provides dozens, hundreds or thousands of relatively low value items. The car buyer does not see the summation of thousands of components, he sees only the one end product. A power generating company may go for partnership sourcing for essential components to achieve lower price, very high reliability and after sales services. The end product, amperes down the wires, bears no resemblance to the generating components and the user, whether industrial or consumer, sees only that his air conditioning plant or television works.

Partnership sourcing is also at its best when there are potentially many suppliers from whom a smaller number of 'partners' can be selected. Partnership contracting on the other hand has the supplier and buyer working much more closely in concept towards meeting the end customer's needs. This is more appropriate where a single customer has a large unique order for a single special requirement, particularly where a high level of research, design or development is required. A new weapons system, a new satellite ground station, a new aircraft, all can benefit from partnership contracting as the intimacy between buyer and seller so necessary on projects of this nature can evolve into a more effective commercial entity.

In moving away from arm's-length contracting the choice between partnership sourcing and partnership contracting can be characterized as follows:

Partnership Sourcing	Partnership Contracting
• Many potential suppliers	• Possibly sole source suppliers
• Many end customers	• Single end customer
• Many supplier products	• Single/few products
• Off the shelf products	• High development content

In both varieties a single supplier may provide a product which is critical to the successful performance by the buyer of his contract with the end customer. However, in partnership sourcing the supplier product, although critical, is either not used at all in the end result (eg pumps for power generation) or is only a minor component (eg the brake pads in a car). In partnership contracting the supplier contribution is a major element of the end result (eg the undercarriage and control system in an aircraft). Indeed, in some examples of partnership contracting the supplier element may be of higher value than the buyer content (see following diagram).

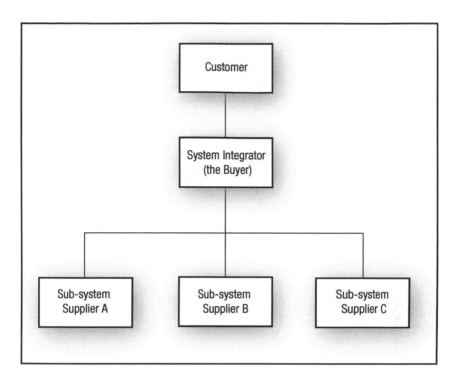

Major Supplier Content

In this scenario the monetary value of the system integrator's work may be quite low in comparison with the work of the sub-system suppliers and yet, as between himself and the end customer, he takes the entire risk in the performance of the system. In this situation the advantages of sharing that risk with the major suppliers is obvious.

Approaches to partnership contracting

The principle of partnership contracting in comparison with alternative commercial relationships can be seen in following diagram.

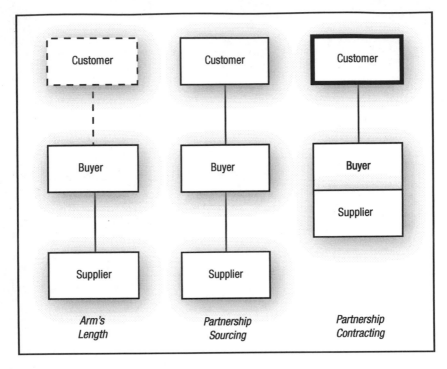

Commercial Relationships Compared

The progression can be seen as the level of importance of satisfying the end customer. In an arm's length relationship the supplier is little concerned with the end customer. His vision is narrow and limited to completing his order. In partnership sourcing the supplier has a wider vision and understands that his endeavours will help the buyer to perform well, but his main focus is still in satisfying the terms of his order from the buyer. In partnership contracting the end customer looms larger and the supplier focus has shifted towards contributing to the performance of the end customer order.

There are three ways for the parties to organize themselves in order to achieve a partnership contracting arrangement (see following diagram).

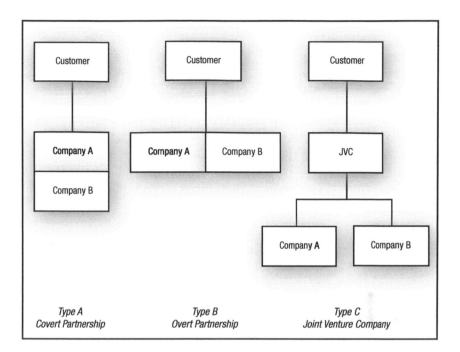

Type A
Covert Partnership

Type B
Overt Partnership

Type C
Joint Venture Company

Commercial Relationships Compared

In a covert partnership the parties would conduct themselves as follows:

a) A would negotiate with the customer.

b) A would provide B with sight of all or part of the draft contracts and invite comments.

c) The contract between A and B may require B to participate in the performance of the contract between A and the customer or of a particular part only (eg a specification).

d) The contract between the customer and A would be accepted and signed by A but with the prior agreement of B.

In an overt partnership the approach is somewhat different:

a) A and B would jointly negotiate with the customer.

b) A and B would jointly review and comment on the draft contract.

c) Performance of the contract would rest with them both.

d) The contract would be jointly accepted and signed by A and B.

The third option is for A and B to create an entirely new company on a joint venture basis whose sole purpose would be to execute the one project (or series of projects) with the customer and would thus negotiate and sign the contract with the customer in the normal way. The JVC may be constituted with the minimum assets and staff and, hence, the JVC may then need to place orders with A and B for further goods or services as the diagram shows.

The choice of approach needs careful thought and the extent to which the parties actually 'trust' each other needs to be considered in the context of their partnership contracting agreement. While overt partnership or JVC may suit their wishes neither may be liked by the customer: the former because the customer may prefer to avoid the confusion of signing with two companies, it being easier perhaps to sue only one company if it all goes wrong, and the latter because the customer may judge the JVC to be too relatively insubstantial to carry the burden of his project. However, he may be prepared to accept this if his risk is mitigated by A and B and/or a third party, such as a bank providing a financial guarantee of performance.

A potential pitfall for the parties in both covert and overt partnerships is that a clear definition is still required as to the parts of the work which each will do. Once that is done it tends to drag the relationship back towards conventional arm's length, under which a failure by one party could lead to a claim against it by the other party in respect of delay and additional cost. To avoid this the parties may decide in their partnership contracting agreement to agree to waive all such claims against each other. This certainly motivates them to work together as though they were a single company, but it is a very big decision for each to make and hence the reference to the degree of mutual trust. The good thing about a conventional contract is that it is fairly straightforward to establish liability and remedy if things go wrong. It is less than easy to legislate for the difficult times when the whole premise is mutual success. Rather like those who seek a divorce settlement, agreement as part of the contract of marriage, the very act of talking about possible problems can introduce uncertainty in the first place. However, this threat of loss of confidence, like any other risk, is there to be overcome and is not in itself a reason not to proceed.

It should also be borne in mind that both parties may see disadvantage as well as advantage in moving into partnership contracting (see following diagram).

	Advantages	Disadvantages
A	Risk Sharing More Status	Loss of Status
B	Involved in control, management and decision making	Less Control More Risk

Advantages and Disadvantages of Partnership Contracting

Partnership contracting is fairly novel, involves a high level of mutual trust and commitment and demands some big decisions of principle. Nevertheless, it is a sound, productive approach for major, high risk projects.

Exclusion clauses

Returning from the sublime considerations of partnership contracting to the conventional contract between buyer and seller, it is necessary to examine one of the blunter instruments of commercial risk management: the use of exclusion clauses to limit or exempt one party from a liability which might otherwise fall to it.

The basic source of authority on such matters is the Unfair Contract Terms Act 1977, which prevents the exclusion of liability for personal injury or death arising from negligence in all forms of contract. However, in non-consumer contracts the parties are allowed to exclude the following subject to a test of reasonableness:

a) Liability for breach of contract.

b) Liability to perform as expected.

c) Liability for complete performance.

d) Liability for other results of negligence.

e) That the goods correspond with description or sample given.

f) Satisfactory quality.

g) Fitness for purpose.

The seller is also prevented from excluding the implied conditions that the goods are unencumbered and that the seller is free to sell them.

The onus is on the party relying on the clause to exclude liability to show that it is reasonable. The reasonableness test is based on:

a) The exclusion being fair and reasonable in the circumstances known or contemplated by the parties when the contract was made.

b) The relative bargaining positions.

c) The existence of any inducement.

d) Whether goods were manufactured, processed or adapted to order.

e) Whether the buyer had reasonable notice of the condition.

If the liability is financially limited then also taken into account would be the resources available to meet the liability and the availability of insurance.

For an exclusion clause to be effective, then:

a) Notice of the clause must have been given at the time of the contract, unless the prior course of dealings or trade practice provide evidence of its existence.

b) Notice must be in a contractual document.

c) Reasonable notice must be given.

d) The clause must apply to that which was intended.

In practice it can generally be assumed that in any business contract that is negotiated (ie as opposed to blind acceptance of a standard form contract), the above provisos regarding notice would be deemed satisfied.

An inducement from seller to buyer to accept an exclusion clause may simply be a discount on price. All risks have at least a notional value and the device of an exclusion clause just moves a risk around. If there is valuable consideration, then it should be reasonable that if the buyer has the benefit of a lower price he should not later be able to avoid the exclusion clause under one or more of the foregoing rules. Frequently it is the satisfactory quality and fitness for purpose undertakings implied (unless they are expressly excluded) by the Sale of Goods Act which suppliers seek to exclude. The argument is that these were intended principally to protect the consumer who buys on the basis of seeing the goods on a shelf, unlike the business purchaser who is 'intelligent' in the sense that he specifies his needs in detail and conducts a thorough appraisal of the utility of the goods before commitment. In such a situation why should the seller carry the imprecise (in scope, extent and time) liabilities of these undertakings? The seller will aim to include clauses such as the following:

'All representations, warranties, guarantees and conditions (other than as to title and those herein expressed or specifically referred to), and whether statutory or otherwise are hereby expressly excluded. Without prejudice to the generality of the foregoing the Company will not be liable for consequential loss or damage, however caused, resulting directly or indirectly from the sale or supply of goods or services by the Company or for any loss or damage caused directly or indirectly by any of the goods or services or in any other way for the performance of any of the goods or services.'

Wow! This is typical of such all embracing clauses which would leave the buyer with very few rights against the seller. Everything from representations made before the contract to problems arising after the contract are excluded from the seller's liability. The courts have been keen to find deficiencies in such clauses so as to preserve natural justice, however, where the clauses have been found legally watertight, then they have been enforced no matter how unreasonable they might seem. So whether in the role of buyer or seller care should be taken in the use of exclusion clauses as a means of moving risk around.

Insurance

Commercial Risk Management is about the allocation of risk between buyer and seller. However, once a particular risk has fallen to one side or the other it does not mean that the carrier has no other option but to hold the risk unto himself. As well as allocating risk the aim is to mitigate risk by passing it on in whole or in part to a third party (see following diagram).

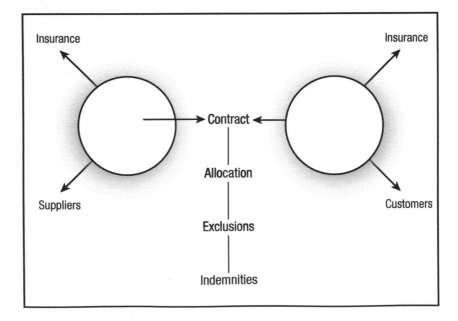

Risk Distribution

In this chapter so far the idea of using the contract as the vehicle for risk allocation has been explored. Exclusions have been discussed and it should be said that, although certain liabilities cannot be excluded, there is no reason for the party carrying the liability not to be indemnified by the other party regarding the financial consequences of the liability materializing.

In the transaction the seller may seek to distribute his risk amongst his suppliers just as the buyer may attempt to distribute his risk amongst his customers. Nevertheless, both may attempt to lay off some of their respective risks through insurance.

Not all risks inherent in a commercial transaction are insurable. At the heart of such a deal is the prospect of gain for which reason the risk is taken in the first place. If failure of the enterprise were to be insurable as far as the loss of that potential gain is concerned, then there would be no incentive to work to achieve that gain and insurance companies would forever be paying for lost anticipated profits which result from no more than the company failing to strive for that goal. However, if 'the failure were to result from a fortuitous event (such as fire), then provided there is sufficient number of similar risks to allow a sensible prediction of the loss to be assessed and a reasonable premium to be calculated, then such risk is insurable. For a risk to be insurable the insured must also have an 'insurable interest in the risk'. The Marine Insurance Act 1909 explains this as:

> '(the insured) stands in a legal or equitable relation to the insurable property at risk, in the consequence of which he may benefit by the safety of the property, or may incur a liability in respect thereof.'

For example, company X cannot insure the property of company Y if X stands neither to gain nor lose from the destruction of Ys property.

There are many risks inherent in carrying on any business and those which are insurable include the following:

Type	In respect of
Property	Loss/damage to plant, buildings, materials, stock due to fire, storm, flood etc.
Business interruption	Financial cost of remedial work, new premises, overtime wages etc.
All risks	Property loss/damage not otherwise covered (eg an overseas construction project).
Engineering	For example business disruption due to a computer system failure.
Fidelity guarantee	Theft by employees.
Crime	Theft by third parties.
Product liability	Injury, death or damage caused by defective products.
Public liability	Injury, death or damage to third parties caused by eg the spread of fire.
Directors and officers liability	Personal liability of directors and officers in respect of liability business duties.
Goods in transit	Loss or damage to goods while in shipment, whether road, rail, sea or air.
Employer's liability	Injury or death to employees suffered in the course of his employment
Credit	Customer failure to pay.
Aviation	Injury, death or damage eg caused by aircraft crash resultant from defective equipment.

Many of these are general to the good conduct of the business. Some are required by statute such as public liability and employee liability. Some make good sense such as 'engineering' provided the premium is not excessive in comparison with the perceived potential loss. Some may result from a particular contract. For example, a company supplying for the first time products that will be built into an aircraft should examine the possibility of aviation insurance, especially so if the products are hazardous or critical to aircraft safety. Others such as credit and goods in transit may be geared to one or many contracts.

It is good commercial risk management when identifying the potential risks in a particular deal to consider special insurance, or at the very least to determine whether existing insurance policies cover the appropriate insurable risks in scope and value without unreasonable exclusions applying. One of the drawbacks of insurance is that once a risk is insured people stop thinking about it and, if they think about it at all, they tend to dismiss the risk as 'not to worry, it's covered'. As each invitation to tender or contract crops up there are several stages to consider:

a) Review the document, the implications of expressed and implied risks and identify the insurable risks.

b) Check that existing insurance policies cover these risks.

c) Identify additional cover required and ensure that the premium represents value for money against the protection provided.

d) Ensure that the contract price embraces any necessary additional premiums or that their cost is otherwise provided for

e) Ensure that project and contract managers are aware of the insurance position and in particular that exclusions, limitations and 'excesses' are understood.

Any insurer is only going to pay out if the risk is covered, if the cover is adequate and provided the insured has reasonably acted to prevent or mitigate the effects of the event. In any event, insurance can only provide financial compensation for the event and not for the other consequences to the business. For example, if the company is able to insure against the risk of failure by a key supplier, financial compensation in respect of additional costs or other financial penalties resulting from supplier failure is little help in preventing good customers from going elsewhere. The company should work hard to avoid any risk materializing regardless of whether or not it is insured.

Customer characteristics

The whole subject of commercial risk management is about managing the risk that lies across the contractual interface between company and customer, between company and suppliers and embracing the effect of extraneous influences such as 'force majeure' events that intrude into these essentially private arrangements. In the analysis, however, it would be easy to assume that in the crucial contractual interface between Company and Customer all customers are the same. A thorough description of a particular customer would have to include the following:

a)	Status	Public or private
b)	Location	UK or overseas
c)	Nationality	British or foreign
d)	Culture	Western or not
e)	Language	English or not
f)	Religion	Important or not
g)	Size	Employees, sites, turnover
h)	Substance	Assets, credit status
i)	Reputation	Good faith dealings
j)	Procurement policy	Strict competition – 'Dutch auction' etc
k)	Personnel	Quality and integrity

Good customer relations demand that these characteristics are identified, understood and responded to sympathetically by the company, particularly on matters such as culture and religion. However, these considerations are just as essential in risk management as in customer relations. Failure to understand the essence of the customer is to expose unnecessary risks.

If the customer says the draft contract will be issued in a week, the company must know whether this means what it says or whether it means that the customer is just stringing the company along while formal negotiations have already opened with the opposition. If the customer says it is contemplating a £50 million contract, the company should know not only that the customer has the money/credit to proceed, but that it has the numbers and quality of personnel to handle a major order and that its approval procedures are of a realistic timeframe.

Commercial Risk Management starts with knowing the customer.

Company culture

If knowing the customer is important then the culture and organization of the company is paramount if risks are to be avoided. Established companies arrive at their organization not so much by clear design but by evolution, taking into account company, local and national politics (eg setting up operations in areas of high unemployment to attract subsidies and cheap labour), geography (eg the location of customers, suppliers, airports and other communications), different cultures and practices (eg when companies merge or are taken over) and other such diverse and possibly conflicting influences. The net effect can be to produce an organization which may look sound to the outside world but which at the same time is inherently not optimized for risk management. The manifestation of this phenomenon can be on the macro scale (eg the way in which the company is structured by different operating divisions) and on the micro scale (eg inconsistent procedural arrangements).

Good examples of this type of problem are:

a) Geographical separation of design and manufacture
This produces an 'us and them' attitude. The designers create what they think is a good design and blame the factory for not being able to make it. The factory complains that the design is not geared for manufacture and cannot be made cheaply. The result is a poor, expensive product that is always delivered late.

b) Functional separation of selling and buying

If there is no functional linkage between those responsible for negotiating terms with customers and those responsible for negotiating with suppliers, there is inevitably a mismatch between the respective terms, possibly leaving the company holding a liability which should properly belong to a supplier.

c) Allowing 'non buyers' to buy

To save time and money companies allow personnel who are not expert buyers to purchase apparently innocuous things. Engineers buying software, administration staff buying photocopy services are examples where important commercial and financial issues are overlooked through ignorance.

d) Following a strict 'buy cheap' policy

'Lowest price wins' is not usually the invariable recipe for success if short and long term risk are not considered.

e) Management attitude

The concept of Total Quality Management (TQM) teaches that everybody should aim to:

    a)   Do things right first time.

    b)   Make sure only the right things are done.

    c)   Challenge the way things are done.

And yet the single biggest problem is to get senior management away from the idea that 'everything we do is right, it's all those other people who are fouling up'.

If TQM is a sound philosophy (which it undoubtedly is) then it should be backed by a Total Risk Management (TRM) culture. The TQM company takes care over everything that it does. The TRM company goes further and ensures at all stages of its commercial operation that:

    a)   Risks are identified.

    b)   Risks are 'owned' (ie allocated to individuals).

c)   Risk are avoided, delegated, shared, insured.

d)   Risks are mitigated by pro-active management.

Achieving TRM means the company must be prepared to alter its organization and culture in order to put the necessary facilities and disciplines
in place.

Post-delivery risk

Is there life after delivery?

The seller wants to deliver, take the money and run. The buyer wants the goods, doesn't want to pay and hopes to have a stranglehold on the seller forever! Somewhere between these two extremes there is a reasonable position regarding post-delivery obligations. In a clinical sense both sides should be seeking certainty as to the point at which the contract has been wholly performed in return for which the full contract price is payable. There may well be residual obligations on the seller after this point in terms of supporting the delivered products, but the real risk lies in the question as to whether all liability in the material work has or has not passed to the buyer.

Key contractual milestones

There are several important points to consider:

Inspection
The opportunity for the buyer to verify that goods offered in the performance of the contract comply with the requirements of the contract.

Delivery
The point at which the contract is performed (regardless of the passage of property and risk), whether by physical movement of goods or by paperwork transaction.

Passing of Property
The transfer of legal title in the goods from seller to buyer.

Passing of Risk
The transfer of liability from seller to buyer for loss or damage to the goods.

Rejection
The right of the buyer to reject goods which do not comply with the requirements of the contract.

Acceptance
The point at which the buyer concurs that the contract has been performed, forever extinguishing his right to reject.

Warranty
A period after delivery during which the seller has express or implied liability to the buyer for defects in the goods.

Payment
Settlement of the contract by the buyer in return for the contract having been performed.

Not surprisingly, buyer and seller have exactly opposing views in each of these principles (see following diagrams).

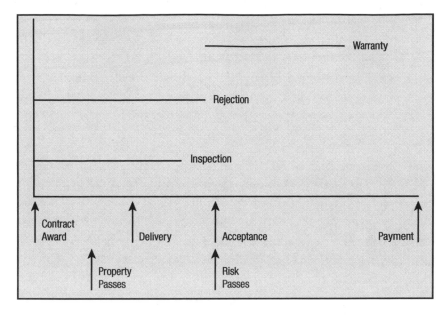

Buyer's Preference

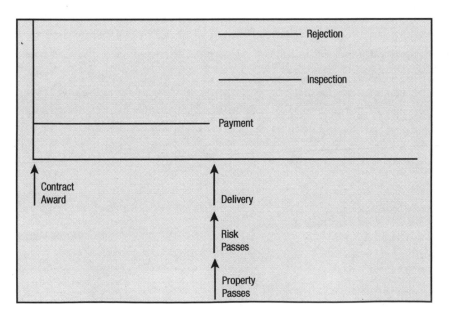

Seller's Preferences

So the buyer likes the ability to inspect the work throughout the period of the contract exposing a risk of rejection even before the seller has offered performance. He wants early title to parts, materials and finished goods and wants to pay way after delivery, having delayed acceptance and adoption of loss/damage risk as long as possible. The seller on the other hand sees performing the contract as his private business until he offers performance, where transfer of property and risk should transfer simultaneously with acceptance immediately thereafter (if not concurrently with) and having enjoyed payment over the life of the contract achieving 100 per cent of the price on or before delivery.

These things must all be worked out in the detail of the contract negotiation. The inter-linking of delivery, property and risk are all dealt with in the choice of arrangements set out in 'Incoterms' which are particularly useful for export contracts. Probably the most important event from the seller's perspective is achieving contractual acceptance. This is because, if goods are legitimately rejected then, unless compliant goods can be offered within the period allowed, the seller is in fundamental breach and risks the contract being terminated for default. Once acceptance has occurred then the right to reject has disappeared, the risk of termination has evaporated and the buyer can only pursue the seller under express or implied warranties if there are any problems with the goods.

Thus the definition, scope and timing of acceptance is something upon which to focus much attention in contract negotiation and in execution of the contract. Getting the customer to 'accept' things is good commercial risk management, such as the classic separation of 'design' and 'make' whereby if the customer accepts the design prior to the make/build/implement stage, he will have much greater difficulty in seeking redress from the supplier at the later stage if there are problems associated with the design.

Residual obligations and risks

Depending on the construction of the agreed contract, primary post-delivery risks may therefore include (if reference is made to Figure 2.1):

1) Rejection of the goods.

2) Goods lost or damaged.

3) Deficiencies discovered under warranty.

4) Payment not made.

These are dealt with later on in this chapter. However, the question remains as to what other risks remain with the seller even once the primary risks identified above have been eliminated. Such residual obligations typically cover:

1) Supply of additional goods under contract options.

2) Delivery of technical data and licences for the use thereof.

3) Settlement of outstanding purchase orders, subcontracts, rental agreements, lease agreements etc.

4) Disposal of residual material within the terms of the contract.

5) Resolution of outstanding claims and disputes.

6) Disposal of customer owned property made available for the purposes of the contract.

7) Cancellation/closure of outstanding bonds, credit facilities.

8) Termination of teaming, collaboration, agreements, guarantees, consortium agreements.

9) Final negotiation and conclusion of any special pricing arrangements (eg cost risk sharing schemes, VOP adjustments).

10) Establishment of contractual, management and procedural arrangements to provide support services and maintenance of technical skills and data.

11) Application for patents and other forms of intellectual property protection in respect of the work of the contract.

Secondary duties such as these, which do not go to the heart of the contract but nevertheless form part of the entire set of contract obligations, are very important. Whether they relate to obligations owed directly to the customer or to other parties they can be-easy to overlook. The arrival of a letter from the customer two years after the contract is finished, legitimately exercising a contract option for more goods which the company had entirely forgotten about, can be an alarming experience. This is particularly so if the goods are no longer in production or no longer capable of economic production. Similarly, a late but proper invoice from a supplier which arrives after the books have been closed on the contract and the profit released to the Profit and Loss Account can be disappointing and certainly risky for the project or contract manager, who must explain this to the finance director!

Just as it is important to plan the start up and execution of a contract, so it is important to plan the closure of the contract. Good administrative procedures should ensure that these residual obligations are not forgotten and positive action should be taken to discharge or eliminate them. For example, the contract option which survives completion of the main work should be examined for viability and if there is a risk that the option could not be performed at all, or not at a profit, then early action should be taken to persuade the customer to agree that the option right is deleted or perhaps to reduce the length of the period during which the option can be exercised.

In business, as in life, there are more people who are good at starting things than there are people who are good at finishing things. This is a characteristic which is also true of companies. Therefore, great attention must be paid to ensuring that residual obligations are effectively dealt with one way or another.

Pricing

When a price is formulated for a potential contract usually only two things are considered. Will this price win the contract? Will this price cover the cost, leaving something for profit? The 'top down' examination of price in terms of perceived competitiveness against the opposition needs to converge against the 'bottom up' approach to estimating cost, together with the business expectation as to the level of profit. However, part of the process of pricing must look at what allowances should ideally be made for risk being both technical and commercial in character. As with all risks the key questions are impact and probability. The probability axis includes a time dimension in terms of the period for which the company is exposed to the risk. Thus, risk allowances should include consideration of the timing of acceptance, the period of rejection, the start and length of warranty. In addition to considering the timing, scope and scale of the primary post-delivery risks are important. So, too, is the taking into account the scope, scale and risk dimensions of the residual obligations.

Account management

Every risk is an opportunity. The primary and residual risks that lie at the tail end of the contract are very real and need to be carefully managed. Eliminating the risks, for example, of late delivery and deficient goods means not only a greater chance of completing the contract at the anticipated level of profit but it also means a satisfied customer. Needless to say, satisfied customers are more likely to come back for more and the company's reputation will have grown in the market place. Thus the contract should not only be seen as the mountain of obligations and risks but as the opportunity to make profit and secure further orders. This much is a blinding glimpse of the obvious but many companies fail to take the opportunity at the start of the contract, or even beforehand, to work out how the particular contract can be used to generate more business. A 'product plan' may look at the technical evolution of a product, how and when it will come to the market, the investment needed, the likely customer base, target selling prices and margins, the volume, time frame and phasing of orders and particular major potential orders may feature as key milestones, but this is inevitably a little bit too general. What is needed is a specific plan for the exploitation of the particular contract which looks at the tactics and timing of introducing to the customer ideas for improvements, enhancements, upgrades, maintenance and other support services. Indeed, these opportunities may grow out of problems and risks encountered during the contract, or anticipated to emerge post-delivery. The problem at the end of the contract of holding open an option for the customer to purchase more goods which at that time (unlike at the time of the contract, some years earlier perhaps) are expected to be uneconomic of further production, can be turned into the opportunity to have the customer consider newer, better products as an alternative – subject of course to some re-negotiation of the prices!

The do's and don'ts of post-delivery risk

RISK – the goods are not accepted

Do

a)   Ensure the contract has an acceptance clause.

b)   Ensure acceptance occurs on

   i)   A specific event or

   ii)   The elapse of a stated period of time from delivery.

c)   Seek acceptance in stages.

d)   Ensure that events are clearly documented to evidence acceptance.

Don't

a)   Agree to acceptance occurring when

   i)   The customer says so or

   ii)   The goods are taken into use or

   iii)   The elapse of a 'reasonable' period.

b)   Agree to 'delayed' acceptance.

c)   Agree to acceptance being linked to payment.

In all contracts it is as well to have an express acceptance. It is such an important milestone that the contract must make it absolutely clear when, where and how acceptance occurs. The best approach is to hang acceptance on to a key event or series of events which are objective and susceptible to clear yes/no, pass/fail criteria. For example, a contract for a complex system could specify a set of 'acceptance tests' the successful completion of which conveys contractual acceptance. The tests may be testing a representative sample of the features demanded in the technical, performance or other specifications which establish the basic requirements of the contract or they may test every feature.

Testing is expensive and in some situations 100 per cent testing is not feasible. Hence, once again the principle of risk sharing applies. In the situation just described, the customer takes the risk that, in accepting the work of the contract in the absence of 100 per cent testing, some shortfalls against the contract may exist which are not detected at the acceptance testing stage. Once the work has been accepted his bargaining power and remedies against the seller are much weaker. However, for taking that risk he will have had the benefit of a lower price and perhaps quicker completion, and hence the bargain is balanced.

If acceptance testing or something similar is not appropriate the best approach to acceptance is for it to be conveyed at the end of a stated period of time from physical delivery. This simple approach is objective and the length of the period can be negotiated on a case by case basis. A balance will always be struck between the two extremes where the seller would want acceptance to occur concomitantly with delivery, while the buyer would want to suspend acceptance for several years!

We should also consider the concept of partial performance. If the contract is so constructed to allow for this then it is important that acceptance is conveyed in stages. Thus it is important to spell out in the contract the acceptance arrangements for every item of the contract or every stage of the work. From the seller's perspective the lightest burden of acceptance is clearly preferable and he should look for the simplest approach, certainly as far as an opening position is concerned. For example, he might suggest that acceptance occurs on delivery provided he has submitted a certificate of conformity with the goods.

To back up an objective approach to acceptance it is crucial that the events upon which acceptance depends are thoroughly documented, so as to prevent disputes as to whether acceptance has or has not occurred.

The goal of objectivity is completely frustrated if acceptance is effectively left to the customer's discretion. And yet this is the effect of clauses which say 'the seller shall complete the work in accordance with the contract specifications and to the satisfaction of the buyer'. Acceptance should be capable of determination without any element of judgment on the part of the buyer or anybody else. Nor should a special piece of paper be needed, such as an acceptance certificate from the buyer. If an 'acceptance certificate' is required to complete, confirm or formalize acceptance then the implication is that the certificate is an essential component of the process or act of acceptance, without which acceptance cannot have occurred. Hence the buyer is hardly going to be motivated to issue a certificate since it is in his interests to delay acceptance for as long as possible.

The uncertainty of the customer 'saying so', is matched by the uncertainty of clauses which provide for acceptance when the goods are taken into use or the elapse of a 'reasonable' period from delivery. Although in the former case, if it is certain that the goods will go into use very quickly (probably so), then it would be beneficial and safe for the seller to agree to acceptance on that basis. In any other circumstance the uncertainty represents a risk. Similarly, references to a reasonable period are inherently risky and only guarantee disputes between the two sides regarding what may be considered a reasonable period in the prevailing circumstances.

The customer's wish to delay acceptance can sometimes be manifested as a clear policy as opposed to a natural instinct. He may specify that acceptance can only take place following extensive use of the goods so that their true utility or performance can be assessed. Clearly this would represent a much greater risk to the seller and one which should be avoided if at all possible.

Finally, it is preferable to avoid the contract linking acceptance to payment. If the arrangements for acceptance are well defined, resistant to dispute and the criteria represent no major hurdle, then such a linkage is perfectly fine. However, if the burden is onerous it is better that clearing the hurdle does not have the additional complication of cash flow issues surrounding it. However, at the fundamental level, if acceptance is not attained due to some deficiency on the part of the seller then the contract has not been performed and the buyer can hardly be expected to pay, although the question of the actual remedies (termination, damages) must depend on the circumstances and the terms of the contract.

RISK – the good are rejected

Do

a) Avoid the contract giving rights of rejection.

b) Link rejection with acceptance.

c) Limit the period within which a rejection can be made.

d) Provide a right of appeal against rejection.

e) Require notice of rejection to be in writing.

f) Seek a right to compensation for invalid rejections.

g) Make sure that property and risk in rejected goods is specified.

h) Prescribe responsibility for returning/re-delivering rejected goods.

Don't

a) Forget to lodge appeals.

b) Fail to challenge rejections and interrogate the rejection closely.

In the seller's ideal world the buyer is obliged to accept the work and has no opportunity to reject, thus the correct, if somewhat fanciful suggestion, is that the buyer should have no right of rejection. Assuming therefore that rejection rights must apply the question is how to limit this risk. The concepts of acceptance and rejection go hand in hand and the contract should reinforce the general principle that acceptance extinguishes any right of rejection. Any period within which rejection is allowed should be stated, limited and triggered by some event such as physical delivery. If rejections are allowed, then sensibly there should be a right of appeal as, presumably, if the seller was confident that he delivered conforming goods, there must be some chance that the buyer's purported rejection is invalid. Incidentally, it should be stated that the right of rejection relates only to a belief that the goods genuinely do not conform to the requirements of the contract. There should be no ability to reject the goods on some general grounds of dissatisfaction. A rejection is potentially a very serious situation for the seller and good practice and protocol demand that it is notified formally and in writing within the period allowed.

The consequences of rejection can range from termination of the contract to delay in payment and the additional cost of investigating the rejection. It is therefore reasonable that if rejections are found invalid the buyer should be required to compensate the seller for the effect of these consequences, some of which will have occurred by the time the invalidity is established.

Whether a rejection is ultimately shown to be valid or not, there is a danger that the goods are in a contractual limbo in terms of where lies property and risk and so it is important to make provision for this so that, amongst other things, one side has the loss/damage risk insured. As a corollary the contract should also nominate the party which is to have responsibility for moving rejected goods around.

Sometimes rejection clauses specify a timeframe within which appeals have to be lodged. The seller should ensure that he has in place the procedures to trigger the lodging of an appeal very swiftly after receiving notice of a rejection with which he disagrees. It is no good for rejected items to be returned by the customer and left lying in Goods Inwards for several months before anybody notices! Procedures should also exist for handling rejected goods so they do not accidentally (or deliberately!) become re-mixed with other 'good' goods.

RISK – property does not pass

Do

a) Ensure the contract has a clause on passage of property.

b) Retain property until the last possible moment

Don't

a) Agree to 'vesting' clauses.

The key question in the passage of property is the point or time at which it is conveyed and where the balance of advantage lies. On the one hand retaining property in the goods until payment has been made in full (so called Romalpa clauses) gives the company security in so far as, if payment is not made it still owns the goods and thus its remedy for non-payment would include recovery of the goods for sale elsewhere. On the other hand if the goods are consumable, are inaccessible or likely to have deteriorated since delivery, such a remedy I s not that helpful and if property has passed to the customer then a clearer case exists for legal action in respect of payment of the contract price. So, the choice inevitably depends on the nature of the goods and the characteristics of the customer.

Part of this equation is the degree to which it is reasonable for property to pass to the customer prior to delivery under so-called 'vesting' arrangements. These are usually sought by the customer in return for granting the facility for advance or interim payments. There is sense in the argument that his security for advancing monies is property in the goods or material parts thereof as they are purchased or allocated to the contract. However, it can be argued that if he has already enjoyed the advantage of a lower price in return for promising advance payments, why should he have the additional benefit of early passage of property in such goods or materials. Setting aside the principle there are two main difficulties with vesting clauses. Firstly, there is the problem of identifying materials or goods in respect of which passage has passed to the customer. This is because of the limitations of accounting systems to provide this sort of facility, complicated by the fact that the company may purchase the same items for many contracts and may have several contracts with many different customers, all of which include vesting clauses. Perhaps the best advice is that if a vesting clause has to be accepted then it should be ensured that it does not allow the customer any rights to verify compliance! The second concern is that care should be taken to ensure that property only passes if advance payments are actually made rather than just promised.

RISK – the goods are lost or damaged in transit

Do

a) Ensure the contract has a clause on passage of risk.

b) Seek the earliest possible transfer of risk.

c) Arrange appropriate insurance.

Don't

a) Carry risk in the acts or omissions of the customer.

In this context, risk simply means the risk of loss or damage to the goods somewhere between acquisition of the component parts and materials by the seller through to the point of physical delivery to or acceptance by the buyer. Each party normally wants the risk to be carried by the other side and so, when the point has been negotiated, the key issue is to ensure that insurance cover is arranged for the period and scope of the risk and that any other arrangements to safeguard the physical security of the material are in place. Although insurance policies may cover the risk of loss or damage caused other than by the seller's own acts or omissions, it is always prudent to have the contract state that the acts or omissions of the buyer are within his own responsibility and liability.

RISK – the goods fail after delivery/acceptance

Do

a) Avoid any post-delivery liability.

b) Exclude the provisions of the Sale of Goods Act.

c) Limit the extent and scope of express warranties.

Don't

a)   Assume customer dissatisfaction equates to a contractual liability.

b)   Agree to warranty bonds or retentions.

The primary objective is to avoid any liability once the contract is complete. Contract completion can mean many different things, but here it is used to convey the idea that performance of the contract has been achieved in so far as delivery is complete and acceptance has been attained. Whilst residual obligations may remain, the primary objective has been secured. Setting aside any residual obligations (eg to maintain the manufacturing drawings) the question is what liabilities arise regarding the delivered goods? If the customer can be persuaded by a lower price or other valuable consideration to accept all the risk once the contract is complete, so much the better. To avoid any risk the contract must achieve three things. Firstly, a clear and comprehensive statement on acceptance. Secondly, an express exclusion of implied warranties and undertakings, including those evoked under the auspices of the Sale of Goods Act. Finally, there must be no express warranty of any sort.

Exclusions of liability must be carefully worded but failure to expressly exclude the SOGA implied undertakings as to satisfactory quality and fitness for purpose mean they do apply unless a convincing argument (such as the customer having specified in detail his requirement and how the seller should achieve it) can be mounted to the contrary'. These undertakings are ill-defined in scope and timeframe and, if only for the sake of certainty, are best excluded in favour of an express warranty if the customer is not willing to carry all the post-delivery risk himself.

The aim of anyone on the seller's side who is responsible for drafting a warranty clause is to so restrict its scope and application as to render it virtually harmless and thus of no risk to the seller. The warranty period and the event (preferably physical delivery or contractual delivery if earlier (eg ex-works) and not acceptance, that starts the warranty clock ticking should be stated and the clause should list all the exclusions, of which the following are possible examples:

1)   Goods not covered by the warranty.

2)   Goods for which no warranty claim is received within the warranty period.

3) Goods not returned within the warranty period.

4) Goods exhibiting defects other than those which are a demonstrable failure against the contract specification.

5) Goods where the alleged defect is not reproducible by the seller.

6) Goods exhibiting defects likely to be attributable to

i) Wear and tear

ii) Improper use, maintenance or storage

iii) Defective components.

The warranty should also be clear as to whether design and manufacture are both covered. A warranty on manufacturing workmanship and materials means that one product exhibiting such a defect would be covered by the warranty, but a warranty covering the design may require the seller to remedy a defect in an entire consignment even though only one unit may exhibit the defect. Thus the difference between a manufacturing warranty and a warranty covering design as well is the scope and the scale of the risk. If the seller is to be liable under warranty then he must seek to have the choice of remedy within his control. The option to repair or replace or refund money should be his.

Thus it can be seen that a warranty as drafted by the seller, if given a free hand, will produce something of no practical worth to the buyer! It is all part of the game of moving risk around.

Needless to say, therefore, the prudent seller will carefully scrutinize all warranty claims and never assume that it (the product) must be wrong just because the customer says it's wrong. The wary customer will have his own views on warranty obligations and one way for him to impose his view is to demand a warranty retention or bond. The warranty retention means that some part of the contract price will not be paid until the customer is satisfied that all post-delivery problems have been satisfactorily ironed out. The warranty bond allows the buyer to call upon a third party to impart money in his direction if the seller fails to discharge warranty liabilities, notwithstanding that the contract price may have been paid in full.

RISK – technical data must be handed over

Do

a) Avoid any clause granting rights in intellectual property.

b) If unavoidable, deal with the issue with an eye to the future.

c) Grant rights only in deliverable data.

d) Limit the amount of deliverable data.

e) Grant rights only in that work required under the contract.

f) Grant rights in principle only, leaving terms to be negotiated later.

g) Grant rights in the following order

    i) use

    ii) use and copy

    iii) use, copy and modify.

h) Limit rights to the customer only.

i) Include express provisions regarding confidentiality.

Don't

a) Fall for the trap that because the customer has paid he must own all the IPR.

b) Forget to maximize IPR protection by patents etc.

Intellectual Property Rights (IPR) is the greatest asset the company has. The company's unique ideas, skills and reputation are what gives it its products, profits, position in the market place and its competitive advantage. More so than any other asset, it should be jealously guarded. Tangible assets such as plant and machinery which are stolen, damaged or destroyed by fire can be replaced, albeit with possible disruption to business operation. By contrast the full value of the intangible asset of intellectual property can never be restored once it is lost, either to the customer (who might otherwise have come back for more work which he feels able to do himself if he acquires the company's IPR), or to a competitor (who may well be able to make use of the information without actually infringing the IPR).

Setting aside the daunting prospect of a detailed thesis on IPR, the principal risk lies in possible obligations to hand technical information over to the customer. The company's best position is one where no rights are granted whatsoever. However, care must be taken as a contract which, for example, includes specified design work but which is entirely silent on IPR ma appear to achieve this position for the company. The risk is that the 1988 Copyright, Patents and Designs Act vests ownership of commissioned designs in the commissioner of the work (ie the customer) and not the designer, unless there is an agreement to the contrary. An agreement to the contrary is best recorded in the contract which should therefore ideally include a simple statement that all IPR vests in the company and no rights whatsoever are granted to the customer. This ideal and simple position is not likely to be easy to secure as customers who are paying, for example, for design and development work may want, as a matter of policy, and need, as a matter of practical application, to acquire some rights in the IPR.

In discussing this issue with the customer at the time of contract negotiation, a weather eye should be kept on future business prospects with that customer. A stark unwillingness even to discuss may be enough in itself to make the customer go elsewhere. Alternatively, granting the customer free, unfettered rights in everything is to prejudice the opportunity that might otherwise have existed of the customer having to come back for more. 'Knowledge is power' is nowhere truer than in the minefield of IPR exploitation.

Any grant of rights by the company should be as limited as possible. The first step is to restrict the rights to data which is actually deliverable under the contract and then to limit the definition of what is deliverable. Then, when it is time to deliver the data, the detail put into the deliverable material should be as sparse as possible so as to be minimally compliant with the least onerous interpretation of the definition! 'What they haven't got, they can't use.' In any event, every effort should be made to grant rights only in that IPR generated under the contract. Any pre-existing IPR brought to the contract by the company should be excluded from the grant. Indeed, any and all such 'background' knowledge should be excluded.

If possible, any grant of rights should be in principle only and an express statement should be included in the contract that detailed terms will be agreed later. Apart from the fact that agreements-to-agree are difficult to enforce both legally and in practice, this leaves the door open for future negotiations on the terms (both fees and further restrictions!) at a time when the customer, having become captive, has much less bargaining power than at the pre-contract stage when the full heat of competition is bearing down on the company.

When rights are being granted the extent of the rights should be considered carefully. Supplying software to a customer carries the implied licence that he is free to use it. This is obviously sensible since it is absolutely inherent in the intended purpose of the contract. Nevertheless, that use can be limited to a particular place and to particular machines. The right to copy can again be limited. Sticking with the example of software, the right to copy might be expressly limited to the implied right to copy for back-up and security purposes only. In granting the right to modify there can be an implied obligation that the customer must be put into a position where he can actually exercise that right, eg by handing over all the technical information necessary for that purpose, regardless of whether that information was expressly deliverable under the contract.

A further restriction is to limit the rights to the customer, only denying him the right to sub licence or assign the benefits or otherwise so as to prevent him from passing the information outside of his organization and potentially into the hands of competitors. Whatever the extent of the rights granted, the company should ensure that the recipient of sensitive information or data, (whether just the customer or in the worse situation his subcontractors and other third parties) is bound by obligations of confidentiality. Confidentiality agreements, which are sometimes known as Nondisclosure Agreements, primarily bind the recipient not to disclose the information without written permission, to safeguard it and to use it only for a specified purpose. This last point provides another opportunity to restrict the rights being granted. To enhance the degree of protection the company might consider requiring individual recipients as well as corporate recipients to enter into such agreements. Whether the information is actually disclosed under the terms of the contract subject to conditions of confidentiality, or whether it is disclosed under a full licence agreement, the two over-riding aims are to RESTRICT AND PROTECT. Restrict the rights. Protect the information.

In some ways the greatest danger is that, despite the terms of the contract, many personnel working on the contract who may either be ignorant of or not understand the IPR provisions of the contract, may just give the information away anyway in the naive belief that if the customer is paying he must automatically own all the IPR. Allowing this risk to exist is unforgivable and it can be avoided by including a clear briefing on the IPR position at the Contract Launch Meeting.

Finally, it should be remembered that in addition to protecting the information by the terms of the contract and any supplementary confidentiality or licence agreements, consideration should be given to statutory forms of protection (eg patents and design registration) and to practical measures such as the use of bold (in both senses of the word) copyright legends on documents and software, procedures to prevent unintentional release and an awareness campaign centered on the abiding first principle of IPR:

'It's ours, they can't have it!'

RISK – breach of third party IPR

Do

a)   Identify all IPR issues at the bid stage.

b)   Secure comprehensive licences from subcontractors/suppliers.

c)   Grant specific licences to the customer.

d)   Secure indemnities from subcontractors,/suppliers.

e)   Secure indemnities from the customer.

f)   Insure against the risk.

Don't

a)   Ignore IPR.

b)   Give indemnities.

If protecting the company against the risk of its IPR being compromised is a big enough challenge, then equally demanding is dealing with the risk of infringement of third party IPR. In many projects the IPR situation is a minefield of conflicting interests and requirements (see diagram).

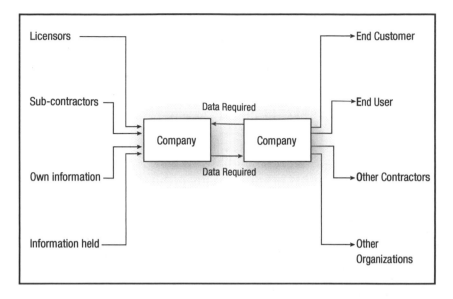

Data Flow

For these purposes the word 'data' is used very generally to describe any information which may be protected or protectable by an intellectual property right. So this might range from copyright material (eg drawings, specifications, computer software) through design information (eg the unique shape or appearance) to patent details (the essence of an invention) and even the use of trademarks/names (eg product names and logos).

Coming into the company will be data from licensors, sub-contractors and perhaps teaming partners, each of whom may be providing data which they own, have licensed from someone else or have stolen (intentionally or in innocent ignorance of a proprietor). The company's own data may be a combination of that which is genuinely the product of its own efforts, that which it happens to possess (ie where the original source is obscure) and that which it possesses as a result of other contracts. Data produced under other contracts may have intellectual property rights vested in the relevant customer(s), the company, third parties or combinations thereof. Data delivered to the customer may be destined for his own use or to third parties under licence or contract, each of whom may have further needs beyond their own use. Each link in the chain may need rights to possess, use, copy, merge or modify the data which it handles. Each may need the right to sub-licence, assign, sell or otherwise dispose of the data. Each may wish to secure intellectual property right protection for its part or parts of the whole work. Each may want exclusive rights in jointly created data. All data transmitted may be governed by confidentiality agreements. Data may have come into the possession of individual parties legitimately, by breach of some restrictive agreement by that party, by breach of some restrictive agreement by another party or because the public domain now includes that data.

Thus, if for the purposes of this discussion, the first and second parties are the company and the customer, then all the other parties shown (ie which may have a contractual relationship with customer or company) plus any others remote from or not ostensibly linked to the chain are the third parties from whom lies the risk of allegation of breach of intellectual property right. Any such third party may allege a breach of intellectual property right. On the basis that prevention is better than cure, the lowest risk approach for the company is to ensure that the entire 'IPR picture' is clear and that all necessary licences and permissions are in place in writing. The sooner this is done the better. It is hardly ideal to supply the customer under contract with copies of subcontractor copyright work, only then to find that the company had no right to make such copies. Apart from the unplanned, additional cost of settling with those parties whose intellectual property rights have been innocently or intentionally (?) breached, there is the much higher impact (although probably lower probability) risk of injunction which could bring the whole operation to a standstill. Take a chance on someone else's intellectual property and you 'bet the company'.

Lack of time and impracticability sometimes prevent full researches being done and the proper measures being put in place prior to bidding or prior to making a contractual commitment to the customer. In these circumstances the company is exposed to the risk of alleged breach of intellectual property rights and, following the principles of good commercial risk management, if a risk is carried then opportunities should be sought to pass to someone else the consequences of the risk materializing. The best approach is to seek indemnities from both 'providers' of data (ie licensors, subcontractors etc) and 'consumers' of data (ie the customer). The logic to use with the providers is that they are the experts in the genesis of their products and data, and must easily be able to offer an indemnity unless there is something to hide! With the customer the logic is surprisingly similar. Only the consumer can know to whom and for what reason data may be disclosed. Hence he too can surely provide an indemnity unless there is something to hide! Notice that the company appears to know nothing about anything! This position of innocence is a good one but for the fact that in most cases of breach of intellectual property rights, innocence is no defence. Hence the importance of the company being protected by indemnities from both data providers and data consumers that pass to them the responsibility for defending claims and the liability for the cost of defence, the cost of settlement and, in the perfect case, the cost of any consequential effects such as the disruption to the company's operation.

If avoiding the risk is not feasible, if passing the consequences elsewhere is not an option, for example because the providers and consumers do not agree to offer indemnities, then the last option is to insure the risk. Indeed, this is a common policy for companies to hold but, nevertheless, this should not be seen as a 'soft' option. 'We needn't worry because it's covered by insurance' is a wholly unacceptable and dangerous ethos.

This essay should be sufficient to show that the greatest risk lies in simply ignoring the problem. Education of all concerned within the company as to the principles of intellectual property rights is in many ways the best form of practical protection. The subject is seen as a black art for obscure experts and while the legal, statutory, procedural and international dimensions of intellectual property matters should not be underestimated for a nano-second, the rules of simple self protection should be understood by all. Returning momentarily to the issue of indemnities, there is a straightforward rule which says that if it is good to be the beneficiary of an indemnity, it must be bad to be the benefactor. The only possible benefit to the company in giving an indemnity would be to limit the scope and monetary value of a liability which might otherwise be by implication an open-ended liability.

RISK – a third party is injured

Do

a) Appoint a product safety officer.

b) Ensure that operating manuals are comprehensive on safety.

c) Use hazard warnings.

d) Seek indemnities from suppliers.

e) Insure the risk.

Don't

a) Dispose of records.

Thanks to the privity of contract rule, in most cases only the customer has a contractual remedy against the supplier in respect of defective goods. Goods which do not meet the requirements of the contract or are not fit for purpose, may allow the customer various remedies designed to rectify the situation. However, these are not necessarily defective goods. A defective product has the special meaning that it is 'a product, the safety of which is not such as persons are generally entitled to expect'. This introduces the idea that defective products are those which may cause personal injury or death. Thus a corporate customer cannot suffer as such but third parties, such as individuals who work for the customer or who are innocent bystanders, may suffer as a result of defective products. Since these third parties, by definition, are not a party to the contract they must look for a remedy other than a contractual one. The law of tort allows an injured party action against the manufacturer but he must prove negligence, which can be extraordinarily difficult. The 1987 Consumer Protection Act overcame this by imposing a so-called strict liability on various entities in the supply chain in respect of injury or death caused by a defective product.

Under the Consumer Protection Act the injured party only has to show that the product was defective, that it led to the injury and that the defendant produced the product or otherwise falls within the ambit of the Act. For these purposes products include goods, electricity and products incorporated in another product, but not immovable things. Injury is death, personal injury and damage to domestic property but the remedy excludes damage or loss of or lack of utility in the defective product and consequential financial loss. Liability for defective products lies with:

a) The producers.

b) Persons who hold themselves out as producers.

c) Persons who, in the course of business, import the product into the EU intending to supply it to another.

d) Suppliers who, after a request by the person injured, fail identify to him within a reasonable time persons listed (a) – (c).

Although the Consumer Protection Act is intended primarily to protect consumers, it is clearly the case that a company not trading in consumer transactions can still be liable to injured third parties if, for example, it produces goods for incorporation into products that find their way into the public domain.

With these risks in mind the company should appoint someone who takes responsibility on behalf of the company for ensuring that in all stages of a product's life – design, manufacture, use – the highest regard is paid to safety aspects. The safety of a product is not limited to its intrinsic characteristics. The packaging and operating instructions are equally important and every effort should be made to draw attention to features or applications which pose a hazard.

If the company's products incorporate the products of suppliers then, although the supplier's products may be at fault, the company's liability is not diminished but protection can be sought in the form of an indemnity from the supplier in favour of the company against the financial consequences of a defective product claim against the company.

Defective product or product liability insurance is also a common form of protection carried by many companies.

The risk in defective products is of long life. Action can be brought within three years of the injury or within three years of the injured party becoming aware of the injury, whichever is the later. However, there is an outer limit of ten years from the date on which the defective product was supplied. If a claim is made, the possible defences are:

a) Development risks, meaning that the company must show that at the time the product was marketed the available scientific and technical knowledge meant the defect could not have been discovered at that time.

b) Products 'not supplied', eg if they were stolen.

c) Contributory negligence. The injured party caused or contributed to the injury.

The longevity of the liability and the means of defence indicate the importance of retaining design and manufacturing information and related material for a long time, perhaps even beyond the time at which the product is no longer made or sold at all.

Part three

PROJECT MANAGEMENT

Planning a project

A large amount of the work of the project manager is concerned with making plans. There are special techniques which make this process easier. Many of these project management tools are now available in the form of computer software, but it is also important to understand the principles on which they work.

This chapter begins by examining the various ways in which one task can dependent on another. These relationships can be represented in flow-charts, network diagrams and Gantt charts. The work breakdown structure is also introduced. This document is central to the planning – and control – of a project.

However sophisticated the visual appearance of your plans, they will only be as valuable as the data on which they are based and the assumptions which you make. This chapter also discusses the principles of preparing budgets and schedules and of obtaining realistic estimates.

Planning and control are two sides of the same coin. The planning tools you select, and the way you use them, are crucial to the effectiveness of your monitoring system. By the end of this chapter, you should have a good understanding of the issues which are at stake.

Dependencies

A dependency is an activity which is connected to other activities.

In any project, there will be some things which cannot happen until other things have been accomplished. The dependencies which you build into your plan may be:

- Internal or external

- Mandatory or discretionary.

Internal dependencies are ones in which all the activities involved are under the control of the project manager. A simple example would be the mailing of a questionnaire which clearly cannot happen until the questionnaire has been printed.

External dependencies occur when project activities depend on something outside the project. For example, if a project cannot proceed unless it receives a grant from the National Lottery Fund, it is impossible to hire the staff and order the equipment until you know whether or not the grant application has been successful. It might, however, be possible to go ahead with other aspects of the project which do not require a major financial investment while you were waiting for the decision about the grant.

Mandatory dependencies are unavoidable. They often involve physical constraints. For example, you cannot tile the sides of a swimming pool before you have excavated the hole. You cannot test a computer program before you have designed it. Some dependencies, however, may not be as unavoidable as they appear:

> 'You may have thought that it was impossible to take publicity photographs of an encyclopaedia before it is printed. But if we waited until we had printed copies before we started our publicity, sales would be delayed unacceptably. We mock up a few pages in advance and photograph them for our leaflets.'

Discretionary dependencies, as the name suggests, are decided on the discretion of the project manager. He or she may decide to follow a standard procedure (if such a procedure exists) or, if there are specific reasons for doing things differently on a particular project, to depart from this standard way of organizing activities.

> *'We normally complete the fitting of the kitchens and bathrooms before we pass our houses over to the sales department. However, we decided on this occasion to make a special selling point of the fact that buyers could choose their own cabinets and bathroom suites. This meant that the fitting had to wait until the houses were sold.'*

If any of your dependencies are discretionary, it is important to document the decisions you have made. This helps you remember that you had a choice about these matters and allows you to change your mind if circumstances alter.

It is often easier to identify dependencies by working backwards. Think about the end result you want to achieve, then consider what has to be done before this can happen.

The most common form of dependency is for the start of one activity to be dependent on the finish of another. This is known as a finish-to-start dependency. It may be possible for the second activity to start as soon as the first has finished, or there may be a time lag. For example, the walls of a house cannot be painted until they are plastered. However, painting cannot take place immediately after plastering – it must wait until the plaster has been allowed to cure.

Three other types of dependency also occur quite commonly:

- Start-to-finish – where an activity cannot finish before another activity has started, or there is a known time relationship between the start of one activity and the finish of another

- Finish-to-finish – where activities must finish at the same time, or there is a known time relationship between the finish of the activities

- Start-to-start – where activities must start at the same time, or there is a known time relationship between the start of the two activities.

An example of a start-to-finish dependency could be the production of business cards for the project team and the installation of telephones.

Although the design of the cards can be settled, the details cannot be final-ized until telephone numbers have been allocated. The finish of the activity 'producing business cards' therefore has to wait until the start of the activity 'installing telephones'.

A finish-to-finish dependency could be the transport of a celebrity speaker to a presentation and the entry and seating of the audience. If either the speaker or the audience has to wait too long, the success of the pres-entation is jeopardized. An example of a start-to-start dependency could be the excavation of a tunnel and the reinforcing of the roof.

Flowcharts

A flowchart is a diagram which depicts a sequence of interdepend-ent activities.

Flowcharts are used in ordinary, operational management to examine processes and look for more effective methods of doing them. In project management, they can be used to map out the general shape of what needs to be done.

In essence, a flowchart is a series of boxes linked by arrows. The direc-tion of the arrows shows the chronological order in which activities must be completed. The shape of the boxes is also significant. Conventionally, these basic shapes are used:

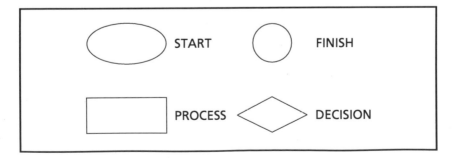

Further symbols are sometimes used to represent data, documents and other elements of the process.

Here is a very simple flowchart which shows the process a company used to handle applications for a training programme:

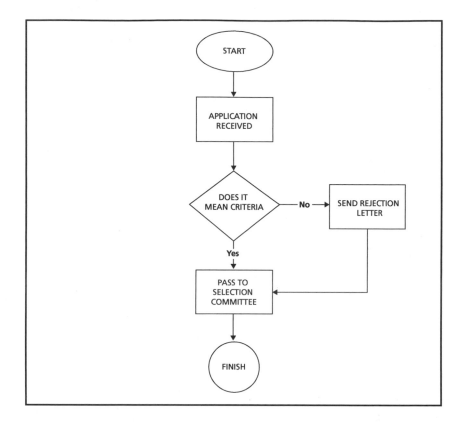

Flowcharts can help you consider whether you are really doing things in the most logical way. For example, the manager who produced the flow-chart above made this comment:

'When I put the process down on paper like this, I realized that the initial screening of applications wasn't quite as simple as I had thought. It often happened that candidates misunderstood some of the questions on the form. In the past, one of our best trainees had not filled in the form correctly. If we used the system I had described on the flowchart, he would never have got on the training scheme. Of course, I would have liked to have redesigned the form, but unfortunately that was something which Head Office had to deal with. In the meantime,

I was stuck with the existing version. So I added another loop to the flowchart, like this:'

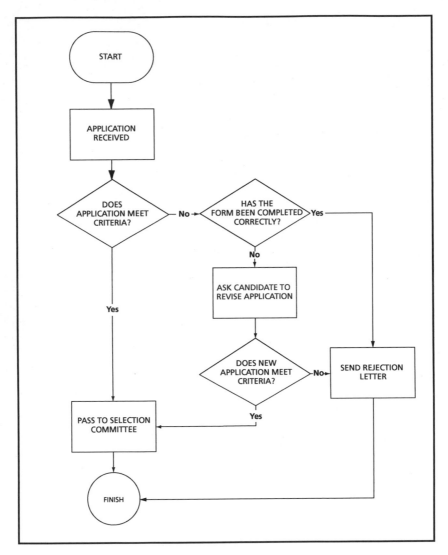

Flowcharts are also a very good way of clarifying which activities cannot begin until other activities have been completed. They can even reveal dependencies which you were not aware of:

'I drew up a flowchart to plan what we had to do to publish a new edition of one of our textbooks. My original idea was to send the old

edition to a specialist editor for updating and then to ask the production department to get some costings for making up the new pages and reprinting. I quickly realized that this was not a sensible way to go about things. I had to get some costings before I invested in the new edition, to know if the project was viable. It seemed like a chicken-and-egg situation. How could I get costings if I didn't know the extent of the changes which were necessary? And how could I employ a specialist to revise the text if I didn't know whether they would make the book too expensive to market? The answer was to split the revision into two stages. First, I employed the expert to advise me on the level of changes which were necessary. Then I got the costings. Then I asked the expert to complete the job and rewrite the passages which needed updating.'

Flowcharts are useful tools when you are trying to conceptualize a project. They will highlight areas where your knowledge is inadequate or where you have not thought through all the implications of your plan. They do not, however, provide all the information you need for detailed scheduling and resource planning. In order to plan these things, you will need to draw up a work breakdown structure and, on a project of any complexity, use some form of network diagram.

Work breakdown structure

A work breakdown structure (WBS) is a method of breaking down a project into individual elements which can be scheduled and costed.

When you begin to plan a project, you are unlikely to know all the details of what has to be done. In fact, if you do have this information, you are probably not dealing with a project at all, but with a repeatable process. Projects are, by definition, unique. You cannot look back in your files and discover how long it took – or how much it cost – to achieve exactly the same outcome the last time around. However, although every project is a one-off, it is almost certain that all of the activities involved have been done before, although not in this exact combination. A WBS is a method of splitting a project up into small parts for which you can predict the resource requirements and which you can build into a schedule.

The first step in constructing a WBS is to identify the main stages of the project. These may correspond to the phases in the project life cycle:

- Initiation

- Design

- Construction

- Operation and evaluation.

The titles – and the number – of these phases may differ, depending on the type of project and the conventions used by individual organizations. The basic structure of the project is often shown on a diagram, like this:

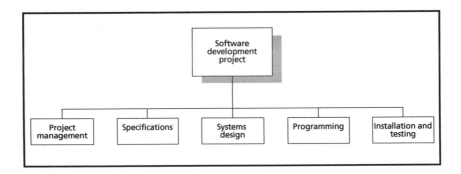

Once the main stages of the project have been established, the second step in developing a WBS is to divide each stage into smaller elements. There is more than one school of thought about what these elements should consist of. Some project managers simply divide the stages into chunks which relate to different areas of the project. For example, here is part of a WBS for the production of a play:

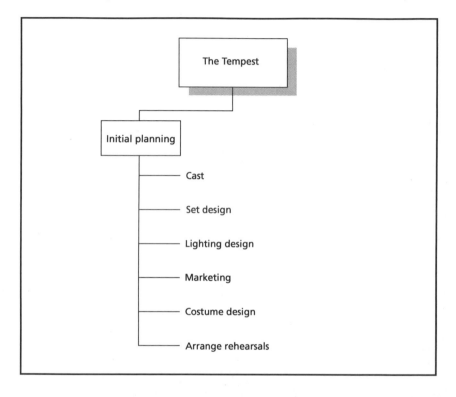

Other project managers insist that each element should relate specifically to a particular project deliverable. This approach has significant advantages, because it focuses attention on the agreed scope of the project and ensures that resources are not wasted on anything which lies outside it. It is also much easier to check that each stage in the project has actually finished.

If the elements were expressed in terms of deliverables, the example above could look like this:

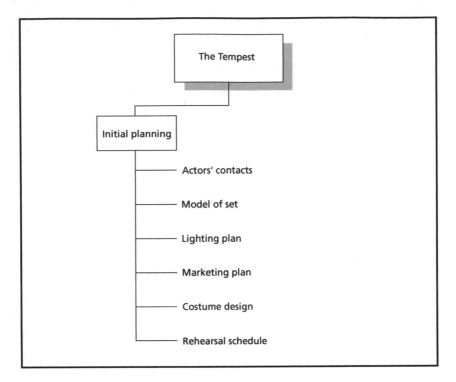

The final step is to sub-divide the items on the WBS into separate activities or tasks. On a relatively straightforward project, this may be done after the second step. On a very complex project, the WBS may need to include several more tiers before the level of individual activities is reached.

The activities listed must meet certain criteria:

1.   They must be measurable in terms of cost, effort, resources and time

2.   They must result in a single end product which can be checked

3.   They must be the responsibility of a single individual.

We will look at these three issues in turn.

Measurable activities

The details of the resources needed to complete an activity, and what they will cost, are recorded. The total cost of the project will be the sum of the cost of all its activities. If costs change, the effect on the final costs can be calculated. The time needed to complete an activity is built into the schedule.

How much detail do you need about the activities in your project?

It is also important that activities are on a scale that is worth measuring. For example, suppose that, at some point in your project, you had to mail 100 questionnaires to potential customers. It would be quite possible to break down the task of posting 100 questionnaires into much smaller components:

- Photocopy questionnaire

- Photocopy covering letter

- Clip letters to questionnaires

- Fold letters and questionnaires

- Fill envelopes

- Attach address labels

- Attach postage stamps

- Put through franking machine.

While it might be useful to mentally rehearse a list like this when considering what is involved in posting the questionnaires, this level of detail is not usually necessary in the WBS. As a project manager, you need to balance the control you get by specifying each part of what has to happen against the resources necessary to monitor activities in such detail. This is an area where the priorities of the project manager and the operational manager are different. If you are in charge of a busy despatch room, where hundreds of letters and packages are sent out every day, it would be important to know exactly how long it took to put 100 envelopes through the franking machine. Your staffing levels and capital costs would be calculated from information of this sort and you would need to make periodic checks that your staff were achieving the expected rate of work. However, if the posting of questionnaires only happens once or twice in the history of the project, it is not important to know exactly how long each stage in the process will take. An estimate for the entire activity will probably be enough for your purposes.

Defined outcomes

Each activity needs a specific end product. This makes it possible for everyone involved to be clear when an activity has actually been completed. It also allows the outcome to be checked against pre-determined quality standards. The aspects of an outcome which it is necessary to define will depend on the requirements of the customer, who may be either inside or outside the project team.

Here are two sets of specifications for activity outcomes. The first is for a set of briefing notes to be handed to casual staff.

The briefing notes should

- Contain clear step-by-step instructions
- Contain a list of do's and don'ts
- Comply with company policy statement HR054
- Occupy more than two A4 pages.

And here is a specification for a press pack issued at the launch of a project:

Specification for press pack

- 500 word press release

- Three colour photographs of exterior of building

- Six colour photographs of interior of building

- Contact list for interviews

- Contents to be presented in project folder

- Copy checked by project manager

- Printed copies available by 3.7.05

The amount of detail you include in a specification will obviously depend on the importance of the outcome to the success of the project:

> 'We wanted to invite 50 key employers in the region to a presentation about a new training scheme we were developing. It was important that these invitations were directed at the right people within each organization, so I specified that the PA telephoned the 50 selected companies and checked on the identity of the individual who was responsible for staff training – and also how his or her name was spelt. We also sent out a marketing shot to a much wider range of organizations. Here, we were expecting a lower percentage response and I simply specified that the PA should extract 2,000 organizations from a database which contained the names of companies with more than 25 employees. This time, the envelopes were not addressed to named individuals but to 'The Training Manager' in each organization.'

As more importance was attached to the mailing of the invitations to the presentation than to the general mailshot, a greater amount of detail and a higher level of specification were felt to be necessary.

Responsibility for activities

Finally, each activity must be the responsibility of a particular individual. This may be the person who actually undertakes the activity, or the person who is responsible for checking that is has been successfully completed. (In many cases, these two individuals can be the same person.) Projects can involve a large team of people working together in new combinations on a wide range of activities. It is therefore essential that everything that must be done is clearly assigned to a specific individual.

Documenting the WBS

As well as the overall WBS, the project manager needs to prepare activity (or task) definition forms. A separate form is completed for each activity, giving the following information:

- Code linking the activity to the WBS

- Name of activity

- Description of deliverable/outcome

- Quality standard of deliverable/outcome

- Dependencies (description, type and who is responsible)

- Start and finish dates

- Resource needs

- Costs (amount and type)

- Individual responsible.

In most situations, a project manager will have to consult with other people, both inside and outside the project team, before describing activities in the detail required on the activity definition form. In a project of any complexity, it is not possible to know the dependencies and start and finish dates of activities before drawing up a network diagram.

Networks

A network is a diagram which shows the dependencies between the activities in a project. It is used to schedule these activities and plan the optimum use of resources.

Like flowcharts, network diagrams show the dependent relationships between activities in a project. Network diagrams also give information about the timing of each activity. This makes it possible to:

- Arrange activities so that the project can be completed in the shortest time
- Make the best use of resources
- Predict how long the whole project will take
- Construct a detailed schedule.

All networks are made up of nodes connected by arrows showing the direction of time. There are, however, two quite different types of network diagram:

- Activity on arrow (AOA)
- Activity on node (AON).

AOA networks

In an AOA network, the activity is, not surprisingly, shown on an arrow:

A
_____→
10 days

Event nodes at each end of the arrow mark the start and finish of the activity:

This shows that Event 1 (the start of Activity A) and Event 2 (the finish of Activity A) are separated by 10 days. The node which ends one activity can also mark the start of another activity:

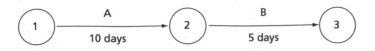

Using nodes and arrows like these, it is possible to construct a network which shows the dependencies between the various activities. In the example which follows, a manager describes a situation in which she needed to schedule several linked activities:

I was planning the writing and production of a technical booklet. After the text was written, it would need to be checked by experts. It would then be edited, desktop published and printed. I also needed to get a rough design done for the booklet. This had to happen before the editing stage. There were also some cartoons to be drawn sometime after the text was written and before the booklet went to DTP. It wasn't necessary for the experts to check the design or the cartoons, but the cartoons should not be commissioned until the experts had been through the text and the general design of the booklet had been settled.

The manager began by preparing a chart showing how long she expected each activity to take and the dependencies between activities:

Activity number	Description	Time (days)	Dependencies
A	write text	10	-
B	experts check	5	after A
C	design	3	after A
D	cartoons	6	after C
E	edit	3	after B and C
F	DTP	4	after D and E
G	print	5	after F

The manager then used this information to begin to draw up an AOA network:

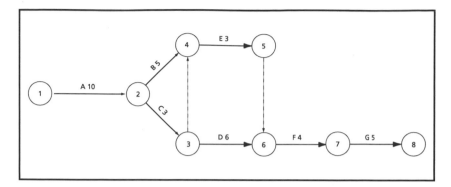

The dotted arrow between Events 3 and 4 is a dummy activity. Although a dummy activity has no duration or number, it is necessary to include it for the logic of the diagram to be correct. This one shows that Activity E cannot start until Activities B and C have both ended. (The editing and the drawing of the cartoons cannot start until the experts have checked the text and the design has been settled.) Similarly, the dummy arrow between Events 5 and 6 shows that Activity F (DTP) cannot start before Activities D (cartoons) and E (edit) have both finished.

When you draw up a network diagram, ask yourself:

- **What has to happen before this activity can happen?**

- **Now that this activity has happened, what else can happen?**

At this point, the diagram shows the logical relationships between the various activities and the time that they will each take. It does not yet show the duration of the whole project or the time at which each activity must start and finish. In order to complete the diagram, more information must be added to the event nodes.

In an AOA network, each event node displays the following information:

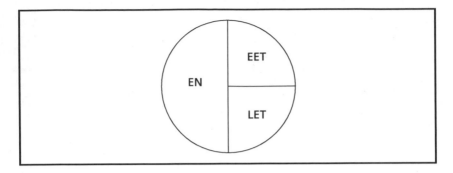

EN = Event Number: to identify the event

EET= Earliest Event Time: the earliest time at which the event can begin

LET = Latest Event Time: the latest time at which the event can begin

The diagram is completed by following these steps:

1. Start by working out the EET for each event. Begin with the node on the far left of the diagram. This is the start of the project and is conventionally given the time 00. It does not matter what unit of time is used on a network diagram. It could be months, weeks, days, hours, or even seconds, depending on the nature of the project. It is, however, essential that the same unit is used consistently throughout the network.

2. Working towards the right of the diagram, find the EET of each event. If an event node only has a single activity arrow leading into it, it is very simple to calculate the EET of the second event. Just add the duration time of the intervening activity. If two or more activities end in the same event node, you have two (or more) EET to choose from. Take the latest time.

3. When you reach the final event node, calculate the EET as usual and then copy this figure into the LET box below it.

4. Now work backwards through the diagram, calculating the LET for each event. This time, subtract the duration of the activity. If two activities begin in the same event node, take the earliest time for the LET.

5. When you reach the first event node again, you should have a LET of 00. If you do not, you have made a mistake (either with your calculations or with the logic of your diagram) and must go back and check where you have gone wrong.

After completing these steps, the AOA diagram shown above looks like this:

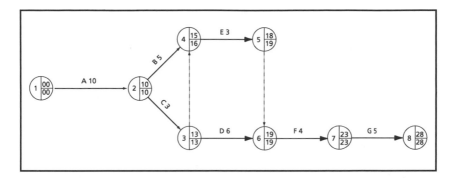

It now shows the earliest and latest time that each activity can begin or end. For some activities, there will be some extra time available. This is known as **slack**, or **float**. For other activities, the time available will be exactly the same as the time the activity will take. These are known as **critical** activities, because any delay here will delay the completion of the entire project. There is a chain of these critical activities through the diagram, known as the **critical path**. It is conventionally indicated with bolder arrows:

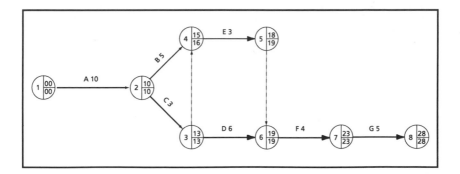

You can locate the critical path on an AOA network by identifying those activities with no float. For each activity, subtract the EET in the node where it begins from the LET in the node where it ends. This is the maximum time available for the activity to happen. Compare this figure with the duration of the activity. If these two figures are the same, the activity is critical.

Critical activities are those with no float.

AON networks

In this type of network, the details of the activities are written on the nodes themselves. The arrows are used to show the dependencies between the activities. Drawn up as an AON network, the basic framework of diagram shown earlier would look like this:

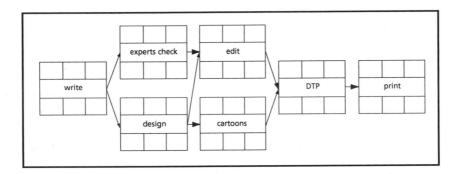

Each node in an AON network carries the following information:

Early start	Duration	Early finish
	Task name	
Late start	Slack	Late finish

Once you have assembled your activities in a logical order, follow these steps to complete the network:

1. Starting at the left hand side of the diagram, fill in the earliest time an activity can start, and its duration. Use the duration to fill in the earliest time the activity can finish.

2. Move on to the next box and do the same. The earliest start time is always the same as the earliest finish time in the preceding box. If two boxes lead into one, take the later time.

3. When you have worked your way across to the node at the right of the diagram, copy the figure for the early finish time into the late finish time.

4. Now work backward through the diagram, using the durations to fill in the latest finish time and the latest start time in each box. The latest finish time is the same as the latest start time in the box connected by an arrow on the right. If you have two latest start times, take the earlier time.

5. Finally, fill in the slack time by subtracting the early finish time from the late finish time in each box. If these figures are the same, there is no slack.

The completed AON diagram looks like this:

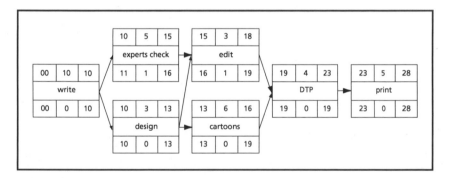

The critical path runs through the activities with no slack.

As you can see, there is no need for dummy activities in an AON network. Another advantage of the AON network is that the slack, or float, is specified on each node. Many people find this type of network easier to construct and understand than an AOA diagram.

Other types of dependency

In the diagrams we have drawn so far, we have made the assumption that an activity can begin as soon as the activity which precedes it in the network has finished. There are also other types of dependency which it may be necessary to represent on a network.

On an AON network, it is possible to add extra information to the arrow. For example, this example shows that 10 time units must elapse between the end of one activity and the start of the next:

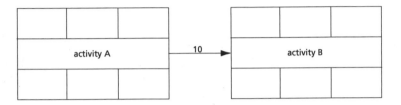

It is also possible to draw an AON network in which the arrows start, or finish, at different ends of the box, indicating finish-to-finish, start-to-start and start-to-finish dependencies.

Gantt charts

Gantt charts have been around since the 1920s. They are a simple, but remarkably effective, method of representing a project plan. They can be drawn up by hand, presented on specially designed wallcharts with magnetic or adhesive strips, or generated by a computer. The basic framework is a chart in which time is measured along the horizontal scale and activities are listed vertically.

	1	2	3	4	5	6	7	8
TASK A	▓	▓						
TASK B			▓					
TASK C				▓				
TASK D					▓	▓		
TASK E							▓	
TASK F								▓

This chart shows a simple project which is scheduled to last eight weeks. It involves six tasks (A – F) which must happen sequentially. The shaded bars indicate the duration of the tasks and the point in the schedule at which they should happen.

It is very easy to show parallel activities on a Gantt chart:

	1	2	3	4	5	6	7	8
TASK A	▓	▓	▓					
TASK B		▓	▓					
TASK C				▓				
TASK D					▓			
TASK E					▓			
TASK F							▓	▓

In this chart, Tasks A and B can happen at the same time. Tasks 5 and 6 can also go on concurrently.

It is also possible to show the critical path on a Gantt chart:

	1	2	3	4	5	6	7	8
TASK A	▓	▓	▓					
TASK B		▓	▓					
TASK C				▓				
TASK D					▓	▓		
TASK E					▓			
TASK F							▓	▓

On a relatively small project, a chart of this kind can be an excellent way of showing what slack there is in a schedule. It is also possible to indicate a variety of relationships between activities. Some may happen sequentially, while others can have common, or staggered, finish or start times. These dependencies are easy to understand on a Gantt chart, especially if it is possible to move the bars which represent the activities. On a complex project, the relationships between the activities may become less easy to understand when represented in this way and it will probably be necessary to link the Gantt chart to a detailed network diagram.

In the past, the main drawback of Gantt charts was the time it took to draw them up and, even more significantly, the time it took to amend them when changes were made to the schedule. Nowadays, however, they can be generated and updated automatically by project management software programs.

Choosing your software

It is almost unthinkable these days to attempt to manage a project without the use of a computer. In this section we will briefly examine some of the options which are available and suggest some of the questions you should ask when considering the purchase of software.

The simplest type of computer programs which you may be offered for project management purposes are little more than a collection of templates to enable you draw your own Gantt charts or network diagrams. It is usually quicker to use a computer than to work by hand, and the results will certainly look more professional. However, the diagrams you produce will not necessarily be 'intelligent'. If you want to revise them at a later date, you cannot update them automatically.

In true project planning software, Gantt charts and network diagrams are linked to databases and spreadsheets. Data is usually entered into a chart and presented automatically in a graphical format. Some of these packages are extremely sophisticated. Among other features, they can offer:

- The ability to schedule thousands of activities

- What-if-analysis

- Automatic coding of activities

- Views of the project at different levels of detail

- Project organization templates which you can adapt to the needs of your own project

- Graphs and charts showing cash flow

- To-do lists, arranged by priority

- Variance reports

- Templates for reports and other project documentation

- Pop-up help files

- Clipart to include in your presentations

- The ability to customize the design of your own charts

- Input from more than one user

- Compatibility with other software programs.

If you enjoy using a computer, you will probably find that some of the project management packages available are extremely tempting. They can give you the freedom to examine your data in a wide variety of formats and produce an integrated set of very professional-looking reports and documents. The danger, of course, is that one selects a package which is too complex for the needs of the project. However user-friendly a program claims to be, it will require a certain amount of familiarity to use it effectively. It is important to consider whether you have the time available to learn to use a program properly, or whether this time would be spent more cost-effectively on other aspects of the project. You should also consider whether the type of charts and reports it produces will be of genuine use to yourself and to other members of the team. On a simple project, a basic Gantt chart may actually be the most effective way of displaying the schedule.

Here are some questions to ask when considering project planning software:

- What specification of computer does it require to run efficiently?

- What specification of monitor is necessary?

- Do I want software which will work in a Windows environment?

- Is a colour printer necessary to get the full benefit of the graphics?

- How many activities do I need to schedule?

- Do I want to use AOA or AON networks?

- Do I want to use Gantt charts?

- Do I want to be able to customize the appearance of my documents?

- Do I want the software to plan and control costs as well as schedules?

- How easy is it to update schedules and budgets?

- What types of relationship (finish-to-start, start-to-start, etc) between activities do I want to use?

- Do I want on-screen help?

- How long will it take me to learn to use this program?

- What other applications, such as word-processing programs and spreadsheets, do I want to use in combination with this program?

- Can I import data from other project planning software?

- How many people will need to use the program at once?

- What reports will I need to print out?

- What other features are important to me?

As well as looking at the publicity material produced by the manufacturers, make sure that you have the opportunity to try out the software for yourself. If possible, it is also a very good idea to talk to managers who have used the program on a similar project to your own. Ask them about their experiences. What were the best and worst features of this software? Did it ever let them down?

When you are talking to other project managers about software, it is important to bear in mind a curious phenomenon which happens to even very computer-literate individuals. Once people have spent a large amount of time working with any piece of software, whether it is a word-processing program or a project management application, they often develop a strong, and sometimes unreasonable, loyalty to it. This loyalty may make them blind to the advantages of other packages which are on the market.

Bear this in mind, and do not expect to get completely unbiased advice from someone who has been using a single program for a long while.

Schedules and milestones

A schedule is a list of dates on which certain activities, or stages of the project, should be completed. It can be presented in the form of a Gantt chart, or simply as text. The following example contains a column for monitoring purposes, where the dates on which events actually happened can be recorded:

	scheduled	actual
Outline to steering group	03.10.97	
Steering group feedback	10.10.97	
D1 to steering group	17.10.97	
Steering group report on D1	23.11.97	
D2 to critical readers	27.11.97	
Critical readers report on D2	03.12.97	
D3 to pilot team	15.12.97	
Focus group	15.01.98	
D4 to steering group	30.01.98	

It is much easier to gain a quick impression of the length of time allocated to each activity when a schedule is presented on a Gantt chart. However, for monitoring purposes, a list of dates is usually more effective. It is usually a good idea to let people know the dates in the schedule which are dependent on their own deadlines. This increases their sense of urgency.

A computer-generated schedule can look impressive, but some people do not take an automatically-produced document as seriously as a more personalized, word-processed or even typewritten schedule. If you update your schedules frequently, especially if you use the same format and simply change the dates, people will soon lose respect for them. If a great deal of human thought and effort has appeared to go into the creation of a schedule, it often has more weight.

Milestones

These are significant dates in the project schedule. They occur at the end of each phase of the project and at other points, on the completion of important deliverables. They may mark the departure of certain members of the team, the beginning of a new type of activity and the time at which interim payments are made.

Milestones are usually moments for reflection and re-assessment. Like the physical milestones you pass on a road, they are points at which you can look around and consider how far you have come – and whether you are going to reach your destination if you maintain the same speed and direction. If you need to make changes to your working methods or perhaps the composition of your team, a milestone is an appropriate point at which to do it.

Milestones also have an important psychological function. On a long project, it can be extremely difficult to maintain momentum. Milestone dates provide interim deadlines, which you can encourage your team and sub-contractors to work towards. They can also provide a reason to bring a geographically distant team together to be congratulated on what has been achieved so far and remotivated for the next stage in the project.

Developing a schedule

So far, we have described how a schedule can be used to present information about the timing of activities. It is also a planning tool. The first stage in producing a schedule is to consider the constraints within which you are working. There may be certain dates which are mentioned in the contract, or dates on which events which are external to the project, but crucial to its success, occur. These dates give you your basic framework. Next, you should consider the various activities which must be completed and the dependencies which link them. The techniques of flowcharts and network diagrams, discussed earlier in the chapter, can be used to prepare a schedule. If you are using project management software, the process will probably be automated for you.

When you look at the first draft of your schedule, you may find that it uses more resources than you have available. You may discover, for example, that you have three separate, simultaneous activities which require the skills of a single member of your team. Or you may find that a particular machine is being used to complete two tasks during the same week, but is lying idle for a month beforehand.

The activities which have priority when you are allocating resources are those which lie on the critical path in a network diagram. They are the activities whose delay will cause the entire project to be delayed. Activities which have slack or float can be moved around, to level out the use of resources. Many project management programs will perform this resource levelling for you. Otherwise, the most intuitive way to visualize and carry out this process is by using a type of Gantt chart.

This diagram represents the first attempt at a schedule. The same series of tasks has to be carried out on three separate elements of a project. The bars represent the tasks, with the shading indicating three members of the team who are involved.

EDITOR

WRITER

DESIGNER

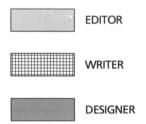

This schedule is clearly unworkable. By looking vertically down the chart, it can be seen that each individual is required to work on more than one element at the same time.

The second diagram was produced by sliding the bars along, so that no individual is engaged on more than one task at the same time. The schedule is now workable. As it does in this example, resource levelling usually involves adding time to the schedule.

P 1											
P 2											
P 3											

Contingency

It is essential to build some contingency time into your schedule. The amount of time you allow will depend, among other things, on the complexity and risks of the activities undertaken. You do not have to tell your team or sub-contractors about the allowance you have made for slippage in the schedule. In fact, the less you say about it, the better. Extra time can be allocated for in-house processes, or activities which you undertake yourself. You can also bring forward deadlines when you present the schedule to the staff who will carry out the work.

Budgets for projects

A budget is an account of all the costs involved in a project. There are several types of cost which must be considered.

Labour costs

These are the wages, salaries and fees paid to the people who work for the project. Some of these costs will be incurred by particular project tasks and are described as direct costs. For example, if you employed an architect to draw up a plan of a building, the fee involved could be directly assigned to that task. Other labour tasks cannot be linked with particular activities. Your own salary as project manager, and the salaries of people who administer the project office, come into this category. These are known as indirect costs and are usually listed separately. If the project is taking place within an organization, these indirect labour costs may be carried by the organization itself and not be counted as part of the project costs. Labour costs, especially direct costs, are liable to be greatest during the implementation phase of the project.

Material costs

These are the supplies which are used up during the project. They may include anything from office stationery to roofing tiles. Material costs are usually highest during the implementation phase of a project. Most material costs can be associated directly with particular tasks and are therefore classed as direct costs.

Equipment costs

These are made up of the costs of hiring, leasing or purchasing any equipment needed for the project.

Other costs

These could include insurance, patent fees and tax.

Direct and indirect costs

The costs which can be attributed to particular tasks are known as direct costs and costs which cannot be allocated in this way are described as indirect costs, or overheads. As a general principle, greater control over costs is possible if as many as possible are linked to specific tasks, so that you know where your budget is being spent. A large burden of overheads may be inevitable, but makes it difficult to produce savings in the budget. Some, or all, of the indirect costs may be taken out of the project budget and accounted for separately. Both direct and indirect costs must, of course, be reflected in the price which the client pays.

Fixed and variable costs

All project costs, regardless of whether they are incurred for labour, materials, equipment or anything else, can be classified as either:

- Fixed costs, *or*

- Variable costs.

Fixed costs are specific amounts of money, while variable costs change, depending on the quantities involved. The purchase of a computer is a fixed cost, but the purchase of paper for the printer is a variable cost, because it will increase as further reams are bought. If a consultant charges a fee of £1,000 to provide a training session, this is a fixed cost. If the same consultant charges his time by the hour, this is a variable cost.

Fixed and variable costs can be either direct or indirect. If a building contractor buys a software program to manage a project, this would be fixed indirect cost. If he buys a central heating boiler to fit into a house he is constructing, this would be a fixed direct cost. Similarly, the weekly wage of an administrative assistant would be classed as a variable indirect cost and the weekly wage of a bricklayer would be a variable direct cost.

The problem with variable costs is that they are open-ended. They can escalate if extra materials are purchased, or the work takes longer than was scheduled. Wherever possible, project managers like to have certainty in their budgets. For this reason, a flat fee is sometimes agreed with consultants and other sub-contractors. In this way, if the work takes longer to complete, the project does not have to bear the extra cost. In other situations, it is possible to negotiate a piece rate with the sub-contractor. If neither of these solutions is appropriate, the cost must be worked out by estimating the quantity of work required and multiplying it by a unit rate. Changes in costs can then at least be predicted and explained, which gives some degree of control.

Preparing estimates

There are two approaches to preparing an estimate. The easiest way to do it is to base your figures on a similar project which took place in the past. Although this method of estimating is quick, simple and cheap, it is not likely to produce a particularly accurate forecast. If very few details are available about the forthcoming project, this approach may be the only one you can use to make a rough estimate of costs. Unfortunately, this is exactly the situation in which it is risky to make assumptions. There may be significant differences between the old and the new projects, which makes a comparison of costs completely inappropriate.

> 'I was once telephoned by a publisher and asked to give a quotation for editing a textbook. I had edited another book in the series two years ago, so I looked back at my records and found how much I had charged. I added a bit on to update the price, and gave the publisher a figure, which was accepted. When the manuscript arrived, I realized I had made a bad mistake. It was half as long again as the book I had worked on previously and was very poorly written. I lost out badly on that job.'

The second approach is to break the project down into the smallest possible components, which are then priced individually. The parts are then added together to produce a total cost. This is a time-consuming procedure, but should produce the most accurate estimate possible. In construction work, estimates are prepared by costing each item on a Bill of Quantities. This document may run to many hundreds of pages and will contain exact details of every operation involved in the project.

The smaller the parts into which the project is divided for costing purposes, the more accurate the resulting estimate is likely to be, and the more expensive and time-consuming it will be to prepare.

In practice, many estimates are based on a balance between these two approaches. Some parts of the project are costed in full, while others, which are more difficult to quantify, are based on educated guesswork.

In many situations, the preparation of costs is a complex information-gathering exercise. You may have to contact sub-contractors and suppliers and ask them to submit formal quotations. Other information will come from colleagues, or other contacts, who have specialist knowledge and can advise you on the time and other resources likely to be required for the project.

You can obtain some of your data from records of previous projects. There are also various formula which you can use to calculate costs. These range from crude 'rules of thumb' to more sophisticated instruments based on a scientific study of historical data:

> *'When I am shooting a film documentary, I expect to shoot about six to eight minutes of film for every minute which appears in the final version.'*

> *'Allow £x a square metre to lay a concrete floor.'*

Where some types of work are concerned, formulae are available in the form of software programs and can be used to produce 'model' costings. Although they can produce accurate forecasts, they need to be used with some caution. It still takes experience of the real world to recognize whether there are any special factors which make a project untypical.

What rules of thumb do you use in your type of work? How accurate have you found them to be?

There are several phenomena which can affect the reliability of your estimates. The first of these is related to an old saying which farmers sometimes repeat:

'One lad's a lad. Two lads are half a lad and three lads are no lad at all.'

Just because you double or treble your workforce, you won't necessarily get double or treble the output. There may be other factors which come into play. Generally, the more people who share a task, the less effort each individual puts in. There are also other costs which are not scaleable. For example, you cannot usually base the cost of small quantities of supplies on the cost of large orders. Some contractors may also be prepared to accept a lower hourly or daily rate than normal in return for a long contract.

If you are calculating how long it will take people to perform a task, you need to take into account their learning curve. The first time someone does a task, they will be very slow, because they are finding out what they have to do, and the best way to go about it. The next time, they will complete the task much more quickly. The learning curve is based on the observation that, for most tasks, people improve their speed by between 80 and 90 per cent each time the number of repetitions doubles. So, if it takes one hour to do a task the first time, it will take, on average:

1 x 0.8 hours to do it the second time (0.8 hours)

1 x 0.8 x 0.8 hours to do it the fourth time (0.64 hours)

1 x 0.8 x 0.8 x 0.8 to do it the eighth time (0.51 hours)

1 x 0.8 x 0.8 x 0.8 x 0.8 to do it the sixteenth time (0.41 hours)

The more times a task is repeated, the quicker people get. The effect starts to tail off after a time, as a larger and larger number of repetitions is required to produce the same reduction in time. Ideally, you do not want to hire people for your project who have to learn how to do their jobs on your time. However, many projects do require new ways of working. For some repetitive and undemanding tasks, it may also be cheaper to hire unskilled labour and provide training than to pay a higher rate to more experienced workers.

You should also remember that people are not machines. They take a little time to reach their peak level of performance and also start to wind down at the end of the working day. If you are using standard work rates, be aware that they may be based on optimum performance, which people are very unlikely to produce 100 per cent of the time.

If you ask people to give you an estimate of how long it would take them to do a job, they may not always give you an accurate answer. There are several reasons for this. They may overestimate their capability, in order to impress you or get the work. They may overestimate how long things will take so that they can have an easier time completing the job. They may simply not know how long a job will take, but not want to reveal their ignorance. They may be naturally cautious and not want to commit themselves to a schedule they cannot keep. Your own knowledge and experience will enable you to distinguish between the estimates you should and should not take seriously, but you may still be left with a range of possibilities.

In this situation, there is a useful formula which has been found to give reasonably accurate answers:

The expected time $= \dfrac{A + 4M + B}{6}$

A = optimistic time estimate

B = pessimistic time estimate

M = most likely time estimate.

Finally, when estimating costs, you should not automatically base your figures on the lowest quotations that you are given by suppliers and sub-contractors. There may be very good reasons not to accept the lowest price.

You may also need to take into account:

- Delivery
- Quality assurance
- Standard of workmanship
- Reliability
- After-sales service.

It may be worth paying a little extra to ensure that the supplies or work you are paying for really will meet your requirements.

Cost and price

It is important to make a clear mental distinction between your costings and the price which the sponsor is willing to pay. If you know that there is a budget of, say, £20,000, available to produce and print a leaflet, it is very tempting to allow this fact to influence your thinking:

'If we've got that amount of money available, we could afford to use x to do the illustrations. At any rate, we can certainly go for full colour.'

To paraphrase Parkinson's Law, it is easy to let the costs expand to fill the budget available.

It is also dangerous to try to make the budget fit an inadequate price:

'I know they will only be prepared to spend £5,000 on this job, so we'll have to cut a few corners...'

If it is impossible to do a job for the price offered, the people who are paying should be made aware of this fact. They may be prepared to increase the budget, or settle for a less ambitious outcome. On the other hand, if you go ahead with an inadequate budget, you may get into serious difficulties when the project is underway.

The project plan

At the end of the planning phase, the project manager puts together a project plan. This is based on the Terms of Reference document produced earlier, but contains much more detail on the cost, timing and specifications of the tasks to be performed. The project plan is the guidebook which will take you through the implementation phase of the project. It will need to be updated and revised as you gain more information and encounter unforeseen obstacles, but it will be a central focus of the project from this point on.

The project plan needs to be approved by the sponsor. It is often the main deliverable at the end of the planning phase. As project manager, you will keep control of the master copy of the plan. You may distribute parts of it to members of the team, or to sub-contractors, but no alterations should be made unless you authorize them yourself.

A project plan can take many forms. It may be recorded in your project software, or be presented as a loose-leaf file of documents. The project plan usually contains these elements:

The contract or Terms of Reference document

This will contain, among other things, a record of the project objectives and project deliverables and an outline of the costs, timing and specifications of the work to be done.

Work Breakdown Structure

This is a detailed WBS, drawn up to a level at which control will be exercised during the implementation phase of the project. It should give specifications for all tasks.

Costs

Estimates of all costs should be given, related to the WBS.

Schedule

Scheduled starting and finishing dates of all activities on the WBS are needed. Major milestones should also be given.

Key personnel

This section should describe the responsibilities of key members of the team. Briefing documents may be included in this section.

Risk management

This should describe the most significant risks to the project and describe the planned response. Any assumptions and constraints relevant to the management of risks should also be described here.

Management plans

This section should contain plans for dealing with specific issues, such as communication with the press, change control or payment of sub-contractors.

Other issues

This section can be used to flag up unresolved issues on which more investigation is needed or where there are decisions which have to be taken.

Additional documentation

This section may include technical specifications, designs, details of relevant legislation or standards and any other important material which will need to be referred to during the implementation phase of the project.

It is important that the project plan is organized in a way which you find easy to use. You should, for example, be able to locate key documents quickly. It should be possible to update and revise the plan and add more information, as necessary. It is also essential to impose a rigorous system of version control, so that it is impossible for out-of-date documents to be circulated.

Building a team

This chapter focuses on the project team. It discusses theories about how people behave in teams and how you can get the best out of the people who are working alongside you. People skills are central to project management. You need to gain and maintain the personal commitment, energy and goodwill of your team. The normal hierarchical roles which apply in many organizations are often inappropriate in the context of a project. You need to develop new ways in which people can work together.

The way in which you communicate with members of your team can have a great influence on their attitudes and behaviour. This chapter also discusses communication skills and suggests a five-point procedure you can use whenever you are planning a memo, meeting or conversation.

Many projects take place within a larger organization. Tact and sensitivity are necessary to manage the interface between the project and the organization. The final part of the chapter examines some of the issues you should be aware of here.

What makes a team?

Anyone who has any interest in team sports knows that a winning team is made up of individuals who excel in different areas.

> 'If I was selecting a fantasy cricket team, I would need strong opening batsmen to wear down the opposition. Then I would pick good stroke players for my middle order batsmen. These are the people who can put runs on, and do it in some style. I would obviously need a wicket keeper, and both fast and spin bowlers. And I would also select some all rounders, who could bat a little and bowl a little.'

In any type of team, whether it is playing for the Ashes, constructing an office block or organizing a conference, different members have different functions. Another defining characteristic of a team is that the individuals within it co-operate to achieve a common goal. In a project team, this co-operation must be sustained for the life of the project and the goal must be aligned with the objectives of the project.

A project team is made up of individuals with different functional roles who share commitment to the project and co-operate with each other to achieve its objectives.

In some situations, teams arise spontaneously. In an emergency such as an accident or a natural disaster, you often find that individuals intuitively share out the tasks that have to be done and focus their energies on a common goal. Heroic deeds can be done in these circumstances. As a project manager, you need a team which will function effectively at all times, not just in a crisis. There are several things you can do to help make this happen.

Building shared commitment

You need to communicate your vision of the project to your team. It is much easier to become committed to something if you are convinced that it is really worth doing. This may involve explaining the history of the project, or the problems it was set up to solve. It may be appropriate to use some of the same presentation techniques you would use to convince potential sponsors of the value of the project. It is important that the team hears about the project from someone who can talk about it enthusiastically. If you are not a charismatic speaker yourself, you could consider inviting someone who does have this talent to address the team. Every member of your team, however humble, should be familiar with what the project has been set up to do and be able to describe its overall objectives.

A project needs a sense of identity. This may be achieved through the use of logos and headed stationery, distinctive procedures and working methods, dedicated premises and equipment, and specialized vocabulary. In a few situations, specialized clothing may even be appropriate. If people are constantly reminded that they are working on project business, they will feel like 'insiders'. However, whatever devices you use to make people feel part of the team, it is important that:

- They are appropriate to the culture of the project and the organization in which you are working.

- They make the work of the team easier, and not more difficult.

- They are not used in situations where they could make other people feel alienated from the project.

- They are explained immediately to new members of the team.

This manager designed a special form for all internal project communications:

'I didn't want odd pieces of paper with incomplete information being passed around the project office. Whenever messages or memos had to be sent, people used a special pad. This had the project logo at the top and a space to write the date and the names of the sender and receiver. The sender had to tick one of a series of boxes to indicate the priority of the communication and note the action he or she wanted the receiver to take. It took no longer to complete this form than to scribble a message on an ordinary scrap of paper, but it improved the quality of communication considerably.'

Another manager developed special techniques for project meetings:

'Our project was based inside an organization. We used the same meeting room that the team used for other occasions. I wanted to make the project meetings distinctive, so I re-arranged the furniture each

time, setting the tables in a large square rather than a long rectangle. Instead of having a conventional minutes secretary, I got a 'scribe' to write up the action points on a flip chart as we went along.'

You should also be aware that some members of your team may not be as enthusiastic as others about adopting the 'project identity'. This does not necessarily mean that they have not committed themselves to the objectives, or that they are not prepared to work professionally. It does not even mean that they are not good team players. Some people just have their own way of working. As long as these people do not undermine the rest of the team, it is often best to allow them some flexibility. This is an area where you will have to make individual judgements.

You can increase people's commitment to a project if you demonstrate that you value their participation. Many projects begin with a meeting which is much more formal than those which follow. This can show the team that you regard its coming together as an important event. As the project progresses, you can prove that you value individual team members by not wasting their time. Do not hold unnecessary meetings or ask them to complete nonessential documentation. And try to make certain that all the equipment and other resources they need are in place for them to begin work.

Commitment to a project can also be increased if everyone involved knows what is happening at any time. There is a balance to be struck here. There may be some things which you cannot share with the team, and you should certainly not burden people with information they do not want or need, but it can be extremely motivating for the team to have a sense of the overall progress of the project. Television appeals, such as Children in Need or Red Nose Day, know that they can raise the flagging spirits of the studio audience by announcing the latest figure for the money raised. You can use different methods to achieve a similar psychological effect. Regular bulletins can remind the team of significant milestones, and congratulate the people involved when they are achieved. It can also help to record progress on a Gantt chart, or other form of easily-understandable display, in a place where all members of the team can see it.

How will you encourage your team to share your commitment to the project?

Encouraging co-operation

The members of your team will come to the project with their own agendas. They may have:

- Volunteered because they fully support the project's objectives

- Applied to join the team because it will help their own career plans

- Been seconded to the project because there is nothing else for them to do.

They may be already committed to the project's objectives, or initially cynical about what you are trying to achieve. They may be ready to learn new ways of doing things, or be determined to carry on working in exactly the same way as they have always done. They may also have pre-conceived ideas about other members of the team.

Negative attitudes in the project team can lead to rivalry, lack of communication and even sabotage. Your job is to bring these people together so that they support each other in achieving the project's objectives. The first step, which has already been discussed, is to create a sense of commitment to the project. This provides a bigger context in which any interpersonal difficulties can be sorted out.

It is also very helpful to set out some ground rules before divisions arise. These may involve:

- The way in which people communicate with each other

- Working procedures

- Lines of command within the project

- Who is authorized to take particular decisions.

Make sure that team members understand and agree to these rules at an early stage in the project. Later on, if problems arise, you can refer back to them. You may have to add to these rules at a later stage in the project, but it is preferable to have the basic principles established at the beginning.

When the project is underway, make an opportunity to discuss the quality of the support that team members give each other. Useful questions include:

- What could x do to make your job easier?

- What extra resources would make it possible for you to work more effectively?

- What could the project manager do to make your job easier?

- How can we avoid a similar problem happening again?

It is important to keep these discussions tightly focused on the project objectives. Do not allow them to degenerate into personal justification or vilification of other members of the team. You must also avoid the tendency which some project teams have for excessive navel gazing. Try to establish as quickly as possible whether there are any changes in procedure which would make the project run more effectively. If there are, assess their costs and benefits and, if appropriate, set them in motion.

Finally, you can often increase co-operation if you exhibit complete fairness in all your dealings with the project team. Do not favour particular individuals above others, or insist on unnecessary restrictions. The more open and honest you can be with the team, the more they are likely to reciprocate.

Supporting different functional roles

The first thing you must do is to make sure that the people appointed to the project team really do have the skills, knowledge and experience necessary for them to fulfil their functional roles. Draw up a job specification and a person specification and make a distinction between essential and desirable attributes.

If a project is happening within an organization, you may find that certain individuals are assigned to the team for internal political reasons. They may be there to support the viewpoint of a particular senior manager. Perhaps they are not very good at their existing job, or it could be that their current role is being phased out. Ideally, the project manager should have a large say in the selection of the project team. If this is not possible, you can avoid many difficulties by being as clear as possible about the specifications you require in your staff.

Once they are appointed, the various members of your team will have different needs. For example, they may require:

- Specialized equipment

- Particular software and hardware

- Information presented in a particular form or at a particular time

- Technical support

- Specific working conditions.

You must find out exactly what members of your team need in order to fulfil their functional roles. Although you are unlikely to be able to provide them with perfect conditions, you can at least ensure that the budget is used to enable them to work as effectively and efficiently as possible. To paraphrase the words of the song, they may not always get want they want, but you should make sure that they get what they need.

What resources would your team like to have? What resources do they need? Can you tell the difference?

Team roles

Much has been written about the combination of personalities that make up the ideal team. You may be familiar with the list produced by Belbin:

- Plant
- Resource investigator
- Co-ordinator
- Shaper
- Monitor evaluator
- Teamwork
- Implementer
- Completer
- Specialist

All these character-types have their own strengths and weaknesses. (Belbin, M, Management Teams: Why they succeed or fail, Butterworth Heinemann, Oxford).

The plant

This is a creative individual who makes his or her own rules. A plant can find imaginative solutions to problems, but is impatient about working out the details. This person may be way ahead of other members of the team and can find it difficult to communicate with them. The plant needs careful handling, but can add a new dimension to the work of the project.

The resource investigator

This individual has boundless energy, especially at the beginning of a project. He or she is a good communicator and can often be the person who makes the contacts and convinces sponsors to support the project. The resource investigator tends to lose interest once things are underway and is less useful in the implementation stage of a project.

The co-ordinator

This individual is a good person to have at the centre of a project. He or she is skilled at chairing meetings and can help people clarify their goals and make sensible decisions. The main strength of the co-ordinator is in assisting other team members to work effectively.

The shaper

This is a dynamic individual who can set the pace in a project. The shaper works best when under pressure and has the drive to overcome obstacles. He or she may be insensitive, however, to the feelings of other people and can upset them with criticism. If you have a shaper on your team, you may have to keep him or her in check at times.

The monitor evaluator

This is the person who weighs up the situation slowly and comes to considered judgements. He or she has a strategic perspective and is able to make decisions which will be in the best interests of the project. As the monitor evaluator has high professional standards, he or she may be very critical of other people's work. Do not rely on the monitor evaluator for creative ideas or expect this person to inspire others. The monitor evaluator may come into conflict with the resource investigator and the shaper.

The teamworker

This individual is happy to work as a member of a team. He or she will listen to other people's opinions work constructively alongside them. The teamworker hates arguments and will do everything possible to avoid them. If you have other, more assertive personalities on your team, the team-worker can be a calming influence. This person is not a natural leader though, and can find it hard to take decisions. He or she may be influenced by other people.

The implementer

Every project needs an implementer. This is the reliable and efficient individual who actually turns ideas into reality. The implementer usually has a high degree of skill and professionalism in a particular area. He or she may be rather inflexible, however, and can be wary about adopting new ideas. The implementer is probably not as extrovert as other members of the team and may be underestimated by them. Make sure that other people appreciate the value of the implementer and do your best to convince this person of the value of the approach you are taking.

The completer

This is an extremely conscientious individual who can be relied on to do the detailed work of the project. The completer is often a worrier and will do extra work rather than trust it to anyone else. Other members of the team can be irritated by the completer's near-fanatical attention to detail. You may have to help this individual to put his or her concerns into a larger perspective. You may also have to intervene to help the completer manage his or her time and resources more effectively.

The specialist

This person has technical knowledge of a particular, rather narrow area. This knowledge is important to the project, but the project may not be particularly important to the specialist, who may only be excited by the demands of his speciality. Although you need the skills and experience of the specialist, don't expect him or her to make much contribution to the project team as a whole.

In combination, these personalities complement each others' strengths and weaknesses and can achieve great things. As project manager, you need to be aware of the areas in which your team members are weak – and also provide them with the resources and support they need to fulfil their potential in the areas where they are strong. Sometimes it may be necessary to alter the composition of the team. If your team is unbalanced by too many shapers or plants, you can provide a steadying influence by introducing further teamworkers, implementers, completers or monitor evaluators. It is often possible to bring in people with these characteristics in a supportive or administrative role. Relatively junior members of the team may have the talents you need to prevent the project going off the rails.

You may also experience the opposite scenario, in which your project team becomes too fixed in its way of thinking. Here, you may need to re-energize your team members by exposing them to the ideas of a shaper or plant. You may be able to arrange a session with one of the people who first instigated the project – or bring in an outside consultant to develop their skills or understanding in a particular area. You may need to plan events of this kind at regular intervals throughout the life of the project.

Some of the personalities described by Belbin are not natural team-players. For example, you may find it difficult to integrate the working style of a plant or a completer with that of the rest of the team. Here is how one manager handled a plant:

> 'The individual who had come up with the design idea for the project was quite brilliant, but absolutely impossible to work with. I would spend hours preparing papers for meetings, then he would come along and turn everything on its head. He was dismissive of the efforts made by other members of the team and upset quite a lot of people. In the

end, I had to take him aside and say, 'Look, we can't go on like this. Your concept for this project is tremendous, but you are making it impossible for us to implement it. You can't put your ideas into action without the team, so please, give us some help here.' Together, we worked out some rules. We arranged to talk before the team meetings and set the agenda. That agenda was then fixed, and he agreed not to change it. For my part, I agreed not to insist on such a rigid structure for the meetings. I also made him aware of the effect some of his off-the-cuff remarks had had on members of the team. To give him his due, he genuinely had not realized that people had been offended by what he had said. I think he was rather shocked to discover that some people were actually afraid of him. Subsequently, he made an effort to acknowledge and praise the work that other people were doing. Things did not always run smoothly, but there was much less tension at the team meetings.'

And here is the tactic that another project manager used to handle a completer:

'If I am honest, Marie was a bit of a pedant. Her attention to detail was a bonus in many ways, but it could be very irritating at meetings, where we were trying to thrash out the overall shape of an idea. I could have cut her out of the meetings altogether, but I felt that it was important that she kept in touch with the big picture. She needed to understand the concerns that other people on the project had. The solution I found was to take much firmer control of meetings. I no longer opened up a topic for general discussion, but asked people very focused questions. In the past, I would have asked, 'What do you think of John's plan?' Under my new system, I asked, 'How long would it take you to put John's plan into action?' By imposing limits on discussion like this, the meetings were much shorter and more productive. Marie was able to make positive contributions on specific points and began to have a much greater appreciation of the general pace of work and the priorities of the rest of the people involved in the project.'

Not all projects require the same mix of personalities. In a high profile project, your team should probably include several outgoing, energetic people who are excellent communicators. In a less visible project, these talents may not be so important. Some projects demand high levels of creative thought. In others, the skills of organization and administration are more significant.

Who would be in your dream team for your present project?

Team dynamics

Teams commonly go through a succession of stages of development. These stages are known as:

- Forming

- Storming

- Norming

- Performing

- Mourning.

At each stage, the team requires different forms of support. The stages can arise over a series of weeks or months – or they can happen over the course of a few hours.

Forming

At the beginning of a project, the members of the team need to get to know each other. Some members may be unsure about what is going to be expected of them – and perhaps whether they are personally capable of fulfilling the brief. Some people may try to impose a structure or way of working that they have used in a previous project. Others may be hesitant about making any contribution until they see the way that the land lies.

As project manager, you must allow time for the group to form. Provide a structure in which people can begin to find out about each other. Do not expect to get any serious work done at this initial stage. The team will be looking to you for direction, so be prepared to give it.

This is how one project manager helped her team through the forming stage:

> 'I organized a weekend workshop to kick-start a project concerned with the development of a major series of training materials. I held it at an hotel in the depths of the countryside, so team members could not escape from each others' company. In the first session, I began by outlining the programme for the weekend. I then asked everyone to introduce themselves briefly. After that, I gave a 45 minute presentation, outlining the project objectives. Then we broke for coffee in the lounge. When people came back into the conference room, I could see that they had started to talk to each other.'

When your team is forming:

- Maintain a high profile
- Clarify the project objectives
- Explain the ground rules
- Allow team members to get to know each other.

Storming

Many teams go through this difficult stage. People may begin to argue about the basic objectives of the project, or the way you plan to organize it. Factions can arise. People may threaten to walk out. Individuals who have not experienced this stage before may be extremely concerned that the whole project is under threat. There is often a lot of emotion around at this point. You may find that you are unable to secure agreement and co-operation on issues which you had assumed to be completely uncontroversial. You may even be verbally attacked by some members of the team.

It is essential to stay calm through this stage. Do not try to smooth over the cracks. Instead, acknowledge the conflicts, but try to express them objectively. Very often, the differences which emerge at this point appear to be much more significant than they really are. Once the issues can be separated from the emotional way in which they have been expressed, they can be examined coolly and frequently resolved. The force with which some people express their opinions at this stage often has much more to do with their own fears and suspicions than with the truth of the situation they are actually in.

This is how the project manager who organized the weekend workshop handled the storming stage:

> 'At the end of the first morning, we broke into three groups, representing the different functional sub-teams. The technical writers and the industry specialists had fairly uncontroversial discussions, but the training officers, who would be responsible for the development and implementation of the project materials, almost came to blows. One individual was insisting that the training programme should only be delivered by specially trained trainers. Another individual was demanding that we came up with a product that could be administered by anyone, without special training. Everyone was aligning themselves with one camp or the other. I had anticipated trouble in this area and had asked my most experienced aide to chair and scribe the meeting. When the three groups came back together, she outlined the discussion to the plenary meeting, taking great care to check that she was relaying the arguments accurately. It was much better to hear these points from a neutral spokesperson than from the protagonists themselves. They would have become too emotional and might have found themselves making statements in the plenary session which they would have regretted later. We then opened the topic up to everyone. After some input from the industry specialists, it became clear that the points of dissension were really very insignificant, and we were able to move on.'

When your team is storming:

- Don't panic
- Try to anticipate difficult issues
- Allow people to express their opinions
- Examine divisions and complaints objectively
- Try to take the emotion out of the situation.

Norming

At this stage, people begin to work together much more positively. A sense of direction emerges and people start to exchange opinions and make plans. You may hear team members using the word 'we' for the first time, showing that they are identifying themselves with the project. You may find that members of the team who have been alarmed or alienated by the previous stage now feel able to make a positive contribution for the first time. It is helpful at this stage to provide definite tasks on which the team can focus. People are generally tired of arguing and want to see some positive progress made.

> 'After lunch on the Saturday, I split the team up again. This time we divided into four subject groups, with industry specialists, technical writers and training officers in each team. The goal was to produce an outline of the materials required in each subject area. I provided each group with a checklist of points which gave them a fairly detailed brief. At the end of the day, we came back together and compared notes. Each of the four groups had produced a viable outline. We ended the day with a real sense of progress.'

When your team is norming:

- Provide tasks on which people can focus
- Give all team members an opportunity to contribute
- Allow a sense of team identify to emerge.

Performing

Now things really get going. The team knows what it is trying to achieve and is working purposively towards its goal. People are co-operating with each other, exchanging ideas and finding solutions to problems. When your team reaches this stage, the best thing you can do is to let them get on with the job. Keep an eye on what is happening, but don't interfere unless you see things going off course. The team is now moving forward under its own energy and usually only needs a light touch on the wheel to steer it in the right direction.

> 'On the Sunday, I split the team into small groups and asked them each to draft a sample unit of the training material. Each group contained

one training officer, one industry specialist and one technical writer. I gave them some specifications for the material and asked them to be ready to present their work at 4pm. Apart from that, I left it up to them. The mood was tremendous that day. I wandered around from room to room – everywhere people were completely focused on the task.'

When your team is performing:

- Monitor events from a distance
- Don't interfere with the momentum of the team unless you have to
- Support the team by facilitating its efforts.

Mourning

At the end of a project, the team will cease to exist. If team members have put a lot into the project, they will probably feel a sense of loss at this point. It is important to have some kind of formal event at the end of a project, when people can evaluate what has happened and think about implications for the future.

'When the groups came back together at 4pm and presented their work, people were amazed at what had been achieved. We had the framework for the whole programme of training materials, which the technical writers could now take away and complete. The rest of the work could be done at a distance. I allowed some time for evaluation of the outcomes, and also of the process that people had gone through. Although the weekend was an unrepeatable event, I knew that some important working relationships had been forged.'

When your team is mourning:

- Provide a formal end-point for the project
- Allow time for evaluation
- Recognize the value of the work that has been done.

Communicating with your team

When you are managing an ongoing operation, methods of communication can evolve slowly, over a period of months or even years. In project management, they have to be set up very quickly – and they have to work immediately.

When you make any form of communication, whether it is a quick message to a colleague or a formal presentation, you need to go through certain steps:

1. Identify your objectives

2. Identify your audience

3. Choose your method of communication

4. Match your message to your audience

5. Get feedback.

We will look at these five steps in more detail.

1. Identify your objectives

The basic question which you need to ask yourself here is:

What do I want to happen as a result of this communication?

There may be several answers to this question. You may want:

- To understand a problem

- To be able to complete a process

- To know how far a process has got

- Somebody else to be able to do something

- To convey your willingness to help

- Somebody else to accept your point of view.

Unless you are clear about your objective, it is surprisingly easy for communications to go off track:

> *'I telephoned the site manager and we chatted for five minutes about progress. When I put the phone down, I realized that I had not pinned him down on the reasons why we were three weeks behind schedule.'*

> *'I dropped in on the lab unannounced to see how things were going. Everyone froze when I walked through the door. I'd intended it as a friendly visit, but the technicians interpreted my presence as a criticism.'*

2. Identify your audience

You must send your communication to the appropriate person. If you don't, you cannot expect it to be successful. This may involve identifying the person who has the information you need, or the power to influence a situation you want to change.

3. Choose your method of communication

Nowadays, the project manager often has a wide range of ways of communicating with the team:

- Face-to-face
- In meetings
- By e-mail
- On the telephone
- By fax
- By voice mail
- In a video conference
- By memo
- By letter
- By standard reports and forms
- In notices and charts displayed on the wall.

Your choice of method will depend on the speed with which you need to communicate, whether you need a written record of the communication, whether the information that will be passed is confidential, the type of feedback you need and the number of people you need to communicate with at once. For example, you cannot expect people to admit to personal difficulties with their work in a general team meeting, but you may be able to find out what is going wrong in a private meeting. If you want to make sure that all members of the team are aware of an important new procedure, it is much better to send them each a memo, rather than assume they will have read a notice you have pinned up on the wall of the project office.

4. Match your message to your audience

The members of your team will have different levels of knowledge on most topics, and different prejudices and expectations. It is important to think about how your message will be received and understood before you send it.

> 'I asked someone new in the office to approach sub-contractors for quotes on the parts of a job which we were not getting done by our direct labour force. I kind of assumed that he knew that the names had to be taken from the list of approved companies and that somebody had filled him in about certain difficulties we had been having with a local firm of electricians. I was wrong. He managed to approach six companies which we would never consider dealing with, including the electricians.'

You may have to send the same message in different ways to various members of your team:

> 'When I speak to my editors, I can be very direct about the changes that have to be made to a book. I wouldn't dream of speaking to my authors in the same way.'

You may sometimes express your message in way that can be understood by all members of the team:

> 'The project management software I use can produce detailed network diagrams. Of course I can understand them, but they are too

complex for many members of the team. Instead, I map progress with a simple chart on the wall, using magnetic strips of different colours. Everyone can understand this.'

5. Get feedback

If you are asking a question or requesting information, you will expect a reply. If you are giving instructions or stating an opinion, it is easy to forget about receiving feedback. This is dangerous, because your message may have been misunderstood or misinterpreted. It may not even have arrived at all. You cannot know that communication has taken place unless you get feedback. When you are circulating large amounts of information to your project team, it is important to build in a method of getting feedback. And once you receive feedback, it is often necessary to alter your actions or perceptions in response to it.

We will now look at three common types of communication:

- Briefing
- Debriefing
- Meetings.

Briefing

You need to tell the members of your project team what you expect them to do. There are some instructions which it is possible to give at the start of a project, while others will have to be added during the implementation phase, in response to unfolding events. In general, only brief people about things they need to know. Too much reading matter at any stage of a project may result in information overload. If people stop reading the material you send them, they may miss vital instructions.

All written instructions should be as short and simple as you can make them.

Here are some guidelines for writing clear English:

- Keep your sentences short.

- Use short words in preference to long ones.

- Write positive sentences rather than negative ones.

- Write active sentences rather than passive ones.

- Explain any acronyms and technical terminology.

- Use headings and good design to help your readers find their way around your document.

There are several devices you can use to convey instructions clearly. A step-by-step list tells people the order in which to do things:

When you receive a quotation

1. Check that the items on the quotation match the details requested.

2. Check the units used are consistent with those on the Bill of Quantities.

3. Convert items into appropriate unit costs, if necessary.

4. Check for extra conditions.

5. Enter the items on the analysis sheet.

A simple flowchart can clarify a complex decision. Here is an example of a flowchart (overleaf) which was drawn up to provide a guide to staff who were responsible for selecting software:

A guide to staff who are responsible for selecting software

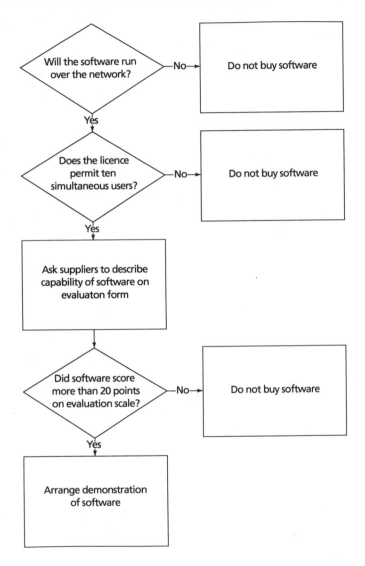

In some situations, a list of do's and don'ts may be appropriate:

DO

- Spellcheck your letters before you send them out.

- Use project stationery for all communications.

- Use first class post.

- Copy all letters to the project manager.

DON'T

- Send colour brochures out in response to telephone requests.

- Use a courier service without checking with the project manager.

The level of detail you give in your briefing instructions will depend on the experience and knowledge of the recipient. If you have put together a competent team, you shouldn't have to tell them how to do every detail of their jobs. You will, however, have to highlight the particular circumstances which apply in the project on which you are working. It is often important, either for legal reasons or perhaps to demonstrate your quality control system to your sponsors, to put certain instructions in writing.

Take a look at the briefing documents used in your last project. Were they adequate? Could you have cut anything out? Could you have explained the process more clearly?

It is also appropriate to give some briefings orally. These can be delivered over the telephone, in one-to-one discussions and in more formal meetings. It is much easier to check that somebody has understood your instructions – and how he or she reacts to them – if you present them orally. You can also convey enthusiasm, urgency, concern (and many other things) very powerfully in speech. And some briefings have to be delivered at a particular location, where you can explain how to operate a piece of equipment or point out the potential hazards of a site. In any project, there are also likely to be some delicate issues about which you want to warn your team, but on which it is unwise to commit yourself in writing. The main disadvantage of oral briefings is that people do not have a permanent record of what was said. You can frequently avoid this problem, however, by following up with a written summary of your instructions. It is also important to consider the time that it takes to gather people together for a team briefing. You must judge whether the benefits outweigh the costs to the project.

Debriefing

You also need your team to give you information on the progress they have been making. It is up to you, as project manager, to decide the way in which this information comes to you. Many managers make use of standardized report forms which are closely linked to the project control system. If you use documents of this kind, make sure that they:

- Give you all the information you need

- Do not ask for irrelevant information

- Can be completed quickly and easily

- Can be interpreted quickly and easily

- Are directed to the appropriate person

- Are circulated at appropriate intervals.

In a project of any size, the business of gathering and interpreting information can take on a life of its own. In some situations, team members may even find that they are spending more time reporting on progress than actually making it. It is important to keep a tight focus on the information you really need. Usually, this will concern the three central issues of time, money and quality. Progress reporting is discussed in more detail in Chapter 10.

You must also distinguish between routine and non-routine information. Provide opportunities to find out about the concerns and worries of your team members, which may not appear on standardized reports.

'The weekly reports from my site manager suggested that we were well up to schedule. I would not have guessed that anything was

wrong. However, when I went to see him, there was obviously something troubling him. When we were talking privately, he came out with the fact that he was very concerned about the behaviour of a key member of his team. Basically, he suspected that the man had a drugs problem.'

'I once ran a large publishing project which was administered by a team of self-employed managing editors working from home. We had a weekly reporting system. When I received the chart from one editor, I saw that he had put back the completion date on one book by eight weeks. I telephoned him immediately for an explanation and discovered that this editor had had a blazing row with one of his authors, who had resigned from the project. I should have known about this much earlier. If the editor had contacted me about it at the time, I might have been able to save the situation. Subsequently, I made it very clear to all the editors that they were to telephone me immediately if they found themselves in a situation which they couldn't handle.'

How will you make sure that your team tells you what is really going on?

Meetings

Meetings can be a way of keeping up the momentum on a project. They are an opportunity for everyone to get up-to-date with the progress being made in other areas of the project and to remember that their own work has implications for other people. Meetings can provide a forum in which solutions to problems can be found. They can also be a tremendous waste of time.

When you arrange a meeting, consider whether there is a better way of sharing the information which will be communicated there. For example, you may be able to summarize progress in a memo, or send copies of a drawing through the post. Meetings are often held to bring together key people to make a decision. However, the same outcome can sometimes be achieved by a series of telephone calls.

If you decide that a meeting is essential, make sure that the right people are there. On some projects, every member of the team is invited to every meeting, even though they may have no real contribution to make. Consider whether it is possible to invite some team members to part of a meeting, allowing them to get on with their work for the rest of the time.

Plan the agenda carefully. It is helpful to express each agenda point in the form of an objective. You can also direct people's attention to particular agenda items by indicating whom you expect to contribute to them.

By the end of this meeting we will have:

- Reviewed progress on prototype E4. **JG, FR, WE**

- Made an action plan for the next stage of development. **ALL**

- Decided the format for the advertising brochure. **AJ, FR**

- Agreed the print run for the brochure. **AJ, FR, PB**

- Discussed the candidates for the administrator's post and selected a short list. **ALL**

- Agreed a time for interviewing for this post. **AJ, FR**

- Discussed the implications of the report in Monday's Daily Telegraph and drafted a press release. **ALL**

During a meeting, somebody should make notes. It is often helpful if a 'scribe' is appointed to write these key points on a flipchart. This makes it clear to everyone when a decision has been taken. When any action is agreed, a particular individual should be given responsibility for it and a date set. These details should appear on the notes and checked at an appropriate time after the meeting.

How useful are your team meetings? Could you make them more effective?

Working within the organization

In the final part of this chapter we will consider the relationship between the project team and the organization. This issue is especially important if your project takes place within the sponsoring organization, within which the members of your team have existing roles.

Most organizations are arranged on hierarchical lines. There is a line of command from the highest to the lowest level. Everyone within the organization knows (or at least, should know) the types of decision they can take themselves and the types of decision they must pass to the person above them in the management structure. Many organizations try to observe the principle of 'unity of command' in their structure.

The principle of unity of command states that individuals' confusion decreases and their sense of personal responsibility increases in relation to the completeness of their reporting relationship to their superior within the hierarchy.

In other words, it is much simpler and more satisfying to work for a single boss. You know what you are supposed to be doing and can take credit for the successes you achieve.

There are several ways in which an organization can be divided up. The divisions are often made on functional lines, or by geographical area. Some companies base their structure on their product range or type of customer.

The lines of command within an organization are often very similar to the lines of communication. People talk to their peers within their own department or unit, their immediate superior and their juniors. They may have very little contact indeed with managers in other parts of the organization. Indeed, in many companies, there is a great deal of suspicion of the activities of other departments.

A project often cuts across the existing structure of an organization. Individuals are seconded from different functional areas and are expected to divide their time (and their loyalty) between the project and their department. This arrangement is known as a matrix structure, in which individuals are subject to vertical (to their line manager) and horizontal (to the project manager) lines of authority and communication. It flies in the face of the principle of unity of control and runs counter to the culture of many more traditionally minded organizations. Here are some typical problems which can arise:

- The departmental manager fears that she may be losing a member of staff to the project, thus diminishing her own authority. She reacts by adding to the workload of the individual concerned, to prove his indispensability.

- The departmental manager is worried about the contacts that the project member is making with people in other parts of the organization and withholds departmental information from him.

- The departmental manager fears that the project manager may, through his work on the project, be about to challenge her own position. She reacts by trying to undermine him.

- The project member finds it difficult to fulfil the demands put upon him.

- The project member finds his work on the project more interesting and fulfilling than his day-to-day duties, which he neglects.

- The project member may try to play one boss off against the other.

These problems can be difficult to deal with because they arise from unspoken, and sometimes unconscious, attitudes. Many of them can be avoided if individuals are seconded full-time for the duration of a project, but this is not always possible. Even if an individual temporarily relinquishes his or her departmental role, some difficulties remain. It can be awkward to move back into the department when the project is over.

The way to tackle these potential conflicts is by setting up effective channels of communication. Talk to your team's departmental managers and explain what you need from their staff. This may help to allay suspicions about the project. Estimate the amount of time that team members will spend on the project – and do your best to keep to these estimates. If you have to vary them, give adequate warning. Find out what other commitments your team members have on their time, and try to work around them. Keep lines of communication open throughout the project. Let the departmental managers know about your successes and setbacks – this will help them to see themselves as stakeholders in the project, and can greatly increase their co-operation.

Working with the culture of the organization

The culture of an organization shows itself in:

- The way people dress

- The way they speak to each other

- Their working methods

- The things they talk to each other about

- The methods of communication they use

- The amount of responsibility they are willing to take

- The amount of effort they put into their work.

It is very likely that the culture you develop within a project will be different from that of the organization as a whole. Because the focus is on specific tasks, rather than on permanent structures and processes, people tend to get more involved and committed to their work. Some people who have held fairly junior positions within the organization may find themselves working at their full potential for the first time. There is often a decrease in formality.

When people inside the organization who are not involved in the project witness these changes, they can feel a number of different things. They may feel intrigued, suspicious or jealous. They may believe that project members are being allowed unfair privileges or that they are not maintaining the standards of the organization as a whole. You need to be aware of these attitudes and may have to warn your project team about the dangers of antagonizing other employees.

Project in progress

This chapter examines the issues which arise when a project is actually underway. At this stage, many project managers suffer from information overload. There is a danger of setting up monitoring systems which are so complex that you are unable to see the wood for the trees. Your monitoring system, however, should be your servant, not your master. When a project is in its implementation phase, your main priority should be to maintain an understanding of the overall direction of events. This chapter discusses how to set up a reporting system which will provide you with information which is relevant, adequate, current and reliable – and allow you to stay in command of the situation.

The next section of the chapter describes how quality management concepts and techniques can be used in the context of a project. In many ways, the project environment is an ideal setting for the application of these ideas.

When a project is in progress, it is important to maintain your relationship with the people who are paying for it. And, as the development of the project deliverables progresses, you also need to seek the views of the end-users. Methods of working with these, and other, stakeholders, are discussed.

All projects involve change of one kind or another, and the principles of leading people through change are described. Another characteristic which all projects seem to share is that, however efficiently they are planned, at some time or another the project manager will be faced with difficult situations. The final section of the chapter discusses some management techniques you can use to deal with problems.

Monitoring a project

The three crucial elements of a project which need to be monitored are:

- Time
- Cost
- Quality.

The project plan, which will have been drawn up at the end of the planning phase, should provide you with the framework to measure these elements. The WBS breaks the project down into activities for which you have recorded an expected finishing date, a cost and a quality specification. As each task is completed, it can be checked off, and any variance in time, cost and quality calculated.

Variance is the difference between an expected and an actual measurement.

Some variances will be within an acceptable level of tolerance. Others will be more serious and may make it necessary to change parts of the project plan. If one activity costs more than anticipated, it may be necessary to reduce costs elsewhere in the project. If an activity is taking longer than it should, this may affect the timing of activities which cannot start until it finishes. As project manager, you need to be aware which variances are significant and demand action.

Earned value analysis

This is a method of measuring how work on a project is proceeding. It involves knowing three figures for each activity:

- BCWS – the budgeted cost of work scheduled – how much you expected to have paid for the work by a particular date

- ACWP – the actual cost of work performed – how much you have actually paid for the work that has been done

- BCWP – the budgeted cost of work performed, also known as the earned value – the amount which you had expected to pay to get this amount of work done.

Using these figures, some useful calculations can be done:

Cost variance (CV) = BCWP – ACWP

Schedule variance (SV) = BCWP – BCWS

Cost variance index (CPI) = BCWP/ACWP

Imagine you are managing a project which involves conducting in-depth interviews with 1,000 residents of a rural area. You have scheduled these interviews to take place over a five week period. You pay your interviewers by the interview and have allowed a total of £10,000 in your budget for their wages. You are monitoring your interviewers' progress by examining the invoices they submit at the end of each week.

At the end of the first week, you receive invoices for a total of £1,500.

BCWS = £2,000

(You expected to have received invoices for £2,000 at this point.)

BCWP = £1,500

(You budgeted £1,500 for the 150 interviews which have been completed.)

ACWP = £1,500

(It has actually cost you £1,500 to get 150 interviews done.)

CV= BCWP – ACWP = £1,500 – £1,500 = 0

(Your cost variance is zero. You are paying what you expected to pay for the work. This is not surprising in this situation, since you are paying your interviewers on a piece rate. If you were paying them on a time-based rate, you could expect to see some variance here.)

CPI= BCWP/ACWP = £1,500 / £1,500 = 1

(Your cost performance index is one. This means that you are paying exactly what you expected for the work. However, if you were paying your interviewers by the hour, week or day, instead of by the interview, you would see some variance here.)

SV = BCWP – BCWS = £1,500 – £2,000 = – £500

(You have a schedule variance of – £500. This tells you that you have spent less than you expected to have spent by this point in time. It is an indication that the project is behind schedule.)

This was a very simple example, but it demonstrates that information on costs can tell you:

a)   Whether you are getting the value you expected.

b   Whether your project is behind (or ahead of) schedule.

You can also do a further calculation to work out the culmulative CPI for a project.

**Culmulative CPI (CCPI) = total of all BCWPs so far/
total of all ACWPs so far**

This gives an indication of how well you are keeping within your budget. A figure which is more than one shows that your actual costs are less than your budgeted costs. A figure which is less than one shows that your actual costs are exceeding your budget. The CCPI can give you an indication of whether you are likely to be able to complete the project within the budget – although it must be interpreted carefully. It is possible for this figure to be distorted by a particular activity which went seriously over budget and for other activities to be showing no variance. It is also possible for activities which are completed for less than their budgeted costs to mask problems elsewhere in the project.

Looking at trends

In order to gain an overview of how a project is going, it can be helpful to look for overall trends. An S curve shows figures for estimated and actual spending in a graphical form.

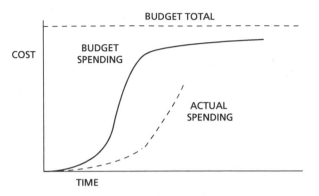

The characteristic shape of the graph is a result of low spending in the early stages of a project, before work commences, high spending during the implementation stage and a tailing off at the end of a project, when work is being checked and prepared for handover. The example above shows that actual spending is occurring later than anticipated. This indicates that work is behind schedule.

The second example shows that money is being spent more quickly than expected. This could be an indication that the project is ahead of schedule. It could also mean, however, that costs are higher than anticipated. It would be necessary to investigate this situation in more detail.

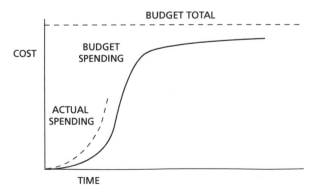

It is possible to display many different aspects of a project on graphs. With the help of project management software programs, you could produce graphs to show, among other things:

- Projected and actual cash flow

- Direct and indirect costs and spending

- Estimated and actual work rates

- Achievement of quality standard.

You can look at the overall situation, or compare and contrast different areas of the project – or even the performance of individual members of project staff. These graphs can yield important information. They can, however, also lull you into a false sense of security. As graphs produced on a software program tend to look extremely impressive, they can suggest that you are in full command of the situation, when in fact you are not. Any graph is only as accurate as the data which goes into it. If your data is based on faulty measurements or unreasonable assumptions, your graphs will reflect these deficiencies. In the next section of this chapter, when we look at progress reports, we will examine some of the problems which can arise, and what you can do to avoid them.

As well as providing an up-to-date and accurate picture of progress, the monitoring system used must also fulfil other functions. It should:

- Allow you to consider the effect of any changes in cost, time and quality on other parts of the project

- Provide a record of the project which can be used for subsequent audit.

Change control

A change in any one aspect of a project can have significant implications elsewhere. Sometimes, the people who are closely involved in the day-to-day work of a project may not be aware of these implications.

'On a publishing project, an inexperienced editor agreed a relatively small change to the text which meant that the extent of the book went up from 96 pages to 128 pages. This had a catastrophic effect on costs. She had not realized that the way the book was printed and bound

meant that it was not possible to add two or three pages to the end. Pages had to added in certain multiples.'

'Because he was unable to obtain a particular raw material, one of our junior staff bought a substitute which was of an inferior grade, which resulted in more machine breakdowns. He hadn't realized that the whole success of the project was dependent on the machines being fully operative 90 per cent of the time.'

Change in any area can have implications for costs, risks, scheduling and staffing. As project manager, you may not even be aware of some of these implications yourself:

'I am very familiar with computer applications, but not with the finer details of programming. I did not realize that, by increasing the number of parameters in one calculation, I was presenting the programmers with a very much more difficult problem to solve.'

The exact implications of any change can sometimes only be appreciated with a combination of expert knowledge and an overall understanding of the interrelationships within a project.

Change control involves gathering information on any changes which occur, or are likely to occur. This information must be passed swiftly to a central control point. The project manager must then consider possible implications, discussing them with people who have specialist knowledge of particular areas. One way to gather information on the effect of changes to the project plan is to issue an Impact Analysis Form. This document is circulated to anyone who is likely to be affected by a change. It asks for the following information:

- Activities which will be affected
- Extra activities which may be necessary
- Changes to the timing of these tasks
- Other dependent tasks which will be affected
- The effect on resources and costs
- The impact on quality or specification

When a change is authorized, the project plan needs to be up-dated. Everyone who is affected by the change must also be informed. All changes to schedule, specification or cost should be communicated in a recognized format, not passed on haphazardly by word of mouth. If you are distributing revised versions of schedules, briefing papers or other project documents, it is essential to consider version control. It should be impossible for any members of the team to be working with out-of-date information.

Here are some pointers for version control:

- Do not update documents more often than you have to

- Date or number each new version

- Highlight the changes you have made – or people may overlook them.

Project records

After a project is over, there are always lessons to be learned. By looking back over the details of what actually happened, similar mistakes and inefficiencies can be avoided in the future. Some records must be kept for legal reasons. In the future, you may have to prove, for example, that:

- Money was paid to certain individuals or organizations

- You took all necessary steps to maintain quality specifications.

Progress reports

In order to monitor and control a project, you need a system which will supply you with information on the progress that is being made. This information should have certain characteristics.

It needs to be:

- Relevant

- Adequate

- Current

- Reliable.

Unless you have quality information of this kind, you cannot make effective decisions. We will look at each of these characteristics in a little more detail.

Relevant information

The information you collect must be relevant. It should relate directly to the aspects of the project which you need to monitor. You will have established standards for cost, timing and quality specification in the planning stage of the project and much of the information you receive will be designed to tell you how your plans are working out in reality. As far as possible, the system you use to gather information during the implementation stage should be based on the same structure, and use the same categories, as you used at the planning stage of the project.

You should also avoid collecting irrelevant information. Do not waste time and resources gathering, processing and storing any information which will not be of use to you. It is comparatively easy these days to analyze large amounts of data, using computers. Information gives power and it is extremely tempting to try to gather as much of it as possible. You should, however, be aware of some of the dangers in this area. If people working on a project are overloaded with requests for irrelevant data, they may be distracted from the work you actually want them to do. They may be late in sending in their progress reports, or fail to complete them properly. And if you have too much information to look at, you may lose focus on the really important elements of the project. These effects can outweigh any benefits you receive from building up a large database for future analysis. Consider the cost-effectiveness of the information you receive.

Adequate information

You need to consider the level of detail that you require for decision-making purposes. Do you, for example, need staff to submit an exact itinerary with their travel expense forms, or is an estimation of their mileage sufficient?

Do you need a group of people who are piloting a product to answer a specific set of questions about it, or is it enough for them to tell you their general impressions? The best way to decide what details you require is to start by considering the decisions you have to take. Think about the criteria you will use to take these decisions – and the questions you need to answer. Base your data requirements on these questions.

Current information

The information you gather should be current. It needs to be collected at appropriate intervals. The frequency of these intervals will depend on the nature of the activities involved and the degree of control you need to exercise. At the start of a project, you may need to check more frequently than you do later on, when you are confident that people know what they are doing. It is also important that the method you use to collect information allows you to see it as soon as possible. The channel of communication (post, telephone, fax, e-mail, face-to-face meetings, etc) can be important here. You should also try to avoid the necessity for lengthy compilation and analysis of data before it comes to you. With the growth of information technology, it is possible for many types of data to be recorded automatically, at the same time as a process is completed. If this is not possible, information should be recorded at the lowest level. Wherever possible, compilation and analysis should be handled by computer, so that they do not delay the arrival of the information.

An effective way of ensuring that information reaches you as soon as possible is to link the reporting system to the payment system. If subcontractors know that an interim or final invoice will not be accepted until they have delivered the information you require, you are unlikely to experience serious delays.

Reliable information

You need to be able to trust the information you receive. The individuals who provide you with data may not deliberately intend to deceive you, but they can sometimes give you misleading information. There are, however, certain things you can do to increase the reliability of the information you receive.

Ask people questions which they are able to answer. If you ask them impossible questions, they may provide you with worthless data. This is more likely to happen if you are asking people to make projections about the future.

Wherever possible, ask for information which is verifiable. Many project managers ask whether a task is 30 per cent, 50 per cent or 70 per cent completed, while others are only interested in knowing whether it is 0 per cent completed or 100 per cent completed. The second approach is safer, because a 100 per cent completed task means that there is a pre-determined deliverable which can be checked off against the schedule, budget and quality specifications.

Construct a monitoring system which has built-in checks. You may have to examine every item of data, but the people who present information to you should know that they will be caught out if they attempt deception. The system of verification should not appear as an attack on the integrity of the individuals involved, but as part of the system to ensure that the objectives of the project are met.

Encourage an atmosphere of openness and trust. If people are frightened that you will criticize them unfairly for failure, they will be unwilling to reveal any problems they are having. Instead, they will try and sort them out themselves and only come to you when they have reached a crisis. While you certainly want members of the project team to show initiative, there are often ways in which you, and the other members of the team, can support people who are experiencing difficulties. If it is tackled at an early stage, there may be a technological or organizational solution to a problem, which the person involved has not thought of. Progress meetings can be a good setting in which to discuss difficulties, but they are not always the best situation in which to bring them up in the first place. It is important that the project manager establishes a range of methods of communication, including ones in which team members can talk informally about their concerns.

Methods of reporting

You need a variety of methods of reporting on progress. Reports on the completion of tasks and on the state of the budget and schedule are usually presented in pre-set formats. The format you use for progress reports should allow direct and easy comparison between expected and actual data. With budget reports, this is usually achieved by basing the report form on the budget forecast, with extra columns for actual figures and variance. Similarly, the WBS provides the framework for task completion forms. The description of the task, the specifications of the deliverable and the individual who is responsible for seeing that these specifications are achieved, should be the same. Scheduled start and finishing dates can also be taken directly from the WBS. There needs to be space on the form to insert data on when the task actually started and finished. You may also require an explanation of any variance, and an indication of other tasks which could be affected. Any other changes, such as alterations to the specification or the process used, which could have wider implications, should also be recorded. When drawing up this part of the form, you need to be aware of the principles described above. Do not ask people questions they cannot answer or for information which you will not use.

Project team meetings are another common method of gathering progress information. These are a good method of bringing together different perspectives. If the members of the team do not see each other on a daily basis, meetings are also a good way of re-aligning and remotivating them around the project objectives. Meetings should not usually be used to report events which could just as easily be communicated on paper, by telephone or by electronic mail. However, if written reports are submitted in advance of a meeting, this can provide a useful stimulus for team members to get their records up to date and settle outstanding issues.

How much do you need to monitor?

In Chapter 9 we described the stages of development that a team usually goes through. It begins by *forming*, then goes through a turbulent period of *storming*. In the *norming* phase, people settle down and agree working methods and relationships. In the *performing* stage, which corresponds to the implementation stage of a project, people should be working under their own steam. They should have taken ownership of the project and be working at their full potential. In an ideal situation, the project manager's role at this point should primarily be one of facilitator. Any unnecessary interference on your part is likely to distract the team or decrease their enthusiasm. You should keep your eyes on the big picture and only step in to make minor adjustments, as and when they are necessary.

Of course, you may not find that you are working in an ideal situation. There may be serious problems with particular processes or perhaps with members of the team. You may have to set up new working procedures, or new forms of monitoring, to deal with issues which you were not aware of at the start of the project. In general, the most effective approach to monitoring is to set up systems which will:

- Run smoothly and efficiently with the minimum of effort

- Enable you to see the overall implications of what is happening

- Highlight significant developments immediately

- Free up your time so that you can concentrate your efforts on areas of the project which really need your attention.

You do not have to justify your existence by the complexity of your routine monitoring system. When a project is actually underway, it is more important to direct your efforts into non-routine events. You can be much more useful as a problem-solver, a mediator and a motivator than as a time-keeper.

Building in quality

In on-going operational situations, quality management techniques are frequently used to maintain stability. Once you know the inputs and processes which are required to produce the results you desire, you stay with them, making only minor adjustments to fine-tune the system.

Techniques such as Statistical Process Control are used to calculate the limits within which processes should be performing. Control charts like the one below are developed by collecting a large amount of data and calculating what kind of variation in the process can be statistically expected. Results which lie outside these boundaries trigger a response from the person in charge of the process.

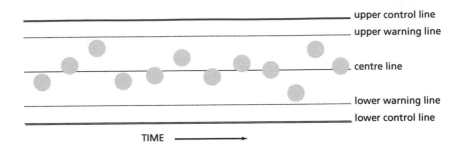

In a project, where resources and processes are used in new combinations to produce a unique end-product, it is not always possible to establish control limits. A process may not take place often enough for it to be worthwhile, or even practicable, to gather data which will tell you the range of results which are likely to occur. There are, however, many other ways in which the principles of quality management can be used in the context of project management.

Tolerances

In a project, specifications for each deliverable are laid down at the beginning. You know, or at least *should* know, what standards each of your deliverables should meet. It should also be possible to establish what deviation from these standards is acceptable. These tolerances may depend on:

- Legal requirements
- Contractual requirements
- Safety requirements
- Practical considerations relating to other project activities.

If these standards are measured in numerical terms – and the processes which result in these deliverables are repeated several times – a graph similar to the control chart above can be a useful tool. Unless you can draw upon historical data, the warning and control lines will not have statistical significance, but they can be drawn at points at which you judge that the process may need adjusting.

Here, for example, is a chart used to monitor the number of errors per 100 entries of operators who were entering survey results into a database:

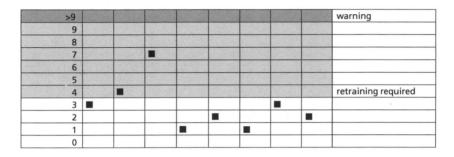

>9								warning
9								
8								
7		■						
6								
5								
4	■							retraining required
3	■					■		
2				■			■	
1			■		■			
0								

Similar charts can be used to monitor any sensitive area of a project, such as costs, or the time taken to complete a task which is repeated several times. They allow you to identify trends and can indicate points at which you have to take action to bring the process back into line.

Quality inputs

Another important concept in quality management is the understanding that quality outputs cannot be achieved without quality inputs. This principle is directly applicable to project management. At the planning stage, quality resources should be selected. These are the raw materials, equipment, staff, information, or any other kind of resource, which are fit for the purpose for which they are intended. In a project, where you are working towards specific outcomes, you are not able to adapt your processes to suit the equipment that is available, or spend a great deal of time training staff whose services you will only require for a few weeks or months. Success often depends on being able to utilize exactly the right resources. The limited timescale and budget within which you are operating help focus your mind on your requirements.

In a project, you are likely to make short-term contracts with your suppliers. This means that you can be very specific about technical specifications, delivery, service arrangements and any other issues which are important to you. Frequently, your suppliers actually become stakeholders in the project. They understand your needs and priorities and may be able to suggest solutions to problems which you are facing. If you can develop a relationship of this kind at the planning phase of a project, it can be of immense help during the implementation stage.

Ownership

Quality can only be achieved if the people who are directly involved in performing tasks take an active interest in the effectiveness and efficiency of what they are doing. In the context of operational management, quality circles and other similar groups are set up to examine processes and look for ways of improving them. In a project, the motivation to get things right – and the organizational structure to develop creative solutions to problems – probably already exist.

The following comments are from a graphic designer working on a multimedia project:

'In my previous job, I never saw the people who used my designs. I just did what I was I told to do by the head of department and had no idea what happened to my work afterwards. I usually only did part of a job, anyway. Somebody would ask me to design a series of buttons or a title screen, and I was not really aware of the whole context. When I worked on a small project, things were very different.

'I was part of a team which consisted of a programmer, a subject expert and a writer. At our first meeting, I was waiting for them to tell me what to do, then I realized that they were expecting me to come up with some ideas. It was the first time since I had completed my training that I had so much responsibility for the end-product.

'The opportunity to work with other specialists was a real eye-opener. Often, in meetings, I would suggest things, and the programmer would say, 'Yes, that's not a bad idea, but it would work better if you could use the same range of colours as you used in the other part of the *screen, then the computer won't have to handle two palettes at the same time.' Or the subject expert would say, 'Your text is too small there. Those are the points which people find really difficult to understand – you need to give them much more prominence.' And sometimes the advice went in the other direction, too. I was able to suggest to the writer that we could dispense with a complicated numbering system and use colour to identify different parts of the text.*

'I no longer felt that I was just doing a nine-to-five job. As the project progressed, it really mattered to me that the final product was as good as it possibly could be. I knew that my name would be on the credits, and I wanted it to be something I was going to be proud of.'

In any sector, people who habitually work on projects know that they are 'only as good as the last job they worked on'. Reputations are built and lost on projects, where the final product is closely identified with the team which brought it about. There is a strong incentive for people to commit themselves fully to a project and perform at a high level.

The limited time scale of a project can also increase a sense of ownership and commitment. People can become very involved with something which they know is only going to last a few months, although they would not be prepared to put in the same amount of effort on a permanent basis. For these reasons, many companies try to organize an increasing number of their activities on a project basis.

Customers and suppliers

Quality management is based on a chain of customers and suppliers, which may be either external or internal to the organization. At each interface, customers and suppliers identify and discuss their requirements. We have already seen how the need to specify inputs, and the contractual arrangements with suppliers, highlight this relationship. There are also other customer-supplier relationships within a project.

The project manager is a supplier to the client or sponsor, whose requirements are clearly defined in the Terms of Reference. Everything which happens in a project is designed to meet these requirements. If changes to the scope, cost or timescale are necessary, these must be negotiated and agreed.

In the implementation stage of a project, the project manager is actually a supplier to the project team. You must provide them with the equipment, raw materials, guidance, working conditions and technical support they need in order to do their work. And the members of the team are also your suppliers. They must deliver work at the cost and time and to the specification which you have set. Because of the dependencies between the various activities which make up a project, individual members of the team also have customer-supplier relationships with each other. A project cannot succeed unless those involved in its various activities are aware of each others' requirements and do their best to meet them, even if this means taking a new and more flexible approach to their own work.

In the last project you worked on, who were your customers? And who were your suppliers? How did you have to adapt yourself to their requirements?

Quality outputs

Within a project, definite standards are set for each internal deliverable. It is the project manager's responsibility to ensure that these standards are set out clearly, so that everyone involved knows exactly what they are supposed to be achieving. When people are working on a contractual basis, payment can be linked to the most important of these deliverables.

It is also necessary to consider the final outcome of the project. If you are working on a new product or service, this will need to be tested on the end-user. In a large project, the reactions of customers will probably be investigated by specialist market researchers. There are some general points, however, which it is useful to remember in other situations.

If you are asking end-users what they think, be prepared to listen to what they tell you. If the feedback you receive is unfavourable, it is very easy to dismiss it as uninformed or irrelevant. The greater your own commitment to a project, the more difficult it can be to accept criticism from outside. For this reason, it is often better for pilots to be conducted by individuals who can put some distance between themselves and the project.

Get the timing right. Do not leave piloting until the last moment, when it will be extremely difficult to make changes to the design or specifications of the product or service. Contact with end-users should be built into a project from the very beginning, so that the original objectives and scope are informed by their opinions. It is often important to talk to end-users, or at least of experts who are familiar with their requirements, throughout the life of a project.

If you are presenting an unfinished product, make this clear. People who are unfamiliar with the development process may expect to see something which corresponds to commercially available products or services and may reject what you are showing them because it does not conform to their experience. If it is possible to do so, it may be advisable to take one example of your product to a finished form.

Ask appropriate questions. Guide the end-user to the areas where you want information. Adapt your terminology to your audience. For example, if you wanted to investigate the effectiveness of the design of a leaflet, your questions might include:

- What pictures can you remember seeing in the leaflet?
- How easy was it to find the information you needed?

In a questionnaire or a formal interview, closed questions, which offer respondents a limited range of options, are often used. The answers to these questions are easy to analyze, but the type of information that you receive is limited by the options you provide. Open questions, where respondents are free to answer in any way they want, can reveal more. They are much more difficult to analyze, however, and also need to be carefully presented. If people are faced with a series of open questions, they may not know what type or level of answer you expect them to give, and fail to respond or only give perfunctory replies. You may only receive full replies from people who feel very strongly about the product, which may distort your results.

Some people may also be unwilling to tell you what they really think. If they have been invited to try out a product or service, they may feel constrained to be polite. Others may be over-critical. There may also be other reasons why people will not reveal their true reactions. Many interviewers use projected questions to get around this difficulty:

- How frequently would you say that most people use a personal deodorant?

- Would a price of £200 be about right, or too much for many people to consider?

- Do you think that parents take enough interest in what their children watch on television?

People are sometimes much more forthcoming about what others think, do or believe than about their own behaviour and views.

Working with stakeholders

It is important to maintain your relationship with the sponsoring organization while the project is in progress. After the initial negotiations are over and contracts are signed, contact between the project and the organization which is paying for it will probably be directed through a single member of staff. This individual can be your spokesperson and champion within the sponsoring organization. If things go badly, he or she can also be instrumental in withdrawing sponsorship from the project.

Consider the needs of this individual. Apart from the progress reports and other forms of documentation described in the Terms of Reference, the representative of the sponsoring organization may also be looking for:

- Personal insight into the work of the project

- Examples of what is happening which can be shown to other managers

- Advance warning of any difficulties which may arise

- Confidence that any assurances that he or she makes on behalf of the project will be honoured.

Once contracts are signed, the sponsor should be your ally, not your adversary. You are, after all, committed to the same objectives.

What actions can you take to encourage a relationship with your sponsor of trust and mutual respect?

Other stakeholders

You can also do a great deal to foster good relationships with other stakeholders. The people who are working directly for the project are likely to be influenced by the following factors:

- Rate and speed of payment

- Acknowledgement of the contributions they make

- Clear guidance

- Support when it is needed.

Here are some comments on good and bad experiences from people who have worked on projects:

'I came up with rather an ingenious solution to a technical problem. It wasn't an earth-shattering development, but it was a neat piece of design. I must say that I was rather flattered when the project manager described what I had done at the team meeting. It's nice to be appreciated.'

'I pulled out all the stops to meet my deadline. I scarcely spoke to my family for a couple of weeks and put all my other work on hold. I was pleased to do it, because I knew that other people in the team were depending on me. However, when I submitted my invoice it languished on somebody's desk for a couple of months before it was finally paid. I was financially inconvenienced by this delay, and I also felt cheated, as though I had been taken advantage of. It left an unpleasant taste in my mouth, somehow.'

'The most irritating project manager I ever worked for had this habit of saying 'Yes, tremendous, fantastic work!' when you showed him what you had been doing. Then he would come back a couple of hours later, or perhaps the next morning, and say, 'Look, I've been thinking. Perhaps there are one or two changes we ought to make...' I hate working for someone who doesn't know his own mind.'

'I was let down by a sub-contractor and telephoned the project manager to discuss the problem. Instead of blaming me for getting into the situation, she was completely practical in her approach. Together, we worked out a rescue plan. She provided me with all the resources I needed and, as I later discovered, took responsibility for the incident on her own shoulders. That is what I call support.'

In some projects, your stakeholders will include local residents. It is often good public relations to supply the local press with stories about current developments. This will increase anticipation for the final product or service and can help diffuse annoyance about any inconvenience you are causing them. In other situations, your 'public' may be an industrial sector or perhaps an academic community. Here too, interim reports in the specialist press can provide good pre-publicity. It is absolutely essential, however, that any information which you release about the project is agreed with the sponsoring organization. They probably have their own plans for publicity.

Earlier in this section, we discussed the importance of consulting end-users. As well as helping you to develop the product, these contacts can also bring other benefits. By issuing a trial version of a new product at a very attractive price, it is sometimes possible to conduct a mass pilot and simultaneously develop a market. If customers feel they have played a part in developing a product, they may feel a sense of loyalty to it later.

Leading people through change

All projects involve change of some kind. This change may be trivial, or it may have a profound effect on people's lives. Many of your stakeholders may be apprehensive about the consequences of your project and oppose it in any way they can. An understanding of the principles of change management can help you avoid some of this opposition.

Force field analysis is a technique which was developed by Kurt Lewin, a social scientist. It is based on the theory that people and organizations act in the way they do because of the combined effect of opposing forces.

Some of these forces propel them in one direction, while others push them in the opposite direction.

The result is a state of equilibrium, in which the both sets of forces are exactly balanced.

The forces which keep the situation in equilibrium can include:

- What people believe

- What people understand

- What people fear

- Costs

- Benefits

- The resources that people have available to them.

As long these forces remain in equilibrium, the situation will not change. If you want to change the situation, three steps are necessary:

1. Destabilize the existing equilibrium

2. Move to a new position

3. Stabilize the new equilibrium.

The current equilibrium can be destabilized by introducing a new driving or restraining force, or by strengthening or weakening any or all of the existing forces. For example, if you wanted to persuade people to accept a change in their working methods, you would start by considering what forces were operating to maintain the present equilibrium:

'I was engaged on a project to develop and implement a new information system within an organization. I wanted to change the current habit that staff had of putting most internal communications

on memos and encourage them to use e-mail instead. I began by talking to staff and considering the driving and restraining forces which maintained the status quo. It seemed to me that the most significant reason why people used memos was:

- *They wanted to stay in frequent contact with other members of staff.*

The main restraining forces, the reasons why they didn't want to move to another system, were:

- *They were unsure how to use e-mail*

- *They felt worried without a written record of their internal communications*

- *They were uncertain about the security of e-mail.*

I saw that the driving force in this situation, the desire for frequent communication, could equally well apply to e-mail. The issues I had to concentrate on were the restraining forces. I decided to remove people's lack of confidence and worries about insecurity by addressing these points in training sessions. The worry about a lack of written records was slightly more difficult. I didn't want to encourage them to print out all their messages for the paper-based filing system. In the end, I decided that the best way forward was to educate them in the use of electronic filing systems. I showed them how, with the use of directories, sub-directories and simple codes, they could have much more efficient access to their documents.'

When people are faced with a change, they commonly go through the following stages:

- Shock
- Opposition
- Exploration
- Acceptance.

Shock

In the initial stage, when the change is first announced, it is important to give information clearly and simply and allow a little time for it to be absorbed. People's initial reaction may be very emotional, especially if they believe that the change is an adverse one. It is important to stay calm and not respond in kind to any emotional outbursts.

Opposition

Once people have collected themselves, they are likely to respond with opposing arguments. These may reflect a desire to keep things as they are. Other people may respond with apathy, cynicism, withdrawal from the debate or anxiety. Self-appointed 'leaders of the opposition' may arise and factions may form, causing internal divisions. Allow people to voice their reactions and treat these views with respect. Provide as much information as you can to avoid the development of rumours. Keep communications as open as possible, so that everyone feels involved.

Exploration

In the third stage, people begin to consider how the changes will affect them. They want to understand the full implications of what is going to happen. People may still be confused, but they are beginning to realize that the change is inevitable. Slowly, they will begin to feel more positive about the future. You can encourage this new mood by involving the people concerned in working out the details of the change.

Acceptance

In the final stage, the change process is almost over. At this point, you should check that the anxieties expressed earlier in the process have been allayed and that any undertakings made while the changes were under discussion have been honoured. This will make people more willing to trust you when you have to introduce another change.

Dealing with problems

However carefully you have laid your plans, it is extremely likely that events will not turn out exactly as you had imagined. A key member of your project team may fall ill, or not be quite as skilled as you had thought. Suppliers may let you down with late deliveries. Equipment may fail. New legislation may mean that you have to revise your specifications or working methods. As the activities of the project become more visible, you may run into opposition from groups or individuals. And the more complex a project is, the more things there are which can go wrong. As a project manager, you must be able to deal with the unexpected. In this section we will examine some of the techniques you can employ to get a project back on track.

Dealing with difficult people

In Chapter 9 we looked at the character stereotypes which combine to make the project team. All these personalities have their strengths, but they also have their weaknesses. We also discussed some tactics you can use to deal with personality clashes, or situations where one individual is holding up the work of the project.

Sometimes, you may have to take drastic action. If a member of the team proves to be totally inadequate, you will probably have to dispense with his or her services. If you have to do this, it is best to recognize the fact as soon as possible and do the deed quickly, before the morale or performance of other people is affected. However, there may be repercussions. The departure of a team member can breed fear and distrust in those that remain. If people feel vulnerable, they may not be quite as eager to come to you with their difficulties. You will also have to find and train up a replacement. Until the replacement is in place, the rest of the team may experience hold-ups or have to do extra work.

Sometimes you can solve the problem by changing people's roles. It is important to do this in a way that does not appear to be a judgement on their own shortcomings. You should focus on the needs of the project, not on personalities. If you introduce new rules, make them apply to everyone, not just the individual who is causing you problems. If you are really skilled, you can convince the person involved that the changes you require in their behaviour or working practices are their own idea:

Project manager: John, I wonder if we could have a quick word before the others arrive. I'm getting a bit concerned about the time it is taking to process purchase orders. Once or twice I have telephoned a supplier to query a late delivery and they have said that they have only just received the order, when I would have expected them to have received it at least a week ago. I was wondering if you could suggest any way in which we could speed the procedure up. Just take me through what happens, could you?

Administrator: Well, the purchase order arrives on my desk and I check it against the budget, and then I get the relevant budget holder to sign it, and then I send it to the supplier, with a copy to accounts.

Project manager: And how many requests do you get a week, on average?

Administrator: It could be 40 or 50.

Project manager: That's a lot. But they are not always for large amounts?

Administrator: Oh no, most of them are for less than £20. Some are under £10.

Project manager: It seems that a lot of effort is necessary on your part to deal with relatively small amounts of money. And it can't always be easy to find a budget holder at short notice.

Administrator: Well, that's the problem. I can't always find someone to sign the order.

Project manager: And we really should be getting the orders processed within two working days. I wonder if we are right to use the same procedure for all orders.

Administrator: We could... Well, how about if I was able to sign orders myself, up to a ceiling of, say, £20?

Project manager: *That's not a bad idea. But I'm still a bit worried about the amount of paperwork you've got on your plate.*

Administrator: *Well, how about if core team members could sign orders themselves, up to £20, and then they were to pass a copy to me, so I could keep the records up-to-date and check that no-one was misusing the system?*

Project manager: *That sounds like a very good suggestion. I'll delegate part of the budget to core team members and draw up some guidelines, so they understand the limits we are working within. And, of course, you will continue to deal with all the important orders in the traditional way. If we set this system up, your desk should be a lot clearer, so what turnaround time do you think you could achieve with the orders over £20?*

Administrator: *Oh, two working days. No problem.*

Project manager: *Excellent. That should speed things up a lot. I'll send a memo round saying that all purchase orders must be sent out within two working days of the original request for supplies being made. Let's have another chat in a couple of weeks and see how the new system is working.*

The project manager handled this situation with great tact. You may not always have the need – or the opportunity – to be quite as sensitive as this. However, if you want to retain the loyalty and enthusiasm of your team, it is as well to avoid upsetting them unnecessarily.

If you need to change the way someone is working:

- Focus on the project, not personalities
- Don't criticize their work in front of other people
- If possible, get the person involved to suggest a solution
- Ratify the solution with your own authority
- Apply new procedures to everyone
- Check that the solution has solved the problem.

Problem solving

It can sometimes be hard to think straight when you are under pressure. If a problem arises, it is tempting to make a snap decision and implement the first solution which comes to mind. However, whenever possible, it is well worth taking the time to go through a simple procedure:

1. Define the **boundaries** of the problem

2. Identify the **cause** of the problem

3. Devise a **range of solutions** to deal with the problem

4. Select the **most appropriate** solution.

Instead of reacting instantaneously when something goes wrong, consider how big the problem really is.

Ask questions like these:

*   How long has this been going on?

*   How wrong were we in our estimates?

*   How much is it costing us?

*   Who is involved?

*   Does it happen all the time?

This will enable you to see how serious the problem is – and which activities or personnel are (and are not) involved.

> 'I had an angry telephone call from a resident who lived opposite the site where we were working. He said that our vehicles were always blocking the road, making it impossible for people to get to work and he had contacted the police. I phoned the site manager and established that there had been a problem that morning, when a delivery lorry had been trying to back through the gates and had held up the traffic for 20 minutes. He was expecting further similar deliveries over the next few weeks.'

Next, look for the causes of the problem. A useful technique to use here is to ask yourself a succession of 'why?' questions:

- Why did the lorry block the road?

  Because it had to back into the gates.

- Why?

  Because it was too big to turn round in the yard.

- Why?

  Because the suppliers sent a big lorry.

- Why?

  Because it's the only one they've got.

This series of questions can often suggest a solution. In this situation, it may be possible to use a different supplier who has a smaller lorry. Other solutions may be possible, too:

- Arrange for supplies to be collected from the supplier

- Ask the supplier to delivery at another time of day, when people are not trying to get to work

- Use another entrance

- Next time you are expecting a delivery, warn the residents the evening before, so they can move their cars to the end of the street.

Finally, when you have assembled a range of options, choose the most appropriate solution:

'I telephoned the manager of the suppliers, explained our problem and asked him to make sure that future deliveries were scheduled for the middle of the day, when local people were less likely to be using the road.'

This was a simple problem to solve. Sometimes, you may be faced with a situation where the causes are much more difficult to identify. In this case, it may be helpful to use an Ishikawa or 'fishbone' diagram. Start by writing the effect in a box, with an arrow pointing to it. Then think of a few categories which the causes might fall into. Common categories are:

- People
- Processes
- Materials
- Equipment.

Set up arrows for each of your categories. Then think of possible causes within each category and write them on the diagram. The fishbone diagram is a good way of analyzing a problem. It can help you to think of causes which might not have occurred to you immediately.

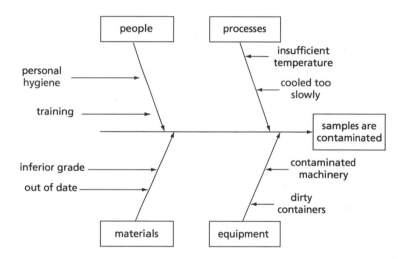

Problems with the schedule

In project management, there are some established methods of solving problems with the schedule.

Bringing in extra resources

If the work is taking longer than anticipated, it is worth considering increasing the resources deployed on the project. This may involve bringing in more staff on a temporary basis, paying staff to work longer hours, subcontracting tasks or using more expensive equipment. A mathematical trade-off is made between the cost of falling behind schedule and the cost of increasing resources. If you assign work to inexperienced individuals, you will probably suffer some loss of efficiency while they learn what is expected of them. If you use people who are already proficient at the task, you may have to pay a great deal for their services, especially if you find them through an outside agency. This latter option, however, is often the best alternative.

Fast tracking

Instead of waiting for a task to be completed before starting the task which depends on it, you can sometimes split the first task into sections and start the dependent task before the first one has finished. On paper, the time savings can look impressive:

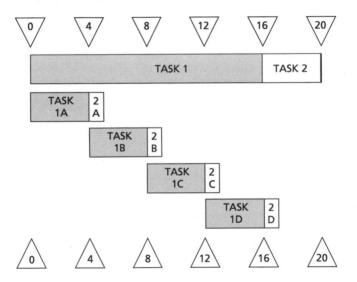

Before fast tracking, tasks 1 and 2 were scheduled to take a total of 20 days. After fast tracking, with task 2 starting before task 1 ends, the scheduled time is cut to 17 days. The savings arise because work is being done on both tasks simultaneously.

The problem with fast tracking is that some of the early work may have to be redone, as issues which affect the whole of the first or second task may not emerge until the whole of the first task has been completed.

> 'To save time on a schedule, I arranged for the statistical analysis of some research results to begin as soon as we had inputted the first batch of data from our questionnaires. Unfortunately, when the third batch of data was put on the computer, I realized that we needed to revise the categories we were using for the analysis. The work on the first and second batches of data was useless and had to be done all over again.'

Other titles from Thorogood

NEGOTIATE TO SUCCEED

Julie Lewthwaite

£12.99 paperback, ISBN 1 85418 153 X

Published March 2000

This book provides accessible, practical guidance and techniques for negotiating, including: useful skills for the negotiator, dealing with 'people issues', negotiation in practice. Written in a straightforward, non-academic manner, this book provides tips and techniques in a clear, easy-to-use checklist format designed for the busy manager.

THE COMMERCIAL ENGINEER'S DESKTOP GUIDE

Tim Boyce

£16.99 paperback, ISBN 1 85418 199 8

Published June 2001

The history of business is littered with great design and engineering ideas which failed to become successful through lack of commercial expertize. Here is a book that shows you how to combine successful design and innovation with effective business skills and acumen. The book explains legal, contractual and commercial matters in straightforward terms; shows how commercial and technical aspects of business agreements are closely inter-related; highlights things that engineers say and do [with the best intentions] which invite commercial disaster.

MASTERING BUSINESS PLANNING AND STRATEGY

Paul Elkin

£14.99 paperback, ISBN(10): 1 85418 329 X

(13): 978-185418329-3

Practical techniques for profiling your business and the competition, analysing the market, mastering strategic thinking, positioning for marketplace success, option appraisal and strategic decision making, as well as implementing and managing change.

SUCCESSFUL BUSINESS PLANNING – ENERGIZING YOUR COMPANY'S POTENTIAL

Norton Paley

£14.99 paperback, ISBN(10): 1 85418 277 3
(13):978-185418277-7
£29.99 hardback, ISBN(10): 1 85418 289 7
(13):978-185418289-0
Published June 2004

"Growth firms with a written business plan have increased their revenues 69 per cent faster over the past five years than those without a written plan." FROM A SURVEY BY PRICEWATERHOUSECOOPERS

Using a real company case history, Norton Paley explains the techniques of building a strategic business plan and how to develop a one-year tactical plan linked to it. Further case studies illustrate successful strategies for countering severe competition. Includes valuable checklists for developing competitive strategies and help topics.

MASTERING PEOPLE MANAGEMENT

Mark Thomas

£14.99 paperback, ISBN(10): 1 85418 328 1
(13):978-185418328-6
£19.99 hardback, ISBN(10):1 85418 138 6
(13):978-185418138-1

How to build and develop a successful team by motivating, empowering and leading people. Based on in-depth experience of developing people and initiating change within many organisations, Mark Thomas provides a shrewd, practical guide to mastering the essential techniques of people management.

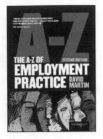

THE A-Z OF EMPLOYMENT PRACTICE

David Martin

£19.99 paperback • 2nd edition
ISBN(10): 1 85418 327 3 • (13): 978-185418327-9
£55.00 hardback • 2nd edition
ISBN(10): 1 854183222 • (13): 978-185418322-4

This book comes at a time when managers are faced with still more new legislation, obligations and potential penalties. It explains what the law is and then what to do, providing expert advice on every aspect of employment practice from recruitment, pay and incentives to maternity/ paternity leave, personnel records, contracts and holidays.

"This book covers everything you need to know about good employment practice... This is a really useful book. Every manager should have one." PROFESSIONAL MANAGER

"This book will be of value to all businesses, particularly perhaps smaller businesses where the director/owner needs to be his or her own personnel or HR manager... a valuable guide for every manager and would-be leader". JOHN SUNDERLAND. CHAIRMAN, CADBURY SCHWEPPES PLC

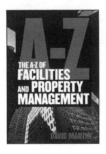

THE A-Z OF FACILITIES AND PROPERTY MANAGEMENT

David Martin

£19.99 paperback
ISBN(10): 1 85418 3133 • (13): 978-185418313-2
£55.00 ringbound
ISBN(10): 1 85418 3184 • (13): 978-185418318-7

A major new reference work, in an easy-to-use A-Z format, covering all aspects of facilities and property management, strategy, administration and control, backed up by a wealth of practical suggestions. Covers all the latest legislation on waste, energy consumption and environmental issues and offers valuable insights into the management of property assets.

THE PEOPLE MANAGEMENT CLINIC

Martin Richardson

£16.99 paperback
ISBN(10): 1 85418 391 5 • (13): 978-185418391-0

A complete A-Z guide to people management – helping managers along the most difficult of paths: leading, motivating and running a team of people. This book takes the form of a clinic during which you can ask an experienced people management consultant how to approach any number of issues and problems that face you on a daily basis. A goldmine of tips, techniques and valuable advice, the guidance throughout is both insightful and pragmatic.

THE FINANCE AND ACCOUNTING DESKTOP GUIDE

Ralph Tiffin

£16.99 paperback • 2nd edition
ISBN(10): 1 85418 309 5 • (13): 978-185418309-5
£55.00 ringbound • 2nd edition
ISBN(10): 1 85418 304 4 • (13): 978-185418304-0

The new edition of this Desktop Guide provides a clear, practical guide to all aspects of accountancy, financial and business literacy. It includes changes to accounting standards and the move to IFRS and is packed with examples, checklists, summaries and special tips.

Thorogood also has an extensive range of reports and special briefings which are written specifically for professionals wanting expert information.

For a full listing of all Thorogood publications, or to order any title, please call Thorogood Customer Services on 020 7749 4748 or fax on 020 7729 6110. Alternatively view our website at www.thorogood-publishing.co.uk.

Focused on developing your potential

Falconbury, the sister company to Thorogood publishing, brings together the leading experts from all areas of management and strategic development to provide you with a comprehensive portfolio of action-centred training and learning.

We understand everything managers and leaders need to be, know and do to succeed in today's commercial environment. Each product addresses a different technical or personal development need that will encourage growth and increase your potential for success.

- Practical public training programmes
- Tailored in-company training
- Coaching
- Mentoring
- Topical business seminars
- Trainer bureau/bank
- Adair Leadership Foundation

The most valuable resource in any organization is its people; it is essential that you invest in the development of your management and leadership skills to ensure your team fulfil their potential. Investment into both personal and professional development has been proven to provide an outstanding ROI through increased productivity in both you and your team. Ultimately leading to a dramatic impact on the bottom line.

With this in mind Falconbury have developed a comprehensive portfolio of training programmes to enable managers of all levels to develop their skills in leadership, communications, finance, people management, change management and all areas vital to achieving success in today's commercial environment.

What Falconbury can offer you?

- Practical applied methodology with a proven results
- Extensive bank of experienced trainers
- Limited attendees to ensure one-to-one guidance
- Up to the minute thinking on management and leadership techniques
- Interactive training
- Balanced mix of theoretical and practical learning
- Learner-centred training
- Excellent cost/quality ratio

Falconbury In-Company Training

Falconbury are aware that a public programme may not be the solution to leadership and management issues arising in your firm. Involving only attendees from your organization and tailoring the programme to focus on the current challenges you face individually and as a business may be more appropriate. With this in mind we have brought together our most motivated and forward thinking trainers to deliver tailored in-company programmes developed specifically around the needs within your organization.

All our trainers have a practical commercial background and highly refined people skills. During the course of the programme they act as facilitator, trainer and mentor, adapting their style to ensure that each individual benefits equally from their knowledge to develop new skills.

Falconbury works with each organization to develop a programme of training that fits your needs.

Mentoring and coaching

Developing and achieving your personal objectives in the workplace is becoming increasingly difficult in today's constantly changing environment. Additionally, as a manager or leader, you are responsible for guiding colleagues towards the realization of their goals. Sometimes it is easy to lose focus on your short and long-term aims.

Falconbury's one-to-one coaching draws out individual potential by raising self-awareness and understanding, facilitating the learning and perform-ance development that creates excellent managers and leaders. It builds renewed self-confidence and a strong sense of 'can-do' competence, contributing significant benefit to the organization. Enabling you to focus your energy on developing your potential and that of your colleagues.

Mentoring involves formulating winning strategies, setting goals, monitoring achievements and motivating the whole team whilst achieving a much improved work life balance.

Falconbury – Business Legal Seminars

Falconbury Business Legal Seminars specializes in the provision of high quality training for legal professionals from both in-house and private practice internationally.

The focus of these events is to provide comprehensive and practical training on current international legal thinking and practice in a clear and informative format.

Event subjects include, drafting commercial agreements, employment law, competition law, intellectual property, managing an in-house legal department and international acquisitions.

For more information on all our services please contact Falconbury on +44 (0)20 7729 6677 or visit the website at: www.falconbury.co.uk.